Liberty, Democracy, and the Temptations to Tyranny in the Dialogues of Plato

THE McDONALD
CENTER FOR
AMERICA'S FOUNDING
PRINCIPLES

MERCER
UNIVERSITY

THE A. V. ELLIOTT CONFERENCE SERIES

The Thomas C. and Ramona E. McDonald Center
for America's Founding Principles

Guided by James Madison's maxim that "a well-instructed people alone can be permanently a free people," the McDonald Center exists to promote the study of the great texts and ideas that have shaped our regime and fostered liberal learning.

Directors
Will R. Jordan and Charlotte C. S. Thomas

PUBLISHED VOLUMES

No Greater Monster nor Miracle than Myself: The Political Philosophy of Michel de Montaigne,
ed. Charlotte C. S. Thomas (2014)

Of Sympathy and Selfishness: The Moral and Political Philosophy of Adam Smith,
ed. Charlotte C. S. Thomas (2015)

The Most Sacred Freedom: Religious Liberty in the History of Philosophy and America's Founding,
ed. Will Jordan and Charlotte C. S. Thomas (2016)

Promise and Peril: Republics and Republicanism in the History of Political Philosophy,
ed. Will R. Jordan (2017)

When in the Course of Human Events: 1776 at Home, Abroad, and in American Memory,
ed. Will R. Jordan (2018)

Power and the People: Thucydides' History and the American Founding,
ed. Charlotte C. S. Thomas (2019)

From Reflection and Choice: The Political Philosophy of the Federalist Papers and the Ratification Debate,
ed. Will R. Jordan (2020)

FORTHCOMING

Will R. Jordan, ed., *On John Locke* (2022)

Liberty, Democracy, and the Temptations to Tyranny in the Dialogues of Plato

Edited by

Charlotte C. S. Thomas

MERCER UNIVERSITY PRESS
Macon, Georgia
2021

MUP/ P623

LIBRARY OF CONGRESS CATALOGING-IN-PUBLICATION DATA
Thomas, Charlotte C. S., editor. | A. V. Elliott Conference on
Great Books and Ideas (2019 : Mercer University), author.
Liberty, democracy, and the temptations to tyranny in the Dialogues
of Plato / edited by Charlotte C. S. Thomas.
Macon, Georgia : Mercer University Press, 2021. | Series:
THE A. V. ELLIOTT CONFERENCE SERIES
LCCN 2020050987 | ISBN 9780881467857 (paperback)
LCSH: Plato. Dialogues—Congresses.
LCC B395 .L45 2021 | DDC 321.8—dc23
LC record available at https://lccn.loc.gov/2020050987

CONTENTS

ACKNOWLEDGMENTS

This collection of essays is based on the 2019 A. V. Elliott Conference for Great Books and Ideas, the 12th annual conference sponsored by the McDonald Center for America's Founding Principles, entitled "Liberty and Tyranny in Plato."

The McDonald Center for America's Founding Principles began as a small conference in the Spring of 2008. It secured initial funding that summer through Mercer University's Academic Initiatives Monetary (AIM) fund and has grown substantially each subsequent year. Neither this volume, nor the conference it is based upon, nor any of the other important work now done by the McDonald Center would have been possible without the foresight of Mercer President, William D. Underwood, the confidence of the AIM committee, the support of then College of Liberal Arts Dean Lake Lambert, and the entrepreneurial spirit of the Center's founders. Anita Gustafson, who now serves as Dean of the College of Liberal Arts and Sciences, has continued in this tradition and shown the McDonald Center consistent support and encouragement.

In the Spring of 2013, the McDonald Center received a generous endowment gift from Mr. A. V. Elliott, for whom our annual conference is now named. Also in 2013, Thomas and Ramona McDonald made an endowment gift to support all of the Center's work, and with it they gave us their name. We are, and always will be, in deep debt to the Elliotts and McDonalds for their support.

Our conference on Liberty and Tyranny in Plato was both a gathering of Plato scholars on Mercer's main campus in Macon, Georgia, and also the culmination of a semester-long reading group made up of Mercer faculty and students. I would like to thank all of the participants in that group by name. Each of them contributed significantly to the excellent conversation that animated our conference and this volume of essays, which it inspired. So, thank you: Will Jordan, Kevin Honeycutt, Elizabeth Harper, Thomas Bullington, Marc Jolley, Garland Crawford, Vasile Stanescu, Erin

McClena-than, Patrick Jolley, Travis Hardin, Lloryn Cylin, Jordan Bracewell, NaShaya Bartolo, Galen Ficklin-Alred, Fredrick Hutcherson, Cheyanne Ingram, Daniel Lentz, James Smith, Yasmeen Hill, Tripp Kennon, Matthew Purlee, Christian Wilson, Devyn Mode, Holly Cooper, Preston Earle, and Cody Moran.

I'm sincerely thankful to Peter Ahrensdorf, Jennifer Baker, Khalil Habib, Kevin Honeycutt, Alex Priou, Richard Ruderman, Nicholas D. Smith, Devin Stauffer, Mary Townsend, Jeffrey Dirk Wilson, and Catherine Zuckert for presenting their scholarly work at the Elliott Conference, for interacting so thoughtfully with our students at the conference, and for submitting their revised essays for publication in this volume. It has been a great honor to learn about Plato from these brilliant, lovely people. I would also like to thank our undergraduate student panelists, who showed great ambition and courage by sharing their research on Plato with all of our visitors and their peers at Mercer who attended the Elliott conference: Holly Cooper, Preston Earle, Cody Moran, and Devyn Mode.

Many, many thanks are due to Marc Jolley and to the whole staff at Mercer University Press, who have been a pleasure to work with. I will be a better person if some tiny bit of their good spirit, thoughtfulness, and diplomacy has rubbed off on me during our collaboration on this volume.

Finally, it continues to be a great privilege to work as co-director of the McDonald Center with one of its founders, Will Jordan. For more than ten years, I have enjoyed the good work of fostering important conversations about great ideas among delightful people. Without Prof. Jordan's energy and foresight, the McDonald Center would not exist. Without his thoughtfulness and good judgment, it would not be thriving. Without his friendship, my work for the Center would be much less fun. So, thanks, Will, for all you do, and for the great grace with which you do it. Everyone who benefits from the good work of the McDonald Center is deeply in your debt.

CONTRIBUTORS

Peter Ahrensdorf
James B. Duke Professor of Political Science
Affiliated Professor of Classics
Davidson College

Jennifer Baker
Professor of Philosophy
College of Charleston

Khalil Habib
Associate Professor of Politics
Hillsdale College

Kevin Honeycutt
Associate Professor of Philosophy
Director of the Philosophy, Politics, and Economics Program
Mercer University

Alex Priou
Instructor in the Herbst Program for Engineering, Ethics, and Society
University of Colorado, Boulder

Richard Ruderman
Associate Professor of Political Science
University of North Texas.

Nicholas D. Smith
James F. Miller Professor of Humanities, Departments of Classics and Philosophy
Lewis & Clark College

Devin Stauffer
Professor of Government at University of Texas at Austin

Mary Townsend
Assistant Professor of Philosophy, St. John's University, Queens,
New York

Charlotte C. S. Thomas
Professor of Philosophy, Director of Great Books, and
Co-Director of the McDonald Center for America's
Founding Principles at Mercer University

Jeffrey Dirk Wilson
Collegiate Associate Professor of Philosophy
The Catholic University of America

Catherine Zuckert
Nancy Reeves Dreux Professor of Political Science, Emerita at the
University of Notre Dame, Visiting professor in the School of
Civic and Economic Thought and Leadership (SCETL) at
Arizona State University

MERCER UNIVERSITY PRESS

Endowed by

TOM WATSON BROWN
and
THE WATSON-BROWN FOUNDATION, INC.

INTRODUCTION

Plato chose to set his dialogues in and around the city of Athens during the life of Socrates. In so doing, Plato immersed his philosophy in the very recent history of his own city, and that recent history was tragic. Not only had Athens recently lost a huge, long, expensive, humiliating war; it had also lost for a brief but brutal time its distinctive mode of self-governance—democracy. Plato's famous critiques of democracy notwithstanding, the loss of self-determination to the Thirty Tyrants was catastrophic for Athens. And, the truly tragic twist of the knife for Plato was that after the terrors of tyranny were curtailed, practically the first significant act of Athens' newly restored democracy was the trial and execution of Socrates. What might have been a moment of celebration as Athens reestablished its sovereignty was transformed into the deepest of philosophical tragedies. It is a wonder, of course, that the philosophy that Plato produced in the process is an unprecedented human achievement that many, including myself, find to be central to our attempts to make sense of ourselves and the way things are in this world that we share. But, it is no wonder, really, that Plato chose to relive the years leading up to these catastrophes—that he interrogated history and his capacious imagination for causes and reasons.

When the Athenians, with a little help from the Plateians, won the Battle of Marathon, "how did we do that?" became the question implicit in every political and cultural project they undertook. There was, after all, absolutely no obvious reason for a little polis to have been able to turn back the army of the Great King. Was it Miltiades' tactical genius that accounted for the win? The discipline of the hoplites who enacted his double pincer maneuver? The prudence of the other generals who gave Miltiades the command out of turn that day? Was it the grace of the gods? Did it have anything to do with the Athenians' weird and distinctive political system?

Each question generated a theory of Athens. And each theory implied a course of action for preparing for the Persians' next, seemingly inevitable, attack. If Miltiades' genius was the key, then Athens needed both to honor Miltiades above all other men and to do whatever it could to cultivate more men in his image. Was military discipline the answer? Then military institutions would need to be affirmed and supported, perhaps expanded. If the generals' prudence was the key, then character education and institutional affirmation of prudential living should be a priority. If the gods deserved credit, then the religious life of the city should be beefed up. And if the Athenians were to credit their victory to their unique political system, then it was time to double down on democracy.[1]

All of this paints with too broad a brush of course, but one can learn a great deal by looking at the rise and demise of Classical Athens as a series of questions about the mysterious success at Marathon and by the various cultural and institutional developments that functioned as hypothetical answers to those questions. At least in the literature of classical Athens that has survived to this day, this is particularly true when we focus specifically on Athenian Democracy. Other Greek speaking cities could claim to have great leaders, be more devout, be better at education, etc., but no one else governed themselves the way the Athenians did. If one was looking for something distinctively Athenian that might explain their capacity to do something no one else thought possible, then democratic governance had to be in contention, at least.

As Plato reconstructs the attitudes of Greek-speaking people before and during the Peloponnesian War, the powers and dangers of democracy are never far from the center of his interlocutors' concerns. Why would one risk the inefficiencies and instabilities of shared democratic governance? What are the alternatives? What are the benefits that could justify those risks? What sorts of institutions

---

[1] One of the clearest expressions of this line of questioning comes in Aristophanes' *Clouds*, where the old *nomoi* of Athens defend themselves against the new *nomoi* by saying they were the *nomoi* that won at Marathon.

would be necessary for democratic governance to work? What sort of people would be capable of sharing in democratic governance? What sort of an education system would support the cultivation of such character? Where could it go wrong? What could be done? These questions are not just interesting in historical terms. When they are translated into the post-socratic world that Plato and the rest of us live in, the questions are not how democracy might go wrong, but how did it go wrong, and how we can avoid making mistakes like the ones that led to the defeat of the Athenian military and the implosion of its political system.

As many of the authors in this volume point out, Plato's critique of tyranny is not also a celebration of liberty. His account does not fall into the categories that seem so clearly to be in binary opposition in contemporary political discourse. For Plato, tyranny is terrible, but so is liberty. Politically, the very recent reign of the Thirty Tyrants in Athens was proof positive of the horrors of being subject to a ruler whose interests had nothing to do with the common good, so the threats of tyranny are real and present. And on a psychological level, Plato's Socrates argues that tyranny is the worst state a soul can be in—a cannibalistic arrangement of animating principles that undermines itself, causing dissipation, self-delusion, and misery.

But, a love of liberty does not seem to be much better for Plato, either politically or psychologically, and not just because liberty opens the door to tyranny. To want what one wants when one wants it is just one small step away from indenturing oneself to a particular desire, compulsion, or addiction, but it is also itself a miserable state of dissipation. The democratic soul is a jack of all trades and master of none. Its inner conflict is fueled by its capacity to be many things, to be unable to choose between them, and always to be aware of how much more accomplished it would be if it could focus. And, politically, Plato's depiction of the democratic institutionalizations of liberty (in *Republic* Book 6, for example) is a terrifying drama of mobs moving randomly and violently, corrupting or destroying virtue wherever they find it—not just failing to choose a focused path through life, but villainizing those who do. To be ignored seems to be the virtuous person's only hope in a democracy.

Plato's Athens existed in what we now know was a tiny historical space of self-determination between the loss of sovereignty to the Spartans in the Peloponnesian War and the loss of sovereignty to Alexander only a few decades later. The Athenian democratic experiment was still alive and, although the execution of Socrates pointed to the likelihood that it was doomed to be unjust, it still seemed to be better than any other present options. In theory, there were several modes of government superior to Democracy; but in practice, especially perhaps for the Athenians, there seemed to be no practicable alternative. Plato was not just a commentator on his own cultural moment, of course, but he did have an audience and we ignore it at our peril. As a philosopher, he pointed to the highest set of possibilities for human beings, including what that might entail for societies and polities. But, as a political theorist, he also wrote to those who might take Athens from where it was, in a dysfunctional and corrupt direct democracy, to where it might actually be able to go. If one could not hope for Athens to become a polity that cultivated virtue, perhaps one could at least hope for a regime that did not squash it.

When one attempts to interpret Plato, reductionism is one of the most serious mistakes one can make. Plato is legion. That legion may all be marching in the same direction with the same ultimate goals in mind (that is certainly my view), but Plato is always doing many things at once. If one thinks that one has found an argumentative thread that is more important than all the others, then one is probably wrong, or at least not right for all times and circumstances. And if one thinks that one has found the thread that refutes all the others, then one is certainly wrong. This is a key principle to have in mind when thinking through what it means to situate Plato's argument in the Athens of his day. There's a deep spring of thought in his writings that hopes for a better world, a world in which the present alternatives were not the only ones. A world in which a person who was committed first and foremost to the good could also hope to have political influence.

When one looks at Plato with a sort of binocular vision, one can see, I think, a version of liberty that Plato not only views positively, but that he presents as a necessary condition for the possibility of living one's best life. In order to see this choice-worthy mode of liberty, one must hold in view at the same time the horrors of Athenian libertinism and the wonders of Socrates' independence within it. One must hold the marvelous thought that Socrates was a product of Athens and that he refused to leave, while at the same time holding in mind the thought that the same city killed him. One can, of course, avoid the paradox by claiming that the Athens that produced Socrates and the Athens that killed him were fundamentally different, but Plato seems to do all he can to block that exit from the dilemma.

In the cosmos that Plato creates within the Socratic dialogues, Athens' dysfunctional political liberty is the assumed starting point for the development of Socratic political liberty. In other worlds at other times, or perhaps in the history or future of our world, a philosopher could emerge from a different political landscape. But, in the world that Plato gives us, there is only one way, and Socrates tries over and over again in the dialogues to illuminate it for his interlocutors and for us. A necessary step on that narrow path is extricating oneself from the authority of convention. If one is subject to convention in Athens, then one is at the mercy of the mob. (Being subject to convention in Sparta or Corinth, for example, would manifest itself differently, and would pose different impediments to philosophical education and political justice.) In order to open oneself to a higher authority (e.g., justice or the good), one first must liberate oneself from the mob. This is real liberty, and it is a precondition for every good thing that follows from it.

Bad things can follow from good ones, though. Liberating oneself from the mob is a necessary but insufficient cause for philosophical education. One who is liberated from convention can stall in that moment and never escape the condition of being free from authority. This might make one an iconoclast—one who knows how to reject things and tear them down, but has no capacity for affirmation or to be constructive. Or, one might become an ancient *iditotes*—one who is removed from the concerns of the city and mindful only of private, present, and individual concerns. This might also make one a tyrant—one who is willing to subject everyone and everything to one's private concerns.

Plato critiques all forms of libertinism and, with it, those who pursue or value liberty as an end in itself. But, rejecting liberty as an end is very different from rejecting liberty full stop. Socrates, in fact, does the opposite in the dialogues. He does everything in his power to liberate his spirited interlocutors from convention and to hold up images of what might be possible for them, individually and politically, if they use that liberty to choose the good.

For that rare (perhaps unique) person who manages to create a life that is free from all authority save the good, there is another sort of liberty promised. Whether you look to the Myth of Er at the end of the *Republic* or Diotima's speech at the end of the *Symposium* or the myth of the Charioteers in the *Phaedrus*, or a dozen other places in his corpus, Plato offers image after image of the pay-off of a philosophical life: the unique capacity—the liberty—to be fully human, to flourish, to be well and joyful.

This volume anthologizes essays adapted from the 2019 A. V. Elliott Conference on Great Books and Ideas, sponsored by the McDonald Center at Mercer University. The Thomas C. and Ramona E. McDonald Center for America's Founding Principles exists to supplement Mercer University's excellent liberal arts program with a redoubled commitment to the foundational texts and ideas that have shaped Western Civilization and the American political order. Our 2019 conference on the theme "Liberty and Tyranny in Plato" brought together eleven philosophers and political theorists from all over the United States and gave them free reign to explore our theme in any part of the Platonic corpus. These papers began as presentations at that conference.

Our first essay, entitled "Plato on the Connection between Liberty and Tyranny," is by Catherine Zuckert. Professor Zuckert looks to the *Republic* and *Gorgias* and shows that Socrates offers a strong critique not just of tyranny, but of liberty as well. The love of liberty is a form of selfishness, on her reading, and "free politics" is collectivized selfishness. She argues that the opposite of tyranny in these platonic dialogues is not liberty, but philosophy.

In "The Socratic Turn to Alcibiades," Alex Priou takes us back to some of the earliest dialogues in the dramatic ordering, the *Alicibiades*, *Protagoras*, and *Second Alcibiades*. Professor Priou focuses on Plato's presentation of Alcibiades as a man thoroughly convinced of his self-sufficiency and of Socrates as one who is committed to systematically dismantling each of Alcibiades's misconceptions. Collectively, these conversations display the myriad ways that human beings understand themselves to be self-sufficient and Plato's arguments for why each of those modes is a different form of misunderstanding.

Nicholas D. Smith goes straight to the heart of one of Plato's most prevalent themes in the dialogues with his piece, "Pity the Tyrant." Professor Smith focuses on the *Republic*, and takes up the paradigm case of the Socratic argument that it is worse to do harm than to suffer it: the tyrant. The tyrant believes that freedom from constraint and authority is choice-worthy, but Plato argues that it is, on the contrary, the most lamentable of human situations. Like Professor Zuckert, Smith argues that there is no explicit account of true liberty in the Platonic corpus. Instead, we get interlocutor after interlocutor enamored of some false promise or corrupted condition. True Platonic liberty, he argues, is self-restraint; and accounts of it can only be discerned indirectly.

Richard Ruderman pushes us deeper into an understanding of how a noble soul could be drawn to a tyrannical life in "Plato on the Tyrannical Temptation." Professor Ruderman highlights the fact that philosophy and tyranny are both beyond the law and that one who is drawn to the former necessarily opens oneself up to the allures of the latter. Both the tyrant and the philosopher seek to be liberated from conventional authority, but the philosopher desires to be ruled by genuine necessity, and the tyrant does not.

Devin Stauffer turns his focus to the moral psychology of the *Republic* and the ways that liberty and tyranny appear when one focuses one's reading on that level of Platonic discourse. In "The Myth of the Tripartite Soul in Plato's *Republic*," he argues that the tyrannical soul is a slave to its desires, not their master. The tyrant's misunderstanding of liberty leads him into the worst form of bondage. Stauffer is in agreement with other contributors to this volume that Plato does not offer an explicit argument for what true liberty would look like in the *Republic*, and this holds for psychological as well as political readings of the text. But, he suggests provocatively near the end of his essay, Socratic critiques of *eros* should be taken with a grain of salt.

In " Socrates' Critique of Homer's Education in the *Republic*," Peter Ahrensdorf invites us to focus on Socrates as a moral exemplar, both in terms of his speeches and in his actions as portrayed by Plato's dramatic framing and character development. Professor Ahrensdorf argues that Homeric and Socratic education share the goal of teaching one to overcome the fear of death, but the Socratic model emerges as a critique of the Homeric educational model which it portrays as a failure. Socrates' actions in the *Apology* and *Phaedo*, in particular, and his arguments in the *Phaedrus* and *Republic* all chart a course for a human being to liberate oneself from the fear of death and shape up one's life in the new space created by that liberation. Freeing oneself from the fear of death is not, on Professor Ahrensdorf's account, the proper end of a flourishing human life, but it is a necessary condition for pursuing the highest possible modes of human life.

Mary Townsend's "Sophistry, Rhetoric, and the Crimes of Women: Plato's *Gorgias* and *Protagoras*, on Female Injustice" brings into sharp focus the tension between the portrayal of the situation of women in the Platonic corpus and the portrayal of the Athenian laws pertaining to women. Women present a difficult set of issues for Plato's Socrates in part because they call into question deep-seated conventions that purport to be, but certainly all aren't, grounded in nature. The question of the nature of women and of their status under the law pushes Socrates into some of the most controversial and important conversations Plato presents. Socrates doesn't offer an answer to the "woman question writ large" in these dialogues, according to Professor Townsend, but they point clearly to the need for an solution better than the one provided by Athenian Law.

In "Notes on the Character of Callicles," Kevin Honeycutt shines a bright light on Socrates' central interlocutor in the *Gorgias*. We know far less about Callicles than we do about most of Socrates' other interlocutors. Plato's text offers a variety of clues about his character, however, and Professor Honeycutt interrogates them carefully. In particular, he looks at four things Plato tells us about Callicles in the *Gorgias*: (1) his deme, (2) his clan, (3) his known associates, and (4) his misquotation of Pindar. Honeycutt then considers Callicles' contributions to the dialogue in light of this context. In word and character, Callicles emerges as an important model of a tyrannical life for Plato—a living, breathing model of the mode of life Socrates spends so much of his energy encouraging his interlocutors to shun.

Jeffrey Dirk Wilson's "*Gorgias* as Reductio ad Absurdum Argument: Socrates, True Politician but Failed Teacher?" focuses on Plato's portrayal of Socrates in the *Gorgias*, with a particular focus on Socrates' failure as a teacher. If one of Socrates' central goals was to turn his interlocutors from tyranny to philosophy and thus, perhaps, also to reform Athenian politics, then the dialogues can be read as a long train of failures. But, Professor Wilson pushes this point further by portraying Socrates' failures as failures of reason itself. Rational argument is insufficient for the task of turning a would-be tyrant to philosophy. One needs to appeal to a non-rational faculty, namely the human imagination. For that, one needs a myth. And, of course, Socrates tells important myths at key moments of many dialogues. Professor Wilson unpacks the importance of mythology for Socratic education in the *Gorgias* and elsewhere in the Platonic corpus.

Khalil Habib brings Plato's teaching in the *Republic* into the modern world by putting it in conversation with Machiavelli's *Mandragola*. The *Republic* and the *Mandragola* both offer very different images of the family, and they level very different critiques of those conceptions. But, both critiques point to the differences between family life and a philosophical life and, by implication, recommend the latter. Professor Habib argues that Plato's vision of the philosophical life comes into sharper relief when we hold Plato and Machiavelli's critiques of the family in mind together.

In "The Worst and the Less Humane Way: The Platonic Condemnation of a Criminal Justice System Like Ours," Jennifer Baker takes on one of the most pressing concerns of contemporary American political life, the patent injustices institutionalized by our criminal justice system, especially in terms of racial bias. Professor Baker argues that one of the reasons criminal justice reform seems so intractable is that social contractarian ethical assumptions underlie our conception of what it means to be a criminal. Plato portrays criminals in a fundamentally different way. She argues that reconceiving criminality according to a conception derived from Plato's dialogues could illuminate a path forward for real reform.

Collectively, these essays take us from the most fine-grained analysis of Platonic philosophy imaginable to attempts to apply Platonic ideas to social and legal problems that vex contemporary policy makers. They look at tyranny and liberty and philosophy from eleven distinct and ingenious perspectives. I am greatly in our authors' debt for their contributions for clarifying my understanding of Plato in myriad and significant ways, and I believe you will be, too, by the time you make it through this volume. My thanks go out to them for their beautiful work and to you, our readers, for your attention to it.

PLATO ON THE CONNECTION BETWEEN LIBERTY AND TYRANNY

Catherine Zuckert

When I began reflecting on the topic of this volume, "Plato on Liberty and Tyranny," I realized with a bit of surprise that Plato seems to have much more to say about the evils of tyranny than he does about the benefits of liberty. Indeed, one might even argue that he does not think that liberty per se is good at all.

We tend to think that liberty is good and that its polar opposite is tyranny. As Mogens Herman Hansen argues, most of Plato's Athenian readers would have held the same essentially democratic view.[1] Nevertheless, in his *Gorgias* and *Republic,* Plato suggests, on the contrary, that it is the desire to be perfectly free from all legal or conventional restraints that leads human beings to want to become tyrants.[2] That is the Platonic contention I propose to investigate further in this essay. One of the great benefits of studying Plato, I believe, is that way in which his works challenge current beliefs.[3]

---

[1] As Mogens Herman Hansen, "Democratic Freedom and the Concept of Freedom in Plato and Aristotle," *Greek, Roman, and Byzantine Studies* 50 (1984): 1–27, points out, the ancient Greeks generally understood liberty in opposition to slavery. As a result, "*eleutheria* was regularly invoked as a basic democratic ideal in debates that contrasted democracy and tyranny. The opposite of this form of *eleutheria* was being enslaved in a metaphorical sense, i.e., being subjected to a despotic ruler" (3).

[2] As Malcolm Scofield, *Plato: Political Philosophy* (Oxford: Oxford University Press, 2006), observes, in the *Republic* Plato does not "accord any explicit recognition to freedom as a fundamental value to be built into the basic design of the *politeia* of the good city" (81).

[3] Believing that liberty is good, but recognizing that Plato does not endorse a modern notion of personal liberty, commentators such as R. F. Stalley, "Plato's Doctrine of Freedom," *Proceedings of the Aristotelian Society*, New Series, Vol. 98 (145–58), Peter Critchley, *The Rational Freedom of Plato and Aristotle* (2001), http://mmu.academia.edu, and Carl Young, "Plato's Concept of Liberty in the *Laws*," *History of Political Thought* 39 (2018): 379–98, seek to extend what Hansen

calls the metaphorical use of "freedom" to the self-control rational human beings or philosophers achieve that enables them to avoid being slaves to their desires. However, in order to extend Plato's understanding of "freedom" to self-control, these commentators have to derive their "concepts" from "themes" in the dialogues, because Plato himself never calls the rule of reason, liberty or freedom. And as Hansen points out, self-rule is still a form of rule or domination. So is the rule of law. Siobhán McLoughlin, "The Freedom of the Good: A Study of Plato's Ethical Conception of Freedom" [2012], https://digitalreposi-tory.unm.edu/phil_etds/15), thus argues that Plato had an "ethical" rather than a "political" understanding of freedom, because he suggests that rational human beings or philosophers achieve a degree of self-control that enables them to avoid becoming slaves to their desires. Likewise, Fred D. Miller, Jr., "Platonic Freedom," in *The Oxford Handbook of Freedom, ed.* David Schmidtz and Carmen E. Pavel (Oxford: Oxford Handbooks Online, 2018*)*, suggests that Plato presents an "aristocratic" conception of freedom in the *Republic* "as the rule of reason over the soul unimpeded by desires," and in the *Laws* where aristocratic freedom entails "willing enslavement to the laws." But both these commentators confront the same basic terminological or textual difficulty. They import and impose terms (and thus concepts) on Plato that Plato himself does not use. As André Laks, "Freedom, Liberality, and Liberty in Plato's *Laws,*" *Social Philosophy and Policy* 24, no. 2 (2007), notes: "Self-mastery does indeed play an important role in Plato's thought. In Plato, however, self-mastery is connected with virtue, rather than with freedom. Indeed, Plato hardly uses the term *eleutheros* and kindred terms when discussing self-mastery or free choice ("liberty")" (133). In Plato's *Laws*, Laks argues, freedom "is neither an independent nor an absolute end. Essential to Plato's project, rather, is that man be a slave (namely to the law), even if he should be a "voluntary slave." As we know, Rousseau and Kant redefined "freedom" in terms of obedience to the law, and this is a conceptual move that Plato could certainly have entertained. He did not, however. This may have something to do with the fact that. . . [Plato thought] "liberty,"…is always prone to become excessive" (143). Laks himself finds two and a half kinds of freedoms in Plato's *Laws*. "There is, first, the constitutional meaning of freedom, which is put to work in Book 3 (and only there) in order to analyze moderately good as well as degenerate forms of historical constitutions. Strikingly enough, this freedom does not play any subsequent role in the shaping of the Platonic constitution itself…There is, second, scattered throughout the *Laws,* the behavioral meaning of 'freedom,' according to which the citizens of Magnesia, who are free in the sense that they are free men, are supposed to behave as such and to be educated accordingly, that is, as 'gentlemen.'…The striking and philosophically interesting fact, however, is that there appear to be no intrinsic or substantial links for Plato between freedom and rationality, as we might expect on the basis of philosophical assumptions whereby freedom is grounded on rationality. Rather, freedom is the condition for

Why the Desire to Be Free Leads Individuals to Become Tyrants

Because the question Socrates asks Gorgias of Leontini at the beginning of the dialogue concerns the power of rhetoric (447c), most commentators have treated the *Gorgias* primarily in terms of what it shows about the power (*dúnamis*) of rhetoric and whether it actually constitutes an art (*technê*).[4] Some commentators have brought out the connection between the use of rhetoric in acquiring political power (especially in a democracy) and tyranny, a connection Socrates also draws in the *Republic*.[5] Only one has observed that all three of the individuals Socrates examines in the *Gorgias* respond to his question about the power (and hence the utility of learning rhetoric) by claiming that learning rhetoric will enable a man to attain or preserve his liberty.[6] Each of these interlocutors presents a somewhat different understanding of the character of the liberty that is so attained and preserved, but Socrates criticizes them all. He argues not only that rhetoric does not have the power claimed for it, but also

---

exercising rationality, because this exercise takes time, and thus requires leisure (*skhole*) from all other tasks, and this is precisely because the exercise of rationality is such a time consuming task. Finally,…in the *Laws*, Plato does on one occasion use the word *eleutheros* to describe self-mastery—something he never did in the *Republic*" (635c–d). However, Laks suggests that the Athenian Stranger's suggestion that a legislator must train citizens to control their pleasures makes "freedom" something negative, to be free from enslavement to the attraction of pleasure, more than a positive quality or good.

[4] E.g., Terence Irwin, *Plato: Gorgias* (Oxford: Oxford University Press, 1979); David Roochnik, *Of Art and Wisdom: Plato's Understanding of Techne* (University Park, PA: Penn State University Press, 1998), 179–231.

[5] E.g., W. R. Newell, *Ruling Passion: The Erotics of Statecraft in Platonic Political Philosophy* (Lanham, MD: Rowman & Littlefield, 2000). Newell argues that the desire to acquire complete or tyrannical political power depicted in the *Gorgias* and *Republic* grows out of a thumotic desire for honor that Plato shows in the *Symposium* can and should be sublimated into an erotic search for wisdom. However, Newell does not connect that desire to liberty.

[6] Arlene W. Saxonhouse, "Freedom, Tyranny and the Political Man: Plato's *Republic* and *Gorgias*, a Study in Contrasts," in Ryan K. Balot, ed., *A Companion to Greek and Roman Political Thought* (London: Blackwell Publishing, 2009), 353–66.

that the securing of liberty as it is understood by any and all of his interlocutors is not a worthy or, in fact, realizable goal. As a goal, "freedom" is an abstraction. What people seek is to be free from the constraints—natural, moral, legal, and political—they think prevent them from getting what they want. They call what they want "good," but if they do not know what is truly good, removing the constraints on their actions will not enable them to achieve what they really desire. Removing the constraints on their actions may, indeed, make it impossible for them to achieve even what they erroneously believe is good.

In the *Gorgias* Plato leads his readers to suspect the integrity of both the rhetorician and his art from the beginning by reporting that Gorgias initially responds to Socrates' questions about the power of his art and what he teaches, by rather coyly, stating simply that rhetoric is about speeches or arguments. (449e) A reader might defend Gorgias by observing that Socrates characteristically urged the rhetorician to keep his answers short—and Gorgias responded by bragging that no one could do that better than he. (449c) But Plato also shows that Socrates prodded Gorgias to give a fuller answer by questioning him further. And we begin to see the reasons that Gorgias might not have answered fully and straightforwardly at first when he finally declares that his art concerns the greatest good for human beings. It enables a rhetorician both to be free himself and at the same time to rule over others in his own city by persuading political assemblies and judges in law courts to do whatever he advocates (452d-e). Gorgias goes even further when he brags that his art gives its practitioners that power without having to obtain expert knowledge of any of the substantive matters under discussion.[7]

---

[7] Saxonhouse, "Freedom," suggests that "Gorgias imagines that this power will be used for benign purposes" (357), even though she also observes that "for Gorgias freedom refers not to the individual unburdened by the control of others, but rather entails rule over others…[when he] explains that the freedom enjoyed by one skilled in the art of rhetoric comes from knowing how to enslave others, to make of them, as he says explicitly, a slave (*doulon*)" (357). As Devin Stauffer, *The Unity of Plato's* Gorgias (Cambridge: Cambridge University Press, 2006), 23–24, sees, the extreme brevity of Gorgias's initial answers indicates his

Rhetoric appears, indeed, to be a substitute for all other forms of knowledge *and* more easily obtained (455d-456c, 459c).

Socrates brings out the problematic character of Gorgias's claim by reminding him that some of the young Athenians listening to their conversation might want to become his students. That reminder first leads Gorgias to exaggerate the power of his art in persuading ignorant people who do not know any better to do as he says. However, Socrates then forces Gorgias to admit that a rhetorician could not persuade an expert who knows what he is talking about (459a). Second, and more significant, Socrates' reminding Gorgias that the topic of political debates generally speaking is what is just or unjust leads Gorgias to see that he may have put himself in a dangerous position. In describing the power of his art, Gorgias had in effect claimed that he could teach anyone who so desires how to persuade the Athenians not merely to elect him as their leader or commander, like Pericles, but to do as he wishes. More bluntly stated, Gorgias claimed the ability to teach anyone willing to pay him how to transform a democracy into a tyranny. Gorgias is a foreigner, and he knows that people generally do not trust foreigners. He implicitly acknowledged that fact when he claimed that a master rhetorician would rule his own city, not any or all cities. If he attracts a young ambitious Athenian student who subsequently uses the rhetorical skills he learned from Gorgias in an attempt to overthrow the democracy, the rhetorician understands, he may be blamed. Having emphasized the great power of his art, Gorgias thus quickly adds that the teacher should not be blamed if a student misuses it (456c–457c). Socrates then asks: since most of the political debates through which a rhetorician acquires influence concern what is just and unjust, will Gorgias teach a student what is just, if that student does not know (459d–460a)? Gorgias is either ashamed or afraid to say that he will not.

Polus objects that Socrates has shamed Gorgias into contradicting himself by promising to teach anyone who does not know what

---

understanding that the power or effect of rhetoric on its listeners could be seen as problematic before Socrates points out the ways in which it is.

is just; Socrates has not shown that rhetoric lacks the power Gorgias claimed for it.[8] But Polus misses the point implicit in the exchange. By reminding Gorgias that he is a foreigner, Socrates pointed to an important condition or limitation of persuasive speech. As Aristotle emphasizes in his *Rhetoric* (1356a4), impressions people have of the character of the speaker affect their willingness to listen and believe him as much, if not more than his words. They follow the advice only of someone they trust. That means they will heed and be convinced only by someone they believe is dedicated to the common good, that is, someone they believe is just.

Socrates responds to Polus' objection by inviting him to investigate the question further with him—but only if Polus is willing to keep his answers short. "Won't I be allowed to say as much as I wish?" Polus protests (461d). Socrates acknowledges that Polus would suffer something terrible if he came to Athens where there is more freedom to speak than anywhere else in Greece, and he alone was denied that freedom. Polus would, in a word, suffer something unjust. However, Socrates adds, he also would suffer something terrible if he were not free to go away and not listen. Granting freedom to one requires recognizing the freedom of others. In other words, considerations of freedom are inseparable from considerations of justice.

Gorgias bragged that learning the art of rhetoric would enable an individual to be free himself and to become ruler in his city. The individual would become free by means of his ability to persuade and thus to rule others. The kind of rule Gorgias appeared to envision is gentle insofar as it is attained by means of persuasion and not by force. However, insofar as the art of persuasion enables its possessor to attain freedom for himself by ruling others—without possessing any other knowledge—it clearly enables a rhetorician to mislead as well as to lead or rule. That ability to mislead or deceive is what makes the power of rhetoric problematic.

---

[8] In a later conversation with Meno, Gorgias thus drops the claim to teach anyone to be virtuous (which would include justice) and states that he simply teachers rhetoric (*Meno* 95c).

Polus explicitly reveals the dirty underbelly—or nasty implications—of Gorgias' claim about the power of his art in responding to Socrates' contention not merely that rhetoric is not an art or *technê*, but, even more provocatively, that rhetoric does not have any power at all. According to Socrates, rhetoric is merely a form of flattery, learned through experience. It is not knowledge properly speaking, because it cannot explain the cause of its effects. "Do good rhetors seem to be esteemed merely as lowly flatterers?" Polus asks. "Do they not have the greatest power?...Do they not, *just like tyrants*, kill whomever they wish, and confiscate possessions, and expel from the cities whomever it seems good them?" (466a–c). The power Polus admires and believes that all other people envy clearly involves physical coercion as much, if not more than persuasion. But Plato brings out the connection between Polus's admiration for tyranny and rhetoric when Socrates observes that anyone has the power to kill another or take his goods, and Polus points out that "it is necessary for someone who acts in this manner to pay a penalty" (470a). For Polus the use and power of rhetoric does not consist primarily in the ability to persuade others deliberating about what policies and laws they should adopt; it consists more in the forensic or defensive skill that enables a criminal to escape punishment for doing what is forbidden by law by persuading the judges either that he is innocent or that he was right to act as he did. If people did not want to murder and steal from others, Polus suggests, there would be no need for laws prohibiting and punishing such deeds. Because people would like to commit such crimes, if they could get away with them without suffering a penalty, they envy tyrants like Archelaus who dare to seize power by murdering their lawful rulers, masters, and relatives.

Socrates responds to Polus's contention that everyone wants to be a tyrant with the power to do whatever he or she wishes, free from any legal (or, we might add, moral and religious) restraints by insisting that what everyone wants is what is good for him or her (466d–468e). He thus points out the difficulty or problem with speaking simply in terms of "power" (as many students of politics to this day continue to do). The question is or ought to be: power to do what? If the end or goal is happiness, Socrates suggests, that end cannot be achieved by obtaining tyrannical power. Tyrants are miserable for reasons Socrates lays out more fully in the *Republic* (to which I will turn later in this essay). Here, Plato shows Polus dismisses Socrates' objection as disingenuous. People do not merely fear tyrants, Polus objects; they admire and envy them. Anyone who could obtain the power of a tyrant would do so. As a rhetorician, Plato shows, Polus considers public opinion to be definitive. But as Socrates points out, human beings admire not merely different, but contradictory things and qualities. Like all animals, human beings are attracted by what is pleasant and seek to avoid pain. Human beings can often be observed to endure pain, however, in order to appear—or even really be—noble rather than base. It is not possible, therefore, simply to follow what "everyone" thinks and achieve happiness, because common opinions are contradictory.

Socrates' point is not merely the importance of not holding contradictory opinions for the sake of logical consistency; he is pointing instead to the impossibility of achieving contradictory goals or desires that lead human beings to act in opposed and thus necessarily self-defeating ways. So long as human beings hold contradictory opinions about what is good and will make them happy, they will not be able to achieve either. They thus need to examine their opinions critically, the way he does.

Rather than rule by shaping or manipulating public opinion about what is good, noble, and just, Plato shows, rhetoricians like Polus appeal to established views and widespread desires. Such rhetoricians are thus followers or servants instead of leaders or liberators. They cannot and do not even try to teach those who listen to their speeches what is truly good, noble, and just, because they themselves do not know. They do not even recognize that they lack such knowledge and need to acquire it.

Callicles jumps into the conversation at this point and accuses Socrates of being a "popular speaker" (482c). The philosopher had been arguing with Polus on the basis of popular opinion, according to which it is bad to suffer injustice, because it is painful, but it is more shameful and thus worse to do injustice than to suffer it. Public opinion is the only authority Polus seems to recognize; but, Callicles charges, Socrates has treated Polus the same way he treated Gorgias by showing that the young rhetorician holds contradictory opinions and thus shaming him. Like Gorgias, Callicles contends, Polus was ashamed to say what he really thought, which is that it is always worse to suffer injustice than to do it (482e).

Callicles acknowledges that it is conventionally or customarily said to be more shameful to do injustice that to suffer it, but he affirms that, according to nature, it is always worse to suffer injustice. And he accuses Socrates of arguing deceitfully and unjustly by shifting back and forth between what is true, according to nature, and what is only conventionally thought or said to be noble and just (483a).

Like Plato's brother Glaucon in the *Republic* (358c–359d), Callicles asserts that laws are made by the weak to protect themselves from the strong, and that the weak persuade the strong to obey them by praising what is to their advantage and blaming the more powerful for seizing more for themselves (483a–484c). Like Glaucon, Callicles thus appears to be openly and indecently arguing in favor of tyranny (although unlike Glaucon, Callicles does not make the argument in the hope, if not expectation that Socrates will refute it). Also like Glaucon, Callicles suggests that the natural right of the stronger (κρειττω) or better (αμεινων) does not arise merely from their having greater physical force, ruthlessness, and cunning. It is a product of their virtue understood as the qualities that make men free.[9] Callicles' position does not, therefore, seem to be as vicious or indecent as it first appears.

Callicles goes on to explain that he considers a man who does not engage in philosophy as a youth to be illiberal. Without having studied philosophy, no one would or could distinguish between what

---

[9] In the transcript of his course, *Introduction to Political Philosophy,* at the University of Chicago, Winter Term 1965, Session 11, 100–111, Leo Strauss observes that the ancient Greeks understood freedom to be a privilege belonging to the non-slave inhabitants of a city; they did not consider freedom to be a natural right.

is right by nature and what is right merely by convention the way Callicles has. However, Callicles insists, when a youth matures, he needs to turn his attention to the things that will make him well-regarded, noble, and just. He needs to concern himself with the laws of the city and learn about human pleasures and desires so that he can talk to others both in public and private. If, like Socrates, he persists in philosophizing in private with a few youths, he deserves a beating (484c–485e). Ironically and apparently unknowingly, Callicles thus adopts the position Socrates had urged in his exchange with Polus: if one perceives himself or a loved one to be acting incorrectly, he should not merely criticize himself or his beloved; he should do everything in his power to see that the malefactor is corrected, which is to say, punished.

As a fellow Athenian, Callicles claims to be Socrates's friend. And he asks: Doesn't it seem shameful to you, Socrates, to be unable to defend yourself, if some base person were to accuse you unjustly in court and demand the death penalty after you were convicted (486a)? As all of Plato's readers would know, Socrates was so accused and condemned.[10]

---

[10] Stauffer, *Unity*, argues that this is the reason Plato shows Socrates specifically going to ask the rhetorician what the power of his art is. That is, Socrates may have approached Gorgias in order to learn how he could save himself by speaking persuasively in a possible future trial. However, in the dialogue, Socrates denies that he could or would have saved himself by learning rhetoric. He maintains that rhetoric is merely flattery—in this case flattery of the *demos*—and argues that such flattery as practiced by famous Athenian politicians such as Pericles made the Athenian people more aggressive and unjust. (Insofar as a rhetorician seeks to persuade an audience by convincing them what he says is good and just he implicitly flatters them by suggesting that they know and can therefore judge what is good, noble, and just.) Plato presents an "apology" or defense of Socrates in his *Apology of Socrates, Crito,* and *Phaedo.* And in the defense speech Plato attributes to Socrates, the philosopher emphasizes that he is giving it because he is required to do so by law. He expects to be convicted, even though he claims to be just, pious, courageous, and wise. The only law he will not obey is one that would forbid him from philosophizing, which he depicts as an attempt to improve his fellow citizens by interrogating and refuting their claims to be wise and just. He explicitly refuses to appeal to the passions of the jurors, particularly to the pity they might feel for him as an old man or the suffering his family might experience

Unlike Gorgias and Polus, Callicles does not urge Socrates to study rhetoric and engage in political activity in order to become free to do whatever he wishes. Like Polus, Callicles understands the function not merely of rhetoric, but of political activity more generally to be defensive. A free man, as Callicles conceives him, needs to study philosophy as a youth, because he needs to be able to think for himself; he does not merely follow the opinions of others or abide by conventions. As an adult, however, a free man must turn his attention to public affairs in order to experience and thus gain knowledge of the passions and opinions of others so that he can learn how to speak persuasively in assemblies and in court, and thus become able to defend himself and those he loves from unjust aggressors.

Socrates first attacks Callicles' apparently indecent contention that the strong have a right to rule the weaker by asking, strong in what respect? Because large numbers of men are clearly stronger than any individual, Callicles' principle would seem to justify rule by the weak—and thus democratically made laws. Callicles emphatically denies that he means physical strength, however; by the strongest, superior, and best, he means the most prudent and courageous (491a–b). He asserts, moreover, that it is right not only for them to rule, but also for them to have more. More of what, Socrates asks. After Callicles contemptuously responds, not of good or drink or clothes, but of wealth and rule, Socrates inquires whether such persons do not need to be able to control or rule themselves, that is, to be just and moderate. Callicles emphatically denies it; the superior people he has in mind are characterized by having the greatest desires. Won't they experience more difficulty in satisfying those desires, Socrates asks. No, Callicles responds; "luxury, intemperance, and freedom" are the definition of human excellence and happiness (492c). However, when Socrates asks whether Callicles considers all

---

as a result of his death, because that would amount to an attempt to corrupt them by urging them to ignore the oaths they have taken to the gods to decide what is legal and just. As Plato shows, Socrates did not convince a majority of the jurors not to convict him.

desires and pleasures to be equally praiseworthy, the young man flinches at the example of boys who accept male lovers. And after Socrates presses him on the fact that the exercise of courage is not always or even usually pleasant, he declares: "As if you thought that I or any other human being did not consider some pleasures better and others worse!" (499b).

Although he initially suggested that he would not be shamed the way Gorgias and Polus were, Callicles reacts vehemently to Socrates' showing that he holds contradictory opinions and wants to end the conversation. He embodies whatever it is that makes human beings resistant to the discipline of reason.

Callicles nevertheless initially agrees to continue answering Socrates' questions in order to gratify Gorgias; but after Socrates leads him through an argument showing that it is better to be punished or corrected than to remain intemperate and unjust, Callicles refuses to go on any further and insists that Socrates present the argument himself. Unlike Callicles, Gorgias is very interested in pursuing the question of the power and limits of *logos,* so he asks Socrates to continue.[11] Inviting Callicles to interrupt him if and when he wishes, Socrates first maintains that, as Callicles has just admitted, pleasure and the good are not the same. Socrates then asserts that the good of anything consists in a certain order, and that in human beings, the order of individual souls consists in moderation. Moderate, self-controlled human beings do what is fitting; they are, therefore, courageous, because they flee what should be fled and do not flee what they should not. For the same reason, moderate, self-controlled human beings are also just and pious, good, noble, blessed and happy (506c–507c). Socrates acknowledges that it would be best if human beings did not need punishment or correction, but, he insists, it is better to be corrected than to remain in error (508b–c).

---

[11] In his *Encomium on Helen,* the historical Gorgias attributed an almost unlimited persuasive power to *logos.* Scholars have since debated whether this was Gorgias' own view or a view he simply incorporated into an epidectic speech displaying his own ability to give a great many different arguments to support the same conclusion. See Joseph Pratt, *Classical Antiquity* 34, No. 1 (April 2015): 163–82.

Because they always want to have more, immoderate human beings are not able to enjoy a common good, become a member of a community, have or be a friend.

Having responded to Callicles' indecent claim that the strongest and most desirous human beings have a right to rule others, Socrates turns to answer Callicles' second, seemingly more decent claim that a man unable to defend himself, his friends, and family from the greatest dangers is in a shameful condition (508c–d). And Callicles re-enters the conversation, emphatically agreeing with Socrates' suggestion that man should prepare himself not to do or suffer injustice by acquiring power—as well as, Socrates adds, art or knowledge. Indeed, Callicles enthusiastically endorses Socrates suggestion that the art of protecting oneself from injustice consists in acquiring rule of one's own city, even as a tyrant, or as a friend of the existing regime (509c–d). Socrates praises Callicles for holding this second, apparently more decent, patriotic opinion to make him acknowledge that this is his true belief (as opposed to his stated conviction that the stronger have a right by nature to rule). But Socrates then shows that Callicles' true, apparently more decent belief ultimately rests on the indecent principle he first articulates.

Socrates first observes that a man who seeks to protect himself and his own by pleasing the ruling party will become like that party or person. So if that person or party is immoderate and unjust, the individual trying to please the ruler will also become immoderate and unjust. Callicles agrees, but insists that will be necessary in order for the individual to save himself (510a–511a). Arts like swimming or piloting enable their practitioners to save lives, but, Socrates reminds Callicles, he does not consider such arts to be noble or good. Callicles admits that is the case, but like the many, he remains unconvinced by Socrates' arguments (513c).

What prevents human beings from agreeing that it is necessary to be moderate and just in order to live well? What makes obviously intelligent young men like Callicles unwilling to examine their own opinions critically so they can discover what it is they truly want and thus become able to seek it? In his depiction of Callicles in the *Gorgias* Plato suggests that it is their love or attachment to their own—

their own lives, families, friends, and country—that makes human beings unable and unwilling to follow the dictates of reason. People generally recognize the nobility and goodness of the courage that leads some, even many human beings to sacrifice their lives for their country. Such people have contempt for cowards; and angered by self-seeking, unjust aggression by others, they band together to protect themselves. However, fear of death, aversion to pain, and shame tends to overcome concern for the common good in such brave men, because they act fundamentally in order to protect themselves and their own rather than to do what is right or just. Indeed, since the best defense is often an offense, these brave "free men" often unjustly seek to seize the goods of others before those others seek to seize theirs.

At the beginning of their exchange Socrates observes that he and Callicles have two traits in common. As Callicles points out, unlike the foreign teachers of rhetoric, he and Socrates are both Athenians, fellow citizens who ought to be friends. But, as Socrates points out, they are also both lovers. Just as Socrates loves philosophy and an Athenian youth named Alcibiades, so Callicles loves the Athenian demos and an Athenian youth named Demus (481d).[12] As Plato's readers would have known, neither Socrates nor Callicles' loves ended well for them. As Thucydides shows, the contradictory passions and opinions Plato depicts in Callicles led the Athenians not merely to deprive other cities of their liberty, but to lose their own freedom in an attempt to expand their empire.[13] And the young man Socrates says that he loves, Alcibiades, played a crucial role in

---

[12] This is the aspect of the dialogue Newell, *Ruling Passion*, 1–5, 12, emphasizes.

[13] E. R. Dodds, *Gorgias* (Oxford: Oxford University Press, 1959), 17–18, argues that it is impossible to establish a precise "dramatic date" for the dialogues, because there are a series of conflicting indications within the text. However, both Seth Benardete, *The Rhetoric of Morality and Philosophy: Plato's* Gorgias *and* Phaedrus (Chicago: University of Chicago Press, 1991), 7, and Arlene Saxonhouse, "An Unspoken Theme in Plato's *Gorgias*," *Interpretation* 11 (1983): 144, point out, the conflicting indications coincide with the duration of the Peloponnesian War.

the defeat of Athens by Sparta, first in Sicily and then at home on the Greek mainland.[14] In several other dialogues—*Protagoras, Alcibiades I & II,* and *Symposium*—Plato relates the way in which Socrates attempted to lead the extremely handsome, talented young man away from his tyrannical desires and ambitions to join the philosopher in his search for what is truly good. However, both Plato and history show that Socrates failed. Socrates himself was, moreover, unjustly accused and condemned to death by the democratic government of Athens. Nevertheless, Plato's Socrates insists, not only that it is better and more noble to suffer injustice than to do it. It is also impossible to protect oneself entirely from the injustice of others; and no mortal can escape death. At most, one can try to prevent oneself from doing injustice by seeking to discover what is truly good and just, and ruling oneself and one's desires accordingly.[15]

---

[14] See Saxonhouse, "Unspoken Theme," 139, on the relation between Callicles and Athens; on Alcibiades' role in Athens' defeat, see Thucydides, *Peloponnesian War* 6.12–13, 16, 28–29, 48, 53, 61, 88–93, 7.18, 8.12, 45–47, 48, 50, 52–53, 56, 81–82, 85–86, 89, 108.

[15] Pace Stauffer, *Unity,* Saxonhouse argues that Socrates would never have learned or agreed to use a form of persuasive speech he thought was flattery that would corrupt his fellow Athenians. I agree. However, in "Freedom," 361, she concludes that the fact that there is no other historical record of an Athenian politician named 'Callicles' shows that Socrates succeeded in persuading him not to go into politics. I, on the contrary, take both Callicles' own statement that like the many he does not find Socrates' arguments persuasive and Socrates' characterization of the story he tells at the end of the dialogue about the gods having learned the necessity of stripping individual souls of their bodies, clothes, and associates to testify on their behalf in order to judge human beings justly as a *logos,* which Callicles will regard as a *mythos,* to show that neither Socrates nor Plato thought that human laws and courts could protect individuals from the injustice of others or that a man like Callicles would be reformed by the philosopher. Like Saxonhouse, I think that Plato shows Callicles values the intelligence and daring for which, Thucydides reports, Pericles praises the Athenians in his funeral oration. As she points out, Pericles later reminds the Athenians that they rule their "allies" tyrannically, and Callicles' first account of the "natural right" of the stronger sounds very much like the Athenians on Melos. She takes the contradiction in Callicles' views to reflect the difference between the freedom, especially the freedom of speech, Socrates recognizes in Athenian domestic politics and their foreign policy. (She thus states that the freedom Gorgias claims for the rhetorician

Why the Search for Political Liberty
Devolves into Tyranny

Through his depiction of Callicles in the *Gorgias* Plato suggests that "free" politics consist fundamentally in collective selfishness, and the selfishness of the collectivity is fundamentally no more just than the selfishness of an individual. Even when political acts are based on persuasion, they are based on speeches directed to groups of people who do not know what is good or right. Socrates does not claim to know what is truly good, noble, and just; he only claims to seek such knowledge. But in seeking such knowledge by examining the opinions of others he claims to be the only person in Athens at his time even attempting to practice the true art of politics (521d–e). However, as Socrates repeatedly emphasizes in this conversation, his "art" operates only on an individual level. It consists in the attempt to bring his interlocutors to agree with themselves. As Plato shows, it is not possible for Socrates or anyone else to practice this art in public, where individuals like Gorgias and Polus feel embarrassed by the revelation of their contradictory opinions and consequently become unwilling to acknowledge what they really think. Yet, if it is not possible even to attempt to learn what true human happiness and excellence are except in a private conversation on an individual basis, any attempt to make people good, happy and virtuous through public action or discussions will necessarily fail.

Wouldn't the best "solution" then be to institute a public order or regime that allows individuals to engage in such private philosophical investigations, like Socrates, if they so choose? Wouldn't it be best to institute a public order that leaves individuals free to live

---

"refers not to the individual unburdened by the control of others, but rather entails rule over others—whether we are referring to life within the city or to one city ruling over another, as the Athenians do with their empire" [357], even though Gorgias claims only that his art enables a man to rule in his own city.) Callicles' name could be taken to mean praise (*kleos*) of the most noble (*kallista*). And, I suspect, there is no historical record of an individual by that name because Plato created him as an embodiment of the corrupting effect Pericles had on the character of his fellow citizens. As Thucydides shows, Athenian foreign policy was originally defensive, but after it succeeded, it became offensive.

as they wish—to practice politics, if they so desire, or philosophy, if they wish? In the *Republic* Plato suggests not.

To be sure, in the *Republic* Plato shows that Socrates convinced Glaucon and Adeimantus that it is better to live justly than to enjoy the reputation, honor, wealth, and pleasure some individuals acquire in great measure by unjust means. Near the beginning of the dialogue Plato's brothers admit that they were not persuaded by Socrates' critique of the rhetorician Thrasymachus' contention that the life of perfect injustice is best. Challenging Socrates to show that he is wrong, Glaucon presents an argument very much like Callicles' that by nature the strong rule, but that the strong have generally been conned by the weak into abiding by conventions which restrict their power. In the *Republic* Plato then shows that Socrates succeeded in persuading his brothers that the just life is best by asking them to discover what is truly just by it "writ big" in a city they construct in speech. But that "city in speech" is no one's idea of free or liberal regime. Birth, education, speech, bodily exercise and the division of labor, family life and property are all highly regulated and publicly supervised. Even the philosophers deemed to be the necessary rulers have to be compelled to rule.

Socrates acknowledges that it is highly unlikely for any such a regime to come into being. No such regime has actually existed. However, he then counterfactually describes regimes that have existed as if they are—or were—degenerations from his "city in speech." He explains the degeneration as a result of an imperfect mixing of the four races Hesiod described—gold, silver, bronze, and iron. (547a–c) These "races" correspond to the four "metals" to be found in the population of the "city in speech" (415a). However, they do not include the age of the heroes that Hesiod described between the bronze and iron ages that corresponds to democracy in the order of the regimes that Socrates presents as degenerations from the best. Might he thus be indicating that democracy is the best possible regime, inferior only to the near impossible "city in speech?"

In describing the regimes that have actually existed, Socrates argues that each seeks to foster a certain understanding of the human good. Just as the "city in speech" is designed to make its citizens as virtuous as possible, timocracies honor victory in war, and oligarchies value wealth, democracies seek to maximize freedom. Because democracies leave their citizens free to pursue whatever way of life they desire, representatives of all the regimes are to be found in them. Democracies are thus the best place for individuals attempting to find and establish a new and better regime to carry out their investigations. In other words, democracies are the best places for people to conduct the kind of philosophical investigations in which Socrates, Glaucon, and Adeimantus are engaged. Because democracies contain representatives of all the regimes, Socrates says that they appear to be the "fairest (*kallistê*)" (557c), and Adeimantus concludes that democracy is "a very noble (*gennaia*) regime" (558c). Nevertheless, Socrates maintains that democracies are worse than oligarchies, which are worse than timocracies and aristocracies, because the freedom they give all their citizens allows those with the greatest desires—the men Callicles most admires—to exhaust all their own economic resources and consequently to seize those of others.[16] The cleverest and boldest of these "drones" become leaders of "democratic" attempts by the poor to become more equal and free by appropriating and redistributing the property of wealthy oligarchs. Although these demagogues initially claim to be acting on behalf of the people and thus appear to be kind and gentle, their unjust redistribution of the goods of their political "enemies" inevitably arouses opposition. To protect themselves, these tyrants then request and are usually granted bodyguards, that is, armed forces answerable directly to them. And to justify the increasingly oppressive measures such leaders find necessary, they also often provoke foreign wars, which further deplete the resources of most of their fellow citizens (*Republic* 544a–576a).

People subject to the rule of a tyrant are generally understood to be miserable, but Socrates extends that misery to the tyrants themselves by arguing that their lives are even more wretched than

---

[16] Stanley Rosen, *Plato's* Republic: *A Study* (New Haven: Yale University Press, 2005), 317–19, presents a similar account of Socrates' argument.

those of their subjects. Recognizing that citizens who are virtuous and just will oppose their oppressive policies, tyrants find it necessary to kill or exile all decent, potentially trustworthy associates and to hire unjust, slavish flatterers and followers. People envy tyrants, Socrates explains, because they are able to act on the forbidden desires—not merely murder and theft, but incest and cannibalism—about which some people dream. However, as a result of their acting on such desires, tyrants become so hated that they fear to venture abroad lest they be attacked and assassinated. Because they cannot trust any of the members of their entourage or household, they become completely isolated (*Republic* 571b–572b).

Most human beings want to live in the company of those they love, admire, and trust; like Callicles, most find it necessary to obtain the assistance of others in attempting to protect themselves and those they hold dear from the unjust desires of others. Unfortunately, Plato suggests in both the *Gorgias* and *Republic,* there is no political "solution," no lasting, reliable defense against the conflicts and harm caused by the immoderate, unjust desires of some. In the "myth" he insists is a "logos" at the end of the *Gorgias* (523a–524a), Socrates explains that human judgments of the acts and characters of individuals accused of crimes are often mistaken, because judges are misled by artful speeches and beautiful appearances; only in the afterlife where the souls of the accused are stripped of their bodies, clothes, and friendly associates, can judges make true determinations of guilt and innocence. Likewise, in the myth of Er with which Socrates concludes the *Republic* he reports that the first soul able to choose his next life selects the life of a tyrant without noticing that it includes incest and cannibalism (*Republic* 619b–d). Having been a citizen of a just regime, this man had acted moderately and justly, because just and moderate deeds were mandated by law; his soul was not truly just, however, because he did not understand why such deeds were necessary in order to live well and happily. On the contrary, he evidently felt that his desires had been constrained and chose a life he thought would enable him to do anything he wished when offered an opportunity to do so.

In sum, Plato's Socrates presents a rather pessimistic picture of the possibilities of securing human freedom by means of political action or power. Because most, if not all human beings have unjust desires, it is necessary to adopt and enforce laws in order to restrain them. As indicated by the need to use force in order to establish and maintain the rule of law, however, all political orders include a measure of tyranny and none is perfectly just.[17] But Socrates is not so pessimistic about the possibility of individual human beings living a satisfying, happy life as Nietzsche suggests in *Twilight of the Idols*. On the contrary, in both the *Gorgias* and *Republic* Socrates holds out the hope that others will follow his example by seeking to examine their opinions in private in order to discover what is truly good and noble. As Plato shows in the *Gorgias*, such discussions have to take place privately, because individuals will not be willing to acknowledge that they have unjust desires and opinions, much less to have those opinions and desires corrected in public. Yet so long as individuals hold and act on their secretly held unjust desires and opinions, they will come into conflict not only with others, but also with themselves. As Socrates tells Polus, people want to be free in order to do what they believe is good for them; but they are obviously not free or able to fulfill this fundamental desire, if they do not know what is truly good. Socrates does not claim to know; he does claim that such investigations are the necessary first step to the achievement of human excellence and happiness. Desiring to learn what is truly good, Socrates is not beset by the fear of death and related desires for ever more wealth and honor that plague his fellow citizens. However, Socrates does not describe himself or philosophers more generally as living a good life because they are free from the passions that move most human beings. On the contrary, upon two occasions, he claims that the only things he knows are the erotic things.[18] He is a philosopher, because he loves learning and seeks wisdom. And in the *Republic* (485a–487a) he suggests that a person who loves the truth above all and has the intellectual capacity to pursue it will

---

[17] See *Laws* 4.709d–712a.
[18] *Symposium* 177e; *Phaedrus* 257a.

possess the other virtues as well. He has no cause to be unjust to others, because wisdom can be shared with others at no cost to oneself.

THE SOCRATIC TURN TO ALCIBIADES

Alex Priou

Funest philosophers and ponderers,
Their evocations are the speech of clouds.
– Wallace Stevens[1]

I. Socrates Before Alcibiades

According to the *Parmenides*, when the young Socrates first arrived on the scene, philosophy's reputation was in shambles. What had begun in earnest as an attempt to answer that exalted question— What is Being?—had devolved into petty, partisan bickering about the number of the beings. The pluralists and monists busied themselves jabbing at one other, each man attempting to prove the other more laughable than the other had just proven him (*Parmenides* 128b7–e4). The inevitable consequence of this battle was that no one emerged victorious, save perhaps the enemies of the philosophic enterprise as a whole (cf. *Parmenides* 127a8–10, 128b3–6). Seeing philosophy in such poor health and standing, Socrates proposed his theory of forms (εἴδη), according to which eponymous speech indicates the variety of natural kinds (*Parmenides* 129a3, 130d5–6,

---

[1] From "On the Manner of Addressing Clouds." All citations without an author are to Plato, all without an author or a text to his *Alcibiades*. All translations are my own. For the text of the *Alcibiades*, I have used Nicholas Denyer, *Plato: Alcibiades* (Cambridge: Cambridge University Press, 2001). For all other citations of Greek sources, I have used the Oxford Classical Texts editions of those works. Some acknowledgements are also in order. When I was a student at St. John's College Annapolis, I had the great pleasure of reading the *Alcibiades* with the late Laurence Berns, whose reputation for generosity and playfulness was, I can attest, much deserved. Many years later, I was also fortunate to attend two seminars on the dialogue by Michael Davis of Sarah Lawrence College. In those seminars, he deftly showed how the question of the self pervades the *Alcibiades* in ways, I fear, I'd never have grasped on my own. His influence on my understanding of the closing argument of the dialogue, in particular, is obvious.

132a1–5, 133c8–d5). As he explained to Parmenides and Zeno, there is no difficulty in the beings being both one and many at once, for each participates in oneness itself and plurality as such (*Parmenides* 128e6–129c1). Rather, such mixing of contraries is a problem only for the contraries themselves, that is, only if oneness itself should prove to be many or the beautiful itself somehow also ugly (*Parmenides* 129b1–c1 with 130b7–10 and d8–9). Socrates thus shows that the contradictions in experience need not be a hindrance to ontology; rather, they are the antechamber to its grand hall. What's more, because his theory takes its bearings by everyday speech, Socrates not only reconciles the schools of philosophy with one another but also brings philosophy as such back into good standing in the city (cf. *Parmenides* 127e9–10, 128b5–6, 129d6). By restoring philosophy to health and respectability all in one stroke, the young Socrates secured his name a permanent place in the history of philosophy.

It is no surprise, then, that Parmenides listened to Socrates' sketch of his theory in silent admiration (*Parmenides* 130a3–b1). Nevertheless, the aged Eleatic discerned in Socrates' prizing of the forms over the things seen (τὰ ὁρώμενα) a tendency to dishonor the latter, so that unity and plurality, sameness and other, and the like are all worthy of having forms, while things like hair, mud, and dirt are not (*Parmenides* 130c5–d5; cf. 129d3–4, 129e5–130a2). But if the forms are revealed by eponymy, then nothing of which we speak generally should lack a form (cf. *Parmenides* 130d5–6). The beautiful or noble, τὸ καλόν, has put Socrates' theory in contradiction with itself. At the heart of this issue is man, whose simultaneous likeness to dirt and access to being give him a peculiar in-between status. For this reason, Socrates hesitates to say whether man has an εἶδος or form (*Parmenides* 130c1–4). What's more, because explaining how the participation of particulars in these forms risks mixing them—for example, should large things be large by virtue of partaking in a small part of the large itself—Socrates' ontology also appears to be incoherent (*Parmenides* 130c12–e2). The greatest challenge awaiting Socrates, then, is that of responding to the skeptic who claims that, because participation cannot be explained, the forms are not or, if they are, they are unknowable to human nature (*Parmenides* 133a8–c1, 134e9–135b2). Parmenides thus challenges Socrates to sort out man as a moral and intellectual being, how τὸ καλόν shades his understanding of being. In this way, among others, he initiates Socrates' turn to political philosophy.[2]

One would expect that the next dialogue in Plato's dramatic chronology would be the *Protagoras*, as its titular character famously advanced a moral and epistemological relativism that made him the skeptic *par excellence*.[3] Instead, we find Socrates initiating a

---

[2] The above is an incomplete account of my reading of the *Parmenides*, which I elaborate more fully in Alex Priou, *Becoming Socrates: Political Philosophy in Plato's* Parmenides (Rochester: University of Rochester Press, 2018).

[3] The particulars of why I take the *Protagoras* to follow the *Alcibiades* are covered in the body above. Still, I will discuss here the scholarly controversy about whether the dramatic date of the *Alcibiades* precedes or follows that of the *Protagoras*, in anticipation of my more thorough reading.

Some scholars have claimed that the *Alcibiades* precedes the *Protagoras*, because in the *Alcibiades* it is clear that Socrates and Alcibiades have never conversed, as they seem to do in the *Protagoras*. Lampert and Zuckert rightly point out, however, that they don't actually converse therein (cf. Laurence Lampert, *How Philosophy Became Socratic: A Study of Plato's* Protagoras, Charmides, *and* Republic [Chicago: University of Chicago Press, 2010], 143; Catherine Zuckert, *Plato's Philosophers: The Coherence of the Dialogues* [Chicago: University of Chicago Press, 2009], 217–18 n. 5). Lampert adds that in the *Alcibiades* "many points large and small…repeat and enlarge what Alcibiades heard in the conversation between Socrates and Protagoras" (Lampert, *How Philosophy*, 144). Yet why should we take the more thorough to be the later? Most persuasive to me is Helfer: "that Alcibiades is still quite unfamiliar with Socrates' '*pragma*' in the *Alcibiades* (and not in the *Protagoras*) seems undeniable" (Ariel Helfer, *Socrates and Alcibiades: Plato's Drama of Political Ambition and Philosophy* [Philadelphia: University of Pennsylvania Press, 2017], 199–200 n. 12). As he elsewhere puts it, Alcibiades has "strayed beyond the traditional and respectable Athenian curriculum" in the *Protagoras* but not in the *Alcibiades* (Helfer, *Socrates and Alcibiades*, 144). To elaborate on Helfer's point, in the *Alcibiades* Alcibiades says that he thinks answering questions is easy (106b5–8). Indeed, he seems altogether unacquainted with Socratic conversation, specifically with the contention that the one answering bears the brunt of the refutation (112d8–113c4). But how could this be, if he had already witnessed how Socrates' questions frustrated and angered the greatest of

conversation with Alcibiades in the eponymous dialogue *Alcibiades*. Then again, the *Alcibiades* might fit better, if the ancient and medieval commenters were correct to deem "human nature" its subject. But why, we wonder, would Plato consider this atypical man, Alcibiades, a fitting entry into human nature? How could he ever serve, to use Alfarabi's term, as a "model" for man as such?[4] It only adds to our perplexity that therein he converses with Socrates, a man

---

sophists and heard Socrates emphasize the burden of answering questions in the *Protagoras* (cf. *Protagoras* 335a4–8, 338e2–5, 360d6–e5)?

More substantively, however, the *Protagoras* constitutes the next step in Socrates' education of Alcibiades, inasmuch as it shuts a door to Alcibiades' political ambition that was first opened (and left open) in the *Alcibiades*. At one point, Alcibiades proposes following in Pericles' footsteps by going to those reputed to be wise, among whom one would include the sophists (118c3–6). This thought only occurs to Alcibiades, however, because Socrates has just shown him that he lacks the knowledge necessary to approach the Athenians (118b5–c2). That is, Alcibiades would not have gone to the sophists had he not already been convinced (whether by Socrates or another) of his own neediness in point of knowledge. What's more, Socrates' argument is wholly circumstantial, so that Alcibiades still holds hope that with better teachers and greater effort he could learn from such men (cf. 118e8). In short, prior to meeting Socrates, Alcibiades believes that his lack of preeminence in the city is to be ameliorated not through study but through action. He is simply inexperienced and uninterested in Athens' intellectual life, Socrates and the sophists included. This is, I think, part of his attractiveness. After Socrates, however, matters are considerably different, and the conditions of the *Protagoras* reflect this change.

[4] For Alfarabi's view, see Muhsin Mahdi, *Alfarabi's Philosophy of Plato and Aristotle* (New York: The Free Press of Glencoe, 1962), 53–54; for Proclus' view, see William O'Neill, *Proclus: Alcibiades I* (The Hague: Martinus Nijhoff, 1971), 4–5; and for Olympiodorus on how Damascius' view differed from Proclus', see Michael Griffin, *Olympiodorus: Life of Plato and on Plato First Alcibiades 1–9* (London: Bloomsbury, 2015), 78. Diogenes Laertius says the *Alcibiades*' subtitle is περὶ ἀνθρώπου φύσεως (Diogenes Laertius, *Lives and Opinions of the Eminent Philosophers* III.59). Charles Butterworth informs me that the word Alfarabi uses for "model" is *al-dustūr*, which refers to the register, whether the original or a copy, in which the king's rules and ordinances are collected. See Edward Lane, *An Arabic-English Lexicon* (London: Williams and Norgate, 1864; reprint, Cambridge: The Islamic Texts Society, 1984), I:879a.

atypical even for that atypical type, the philosopher.[5] Their oddity is apparent from the very first. Socrates depicts Alcibiades as a man so vain and ambitious at once as to claim to need nothing yet still remain in want of everything (104a2–c2, 104e6–105c7), while he casts himself as a stalker restrained only by the voice in his head that he claims to be his private divinity (103a1–b1, 105d3–106a2). How could a conversation between two eccentrics be the appropriate means for the consideration of man as such, for the consideration of the εἶδος or look of man? Why did Socrates turn to Alcibiades?

II. Socrates With Alcibiades

Contrary to this initial assessment, there is on second glance something all-too-human in the dynamic between these two oddballs. As Socrates presents it, the oddity of Alcibiades consists in his claim (φὴς) that the things belonging to him—beginning from the body and ending in the soul—are so great as for him to need (δεῖσθαι) no one for anything (104a2–4). It is precisely this λόγος, by which Alcibiades has such grandiose thoughts (ὑπερπεφρόνηκας), that Socrates wants to go through (104a1–2). To entice Alcibiades into conversation, Socrates introduces his own oddity, claiming that, should his private δαιμόνιον prove willing, he could sate once and for all the need that fires Alcibiades' ambition—that it could aid Alcibiades in filling all mankind with his name (ὀνόματος) and his power (δυνάμεως), making him both loved and feared as though a god (105c2–e6). Intrigued, Alcibiades allows his extraordinary lover to test the limits of his varied means to self-sufficiency. Socrates thus sees in Alcibiades' comprehensive vanity a claim to such

---

[5] Consider the *Alcibiades*' chosen reader, that is, the reader most likely to read this dialogue before the others. Presumably he would have known the author and the title. He might also have heard that in this text Socrates woos Alcibiades. All told, then, he would be struck by the fact that Plato wrote a dialogue, in which his teacher seduces his most notorious student. Thus, for an average Athenian the *Alcibiades* would have had the appearance of a celebrity tell-all. Like the *Symposium*, its chosen reader is the gossip. That the dialogue goes on to show the limits of a "tell-all" offers us a glimpse of Plato's genius.

thoroughgoing self-sufficiency as might grant insight into the whole range of human possibilities. Thus, not despite but because Socrates and Alcibiades are so peculiar can the *Alcibiades* emerge as a work on human nature in general.

In addition, Plato's exposition of Alcibiades' putative means to self-sufficiency attains a systematic quality in light of the fact that, aside from being highly ambitious and intelligent, Alcibiades is also uninclined to accept unnecessary obstacles. He is, in a word, impatient. His ambition makes him want to have it all, while his impatience directs his intelligence to the most immediate means to getting it all. Thus, each time Socrates removes one of Alcibiades' many paths to ascendancy, Alcibiades responds by intelligently discerning the next, most readily available path. In this way, Plato is able to display, in their logical order, the myriad ways in which human beings convince themselves of their self-sufficiency. In short, in the company of Socrates, the soul of Alcibiades reveals the contours of human nature as a river's downward determination reveals the contours of a mountain. To understand the *Alcibiades* as a work on human nature, therefore, we must discern each position Alcibiades takes and how Socrates gets Alcibiades to pivot from one to the next.

The *first position* Alcibiades takes is that he will counsel the Athenians concerning those things that he knows better than they (106c5–d1). The distinctive feature of this position is its vagueness. Though he eventually says that he wants to advise the Athenians about matters of concern to them (πράγματα)—more specifically, war and peace (107c6, d3–4)—he has not considered from where this knowledge comes nor in what it consists (107d5–109a5, 109d1–8). He is made aware that, when we want to know something, we typically learn it from an expert so as to develop that expertise ourselves, but also that he has consulted no such expert on the relevant matters he claims to know (109d1–6). Even concerning the other things he knows and has learned from an expert, Alcibiades struggles to articulate in what this knowledge consists (108c6–d8). Alcibiades is thus confident that he possesses knowledge concerning what his city ought to do, a knowledge whose source and content are inexplicable and will of necessity remain inexplicable, so long as his confidence in his possession remains unshaken. His sense of competence in political matters is therefore bare: Alcibiades first dons the guise of the unreflective citizen.

After quite the embarrassing struggle, however, Alcibiades takes his *first pivot* and notices that the knowledge he claims to possess is a knowledge of justice and that he has had no teacher of this. He thus claims to know about the just and unjust things otherwise (ἄλλως), that is, to have learned them differently than from an expert (109e1–2). Guided by Socrates, Alcibiades arrives at his *second position*, namely, that he investigated and discovered them on his own, when at some point he supposed himself ignorant of them (109e3–7). That is, shown not to have learned from an expert, Alcibiades senses that nevertheless he has *somehow* come by this knowledge on his own. His second guise is thus that of the self-made expert, of one who claims that he has, on his own and from his own experience, learned what he knows—it is the guise of the discoverer or inventor.[6]

When, however, Socrates urges him to clarify this "somehow" by identifying the time at which he noticed his ignorance, Alcibiades is shocked to learn that he has always supposed himself to know these things (110c11). Even when he was a child, he supposed he had knowledge of the just and unjust things; in fact, he emphatically *still* supposes that he then did have it (110b1–c5). Alcibiades' *second pivot* thus comes upon realizing that, though he has acquired this knowledge on his own, he cannot say when. It has been with him so long as he can remember. Consequently, when pressed again to identify the source of his knowledge, Alcibiades arrives at his *third position*, that he did not discover the just and unjust things on his own but rather learned them from the same teachers everyone else has, namely, the many (110d5–e1). That is, reminded of the role of justice in his childhood games, Alcibiades astutely discerns that he has learned about justice in the way he has learned to speak or to be

---

[6] As Plato and Aristotle attest, it is a noble guise (cf. *Symposium* 209a5; Aristotle, *Metaphysics* A.1 981b13–17).

Greek (τὸ ἑλληνίζειν) (111a1). In other words, Alcibiades has known about justice so long as he can remember because this knowledge comes from time immemorial: it is his inheritance, an ancestral knowledge dating back to or even before Homer (cf. 112a10–d7, esp. b2: ἀκήκοας with 106a1–2: νῦν γὰρ ἄν μου ἀκούσαις). Thus, in the third place, Alcibiades dons the guise of the conservative or traditionalist, who sees in his people's ways a time-honored wisdom.

Socrates effects Alcibiades' *third pivot* when he brings him to see that the many dispute about just and unjust men and affairs in a manner inconsistent with our expectation of unanimity among experts, so that the ancestral contains within it not knowledge but a confusion—or, rather, its knowledge consists in a confusion (111a5–112d11; cf. *Minos* 316b6–c4). Reluctantly accepting that this confusion is his own (112d11–113c6), Alcibiades comes to his *fourth position*, according to which the Athenians and other Greeks deliberate not concerning the just and unjust so much as the advantageous (113d1–8). Alcibiades sees the advantageous as possessing a degree of clarity not present in the just nor, later, the noble, which are variably advantageous and disadvantageous and thus both good and bad: the good may well be unjust and base (115a1–16). So, in the fourth place, Alcibiades dons the familiar guise of the conniving immoralist, for whom justice is the advantage of the stronger or, alternatively, for whom injustice is the good (cf. *Republic* 338c2–4, *Gorgias* 472e1–3).

The *fourth pivot* occurs when Socrates readily exposes the illusory clarity of the advantageous through the introduction of the noble or τὸ καλόν. Like the just or even more than it, τὸ καλόν appears disadvantageous; unlike the just, however, it has an especially strong grip on those seeking to counsel their fellow citizens about what to do, that is, those claiming some preeminent status among them. As he is among those seeking so to counsel, Alcibiades too finds himself torn between his love of the good and his love of τὸ καλόν. For Alcibiades, the shame of cowardice is worse than death, but for this ultimate sacrifice the nobility of courage offers no reward

(115d5–11, e6–14). In response, Socrates argues that the nobility of courage attends only the deed itself and not the death that might result (115b5–10). Rather, according to this argument, the death is shameful (115e15–116a4). Consequently, the nobility of courage is not highest but rather lowest when resulting in death, a view that might earn our distrust but which nevertheless enthuses Alcibiades. By separating Alcibiades' attraction to τὸ καλόν from his aversion to or revulsion at the risks associated with its pursuit, Socrates lets him have his nobility and enjoy it, too. For Alcibiades, a noble life must be, first and foremost, a life. Alcibiades wants both a name *and* power, not a lifeless reputation.[7]

Unfortunately, the inevitable consequence of this argument is that, contrary to Alcibiades' initial claim, the just is noble and thus advantageous (116c4–d4). So cornered by Socrates, Alcibiades speaks with as much confusion about the advantageous as the many do about the just, even though it was to avoid their confusion that he had pivoted from the just to the advantageous. The prospect of one so confused counseling anyone, let alone the Athenians, is so ridiculous as to make Alcibiades' sense of his condition a strange one, as to render his experience a question for himself (116d7–e5; cf. 114b6–e11). Invoking again the standard of expertise, Socrates elucidates Alcibiades' experience of wandering, with respect to those things he supposes himself to know, as a lack of learning (ἀμαθία) in the greatest things—indeed, as ignorance of this very lack of learning (116e6–118c2). Once Socrates has impressed upon him the severity of his ignorance, Alcibiades arrives at his *fifth position*, according to which he can follow in the footsteps of his guardian Pericles, who "is said to have become (γεγονέναι) wise not from his own effort (ἀπὸ τοῦ αὐτομάτου) but to have associated (συγγεγονέναι) with many wise [men]" (118b5–c6; cf. *Menexenus* 235e3–9). That is, with his reliance on the "knowledge" of the many shown questionable and his own expertise proven lacking,

---

[7] Compare *Second Alcibiades* 141c1–5. This aspect of Alcibiades' character features prominently in his later escapades, in which he alternates between daring political ambition and cunning deceit in seeking his safety.

Alcibiades turns to those reputed to be wise, to men like the cosmologist Anaxagoras and the sophist-musician Damon (118c3–6; cf. *Laches* 199e13–200c6). Alcibiades has not studied with such men but clearly entertains the idea later, as the next time we encounter him in Plato's dramatic world he goes among those gathered around the sophists in Callias' house (cf. *Protagoras* 316a3–5, 317d10–e2). Alcibiades' fifth position is, therefore, a sort of φιλοσοφία, though his love of τὸ καλόν distorts φιλοσοφία into τὸ φιλεῖν τοὺς σοφούς, into the love of those already in possession of wisdom or, rather, those reputed to be wise. Thus, in the fifth position, Alcibiades adopts the guise of the cosmopolitan, whose worldly wisdom travels readily from city to city (cf. *Protagoras* 337c6–e2).

Alcibiades' *fifth pivot* happens when Socrates points out that, whatever wisdom Pericles may have acquired from such men, it does not meet our expectations regarding knowledge, that is, it is not communicable to another or, at least, has not so far been communicated (118c6–119a7). This caveat is important for understanding why we encounter Alcibiades in the *Protagoras* (see Section III). That aside, robbed now of all immediate access to existing expertise, whatever its source, Alcibiades proves to be uneducated (119b3: ἀπαίδευτοι), reduced again merely to Kleinias' son (103a1: ὦ παῖ Κλεινίου).[8] Even here, however, Alcibiades finds a new means for his ambition, and so arrives at his *sixth position*: the lack of anyone educated makes it unnecessary both to practice and to bother (πράγματα ἔχειν) learning; in his nature, at least (γε), Alcibiades will surpass the rest very much (119b5–c1). Alcibiades' sixth position reconciles his incompetence with his ambition (μεγαλοφροσύνη) by locating his exceptionality not in his knowledge but in his nature. With education unnecessary because lineage is sufficient, the phrase "son of Kleinias" is no longer belittling but an honor. That is, without any knowledge available, Alcibiades disposes of its necessity by combining τὸ καλόν with the ancestral into τὸ γενναῖον, into the noble in descent or the noble from

---

[8] Note that it is Alcibiades and not Socrates who uses the term ἀπαίδευτος.

birth (cf. 120d12–e5). Thus, in the sixth place, Alcibiades dons the guise of the aristocrat or the nobleman.

Socrates uses two arguments to effect the *sixth pivot* to wisdom or prudence, a brief argument from the good (120c8–d8) and a much longer and (to Alcibiades) more compelling argument from the noble (120d9–124b6, esp. 120d9–10: ἐκ τῶν εἰκότων σκέψαι, d12: εἰκὸς with 124b7–8: ἔοικας ἀληθῆ εἰρηκότι). According to the first argument, Alcibiades risks harm should he not take trouble over himself. Alcibiades is persuaded but not considerably moved. In the second, Socrates depicts Alcibiades' birth, rearing, and education as utterly deficient in comparison with his counterparts in Persia and Sparta. Consequently, the thought of Alcibiades competing against them in terms of τὸ γενναῖον is so wondrous a bit of insanity as to render him once again a laughingstock—even before the Persian and Spartan women (123c4–124a8).[9] So shamed, Alcibiades arrives at his *seventh position*, namely, that he has no choice but to deliberate about how to become best (124b7–c2). By becoming best (βέλτιστος), Alcibiades means becoming most excellent (ἄριστος) in the virtue (ἀρετή) of the good men (οἱ ἄνδρες οἱ ἀγαθοί), that is, those good in practicing certain affairs (πράγματα), that is, those affairs practiced by men both beautiful and good—by gentlemen (οἱ καλοὶ κάγαθοί)—whose goodness lies in their being prudent (φρόνιμοι) (124c1–2, 124e1–125a3). As the argument's meandering path shows, Alcibiades accepts Socrates' connection of the good with wisdom implicit in his initial argument from the good (and, earlier, in the fourth pivot), but only after taking a detour through political respectability. Stated more precisely, by contesting Alcibiades' claim to exemplify τὸ γενναῖον, Socrates forces him to separate τὸ καλόν from the ancestral and connect it to τὸ ἀγαθόν. More simply, Alcibiades now dons the guise of the respectable or preeminent citizen, of the man both noble and good, the gentleman (cf. 125a6–7).

---

[9] Even the task of going through the nurturing and education of Alcibiades' competitors is too much for Socrates (122b4: πολὺ ἔργον). Compare *Parmenides* 127a6, 136d1 and *Republic* 530e1, 531d4 in context.

Alcibiades' *seventh pivot* attends two problems. He first struggles to explain who the gentlemen are, offering a number of lengthy and largely unhelpful equivocations (125b8–d8). He then contradicts himself regarding the product of the knowledge (ἐπιστήμη) or good counsel (εὐβουλία) such men possess, claiming that it produces like-mindedness (ὁμόνοια) while also observing that justice requires doing one's own things and thus disagreeing or being of two minds (διχόνοια) on the things others do (125e4–127d5).[10] Despite the apparent contradiction, Alcibiades isn't speaking nonsense, as the doing of one's own things presumes some like-mindedness, at least concerning justice; rather, with both problems, Alcibiades seems instead to struggle to articulate his thought in speech (cf. *Laches* 194a6–b6, *Theaetetus* 148e8). Far from being able to introduce like-mindedness into the city, Alcibiades is not even like-minded with himself (cf. 126c11: οὐκοῦν καὶ [ὁμονοεῖ] αὐτὸς αὐτῷ ἔκαστος).[11] Reflecting on this struggle, Alcibiades expresses his extreme shame that he himself (αὐτὸς) does not know what he says or means (λέγω) (127d6–8). It is out of Alcibiades' reflection on the distance between his self and his speeches that Socrates develops the eighth and final position.

Once Alcibiades confesses that he is opaque to himself, Socrates turns their questioning away from the *result* of the care for oneself and toward what they mean by the word "oneself" (127e8–128a3). Their discussion of the self is quite long but relies primarily on the

---

[10] Alcibiades' concern with ὁμόνοια reflects a long tradition concerning the nature of political unity (cf. Jean-Pierre Vernant, *The Origins of Greek Thought* [Ithaca: Cornell University Press 1982], 90–96). But it may also reflect his imperial ambitions.

[11] On the developmental roots for Alcibiades' position here, compare 126e3–5 with 112c2–6, 118e3–4 and *Second Alcibiades* 143c8–d2 against 143e8–144b3. The effect of Alcibiades' upbringing on his ambition is underappreciated. That the renowned Pericles is his step-father and not his father, that his father's own greatness entailed his death, and that these facts detract from his otherwise impeccable appearance and résumé all contribute to Alcibiades' yearning to live a noble life that finds no premature death, to fill the world with his name and his power.

distinction between oneself (αὐτός) and the things of or belonging to oneself (τὰ ἑαυτοῦ). According to this distinction, to know oneself is to know the self in abstraction from any trappings, be those trappings the arts and their implements, the body that uses them, or even the things one says (129b5–e9). Socrates thus exploits Alcibiades' sense of the distance between his self and his speeches to bring him to the conclusion that man is, by this argument, the soul alone (129e10–130c7, c8). Accordingly, Alcibiades must first acquire the moderation that is self-knowledge and, with this virtue, then come to rule himself and the things of or belonging to himself, whereupon he may also come to rule the city and the things of or belonging to the city (133c20–134c9). Following the inward motion of coming to know oneself, therefore, Socrates posits a second, outward motion, in which one exercises the virtue that allows for self-rule and the rule of others in the city. Such virtuous self-rule is that befitting a freeman, while those who seek to rule without this virtue— whether in politics, medicine, navigation, or beyond—exercise the license (ἐξουσία) characteristic of tyranny, though they are rather deserving of servitude (134c10–135c9). Alcibiades' eighth position is thus best characterized as an awareness of the twin poles governing the range of human possibilities charted above, an awareness of man as capable of both freedom and tyranny. As a sort of unadorned openness, this final position is not so much an eighth alongside the preceding seven as it is the psychological root of the rest.

Let us pause to survey the terrain of follies Alcibiades has traversed in the course of the dialogue—follies familiar at times from our experience of others, at times from our experience of ourselves. He was first blindly confident of his competence in political matters, second certain that he had at some point figured out what justice is on his own, third reliant on his ancestral inheritance from his community, and fourth sure of the clarity of private advantage, even when unjust or base. In the fifth place, he sought association with those deemed most wise, be they statesmen or sophists; in the sixth, he united the ancestral with the noble into the well-born and well-bred (τὸ γενναῖον); and in the seventh, he sought such wisdom as

34

would unite the noble with the good, a wisdom that might lend one political respectability. In short, Alcibiades has variously posed as the conventional citizen, the self-made expert, and the conservative or traditionalist, in addition to the conniving immoralist, the cosmopolitan, the nobleman, and the gentleman. And at the heart of these seven guises lies the eighth, which is really no guise at all but rather that part of human nature open equally to the rest—more broadly, to the self-rule befitting a free man and the license taken by the tyrant.

The difficulty with this openness, however, is that the opacity of the self appears to render self-rule *simpliciter* impossible. By stripping the self of all external manifestations, Socrates renders it altogether immanifest in itself. He compares knowing the self to seeing one's own sight in another's eye, but that requires "looking to that place of the eye in which the virtue of an eye happens to come to be" (133b2–5). One never sees one's own sight, but rather always another's eye seeing one's own or something else. Likewise, what we aim to see in the soul—a sort of knowing, thinking, wisdom, or prudence (cf. 133b10, c2, 5)—manifests itself only in thinking someone who is thinking someone or something else. Paradoxically, then, to know the self is to know it as concerned with something other than itself, to know it as that thing that dons guises that occlude the self from itself (cf. *Second Alcibiades* 150d6–e4). For this reason, the self emerged as an abstract, neuter principle—as the self itself or αὐτὸ τὸ αὐτό—unfamiliar to us even though it's what we're all supposed to be.[12] We all, like the tyrant, take license, inasmuch as we insist that we are who we appear to be, inasmuch as we trust that who we appear to be is all we'll ever need to be. Yet in our open awareness that the city and, indeed, we ourselves thrust upon us our various personae and so hide our folly beneath a mask of competence, we exhibit something of the self-possession of the freeman. The

---

[12] Typically, αὐτός can be used as a personal pronoun only in the oblique cases, while in the nominative it can only be an intensifier (cf. Herbert Weir Smyth, *A Greek Grammar* [New York: American Book Company, 1920], §325d). Plato breaks this rule of hiding the self.

Alcibiades thus indicates how liberty and tyranny have a common root in the opacity of the self, cognizance of which constitutes a limited freedom akin to Socratic knowledge of ignorance, a knowledge of how political life exploits our tendency to lay claim to what is not and cannot be our own, and so to act the tyrant.

It seems, then, that Socrates was correct in his post-Parmenidean anticipation that examining Alcibiades would allow him to understand all of man through a single one, a feat possible only given an individual of unusual gifts, access, and ambition. Once Socrates is through with him, however, Alcibiades promises never to leave his side (135c12–d3, d7–11). Though stripped of all trust in his trappings and denied every means to success, Alcibiades treats Socrates as but another adornment, though a peculiar one at that. Socrates would have preferred that Alcibiades turn to the god rather than him, to the will of an immanifest being than to the doting instruction of a particular man (135d3–7). But what's immanifest cannot be put on display, and more than anything else Alcibiades wants to make a display of himself. Alcibiades' response appears to show Socrates that he who spans the range of human types offers a glimpse of each while doing justice to none. Throughout the dialogue, Alcibiades has been so eager to take up his next means to success that he never dwelled on any particular argument more than momentarily. His tendency is never to save a position under attack but to find a new one sturdier than the last. Alcibiades' peculiarity as a type thus prevails over all the other types enclosed within him. And it is in this inclination to save face that Alcibiades betrays his dependence on the attention of others. After his turn to Alcibiades, Socrates is therefore left with two tasks: to complete Alcibiades' education (so far as possible) and to investigate the cause of his teaching's distortion. This he does, as we will see, in the *Protagoras*, *Second Alcibiades*, and *Charmides*.

III. Socrates After Alcibiades

Alcibiades leaves his conversation with two options. He can and will, as he promises at the end, pursue his erstwhile pursuer. But

Socrates also directed Alcibiades to the possibility of learning from those reputed to be wise, among whom one counts the sophists. As it stands, Socrates' argument against the teachability of virtue has been merely circumstantial, that is, based on Alcibiades' experience of and with Pericles (cf. 118e8–119a7). As Socrates confesses, his education of Alcibiades is both incomplete and risky (135e4–8). It remains for Socrates to redirect Alcibiades away from those reputed to be wise and to restore his own reputation, while Alcibiades must attend both to these so-called wise men and to Socrates to consider the question of whether virtue can be taught. The *Protagoras* meets these circumstances precisely. There, Socrates appears to attempt a restoration of his reputation by rushing to tell an anonymous comrade, very much the average Athenian and very much intrigued by Socrates' relationship with Alcibiades, of how he succeeded in saving the impetuous, young Hippocrates from the clutches of the great sophist Protagoras. When they arrive at the home of Protagoras' patron and host, Callias, they encounter those with the greatest reputations for wisdom, that is, those to whom Alcibiades is most likely to attend, besides Socrates yet after his Socratic education (*Protagoras* 337c5–e2 with *Hippias Major* 285d3–e2). Indeed, Alcibiades arrives soon after or even following Socrates, albeit in the company of the poet and eventual tyrant Critias, seen again later in the *Charmides* (*Protagoras* 316a3–5). While there, Alcibiades takes every pain to ensure that Protagoras submit to Socratic conversation, to see whether Socrates can befuddle the greatest of sophists as he had Alcibiades (cf. *Protagoras* 336b4–d5, 347a6–b7, 348b2–c4). Socrates does. For he leaves Protagoras with the conclusion that virtue—what Alcibiades is determined to acquire only after his encounter with Socrates—is knowledge yet not teachable, that is, that the alternative Socrates left open in the *Alcibiades* is rather closed (*Protagoras* 361a3–c2). Socrates thus appears to succeed in completing the argument of the *Alcibiades* while restoring his own reputation, as Hippothales must be disappointed with what he's seen from Protagoras (*Protagoras* 362a4: ἀπῇμεν). We assume that Alcibiades, more competent then Hippothales, would have experienced a similar disappointment.

Perhaps for this reason, Socrates next encounters a dejected Alcibiades in the *Second Alcibiades*, as he is now left either with Socrates, who cannot give him what he wants, or the god, whose failure to answer his prayers leaves him hopeless (*Second Alcibiades* 138a1–b5).[13] In the course of their conversation, Socrates convinces Alcibiades to guard against praying for bad things that seem good (τἀγαθά) (*Second Alcibiades* 148a8–b4). Toward that end, Alcibiades agrees that he needs someone to remove this occluding mist from his soul as Athena did for Diomedes (*Second Alcibiades* 150d3–e2; cf. Homer, *Iliad* 5.375–415 with *Symposium* 190b5–c1). Socrates is silent as to what in the soul allows one to recognize evil and good (ἐσθλόν) (*Second Alcibiades* 150e1–3: δι' ὧν), with the means to such recognition having been presented both in the form of a prayer and as a sort of knowledge (*Second Alcibiades* 142e1–143a5, 144d4–7). But the difference doesn't seem to matter to Alcibiades, who later confessed a concern that he would waste his life beside Socrates (*Symposium* 216a6–8). He was fated, it seems, to turn to the praise of the Athenians instead, whatever contempt he may have developed for them (*Symposium* 215d3–216c3; cf. *Second Alcibiades* 139c6–9). Indeed, so strong was Alcibiades' attraction to their praise that even Socrates' subsequent display of endurance, courage, prudence, and overall excellence at Potidaea and Delium[14] was insufficient to convince Alcibiades that the life of moderation and justice through self-knowledge delivered on its promise of virtue (*Symposium* 219e5–

---

[13] It might seem strange to treat the *Second Alcibiades* in a section titled "Socrates After Alcibiades," but on this point Helfer is helpful: "*Alcibiades/ Second Alcibiades* is not the only pair of Platonic dialogues to feature the same interlocutors, nor is it the only pair with both parts named after the same person. It is, however, the only pair of dialogues in which the title of one suggests that it cannot be understood apart from the other. The *Alcibiades* can stand alone, but the title *Second Alcibiades* implies that the dialogue's purpose and meaning are not fully discernible without reference to the *Alcibiades*" (Helfer, *Socrates and Alcibiades*, 101).

[14] Cf. Zuckert, *Plato's Philosophers*, 237 n. 41.

221c1).[15] Or, rather, it only further convinced him of his own inferiority to Socrates in his dependence on the praise of the Athenians (*Symposium* 221c2–222a6 with 216a8–c3). Whatever the case, Alcibiades' concern that the Athenian generals recognize Socrates for his display of excellence at Potidaea must have shown Socrates that Alcibiades was irreversibly in love with the many and that he himself would forever be associated with Alcibiades (*Symposium* 220e5–7: αὐτὸς...σαυτόν).[16]

It is no surprise, then, that upon return from Potidaea Socrates almost immediately went to his old haunts to examine the current state of philosophy and of the wisdom and beauty of the young (*Charmides* 153a1–6, d2–5). There he encountered the aforementioned Critias, who appears to have taught Charmides that moderation (σωφροσύνη) is doing one's own things (τὸ τὰ ἐαυτοῦ πράττειν) and who, in turn, defines moderation as self-knowledge, namely, as knowing what one knows (*Charmides* 161b4–c1, 162c1–d6, 167a5–8). One hears echoes of Socrates' education of Alcibiades in these formulas, and so suspects that Critias like Alcibiades was among Socrates' students before Potidaea (cf. *Charmides* 156a7–8). Indeed, Critias detects in Socrates' critique of his definition of moderation a desire to refute for refutation's sake, that is, he suspects that Socrates has the very same opinion as he (*Charmides* 166c3–6 with 163e4–5). But whereas Critias sees doing one's own things as a handy formula passed on from Socrates to himself and from

---

[15] When Socrates returns from Potidaea, everyone is surprised that he has survived, while many well-known men were killed (*Charmides* 153a1–d1, esp. b1: ἀπροσδοκήτου, b4, b9–c1, c3). Whatever reputation Socrates had cultivated by this point, it does not seem to have been one of military virtue. Compare the Socrates of Aristophanes' *Clouds*, whose disregard of political things does not mean that he lacks a sort of continence or self-control; rather, he seems exceptional in this regard (cf. Aristophanes, *Clouds* 184–86, 363, 723–26).

[16] Benardete suggests that Socrates actually may have intended all along to send Alcibiades back to Athens with self-loathing at his lack of moderation, so as to urge Athens to restrain herself, as did eventually (though not immediately) happen (Seth Benardete, *The Argument of the Action*. [Chicago: University of Chicago Press, 2000], 185).

himself to Charmides, Socrates sees it as a riddle (*Charmides* 161c8–9, 162a10–11, b4–6); whereas Critias defines moderation as knowledge of knowledge (ἐπιστήμη ἐπιστήμης), Socrates must intervene to include knowledge of ignorance (*Charmides* 166e5–9); whereas Critias grows angry at Charmides for flubbing his lines, Socrates with curiosity reflects back on a conversation in which he saw his education transformed (*Charmides* 162c1–d6, 153a1 ff.); whereas Critias sees moderation as a science similar to calculation (λογιστική) and geometry, Socrates finds this view rather perplexing (*Charmides* 165e3–166a2, 167b6–8); whereas Critias speaks incoherently to hide his perplexity, Socrates wishes rather to further the inquiry (*Charmides* 169b5–d8); and whereas Critias dreams of a science that would allow one to live a life without error, Socrates suspects himself to be a fool and a paltry searcher (*Charmides* 171d2–172a6, 173a3–5, 175e5–176a4). Socratic refutation appears to have made Critias fall in love with abstraction and precision, yet without the accompanying sensitivity to the problem of self-knowledge: Critias of his own initiative hides Socratic stripping below a form of therapy; he does not consider how they may be one and the same, how confusion is the cure (*Charmides* 154e5–b8). In all these ways, Critias unknowingly shows Socrates how his teaching adopts foreign hues in the mouths of others, and how this very process is the key to the specific difference between himself and Critias.

Parmenides sent Socrates back into Athens with the task to sort out man as a moral and intellectual being. To accomplish this task, Socrates examined a single man, Alcibiades. Gifted in nature and circumstance beyond his compatriots, Alcibiades developed a vanity that left no avenue to competence unclaimed, so that he promised to contain within him all other types. But what Socrates does not anticipate is that, just as Alcibiades distorts the world to serve his ends, so too he distorts Socrates. And the inevitable consequence of this distortion is that the perceived sins of Alcibiades are assumed to reflect the sins of his intellectual father. Recognizing this after Potidaea, Socrates returned to see the problem of self-knowledge distorted into a science in the mouth of Critias. Different as this reaction is from that of Alcibiades, who clung in self-loathing first to Socrates and then to the Athenian multitude, still the *Charmides* ends similarly to the *Alcibiades*, with its title character eagerly attending to Socrates (135d7–11 with *Charmides* 176b1–4). That Charmides does so in obedience to the command of his guardian Critias shows Socrates that his attempt to elucidate the difference between himself and Critias has not robbed Critias' scientific veneer of all its sheen, at least for Charmides (*Charmides* 176b5–c4). Perhaps for this reason, then, Socrates rehearses the conversation again by himself or for another. The conversation in the *Charmides* thus confirms and (upon Socrates' repetition) explores what Socrates surmised at the end of the *Alcibiades*, that his public reputation will forever be associated with Alcibiades and, now, Charmides and Critias. The Socratic transformation of Alcibiades seems to have entailed the Alcibiadic transformation of Socrates, or at least of his reputation (cf. *Second Alcibiades* 142b3–c3, *Second Letter* 314c1–4). Socrates acted as though he could treat man without considering his own place in the human order. And with his αὐτός irreversibly limited, Socrates has unwittingly set in motion his own accusation.[17] The *Alcibiades*' final words are σοῦ κρατήσῃ: "It, the city, might master you." They are a serious warning of the city's power that playfully pun on Socrates' name.

---

[17] Compare Aristophanes, *Clouds* 218–19 and context.

PITY THE TYRANT

Nicholas D. Smith

Introduction

We are used to thinking of liberty and tyranny as something like polar political opposites: tyrannies are those forms of government that eliminate individual liberties and thus oppress those governed. On the contrary, the best regimes are those that afford the greatest liberty to the governed, who are thus not simply negatively free from oppression but in the best cases also positively free to pursue their own private interests without interference from or control of the state. Equipped with these assumptions, however, we will find ourselves quite taken aback when we read what Plato has to say about liberty and freedom in the *Republic*.

In Book 8 of the *Republic* he characterizes democracy, with the great liberties it affords to its citizenry, as only the second-worst possible form of government, with the very worst being tyranny. In other words, Plato counts tyranny as only one further step down from democracy, which Plato is very clear is a form of government that is all about liberty. Along with liberty, moreover, Plato also recognizes that the recognition and valorization of liberty also leads to the greatest degree of acceptance of *diversity* among the city's citizens. Modern liberals think of that as a very good thing. For Plato, it is one of the clearest indications of precisely what is wrong with valuing liberty in the way democracy does.

> First of all, then, aren't they free? And isn't the city full of freedom and freedom of speech? And doesn't everyone in it have the license to do what he wants?
>
> That's what they say, at any rate.
>
> And where people have this license, it's clear that each of them will arrange his own life in whatever manner pleases him.
>
> It is.

Then I suppose that it's most of all under this constitution that one finds people of all varieties.

Of course. (*Republic* 5567b–c)

Plato goes on to describe an appreciation for this kind of diversity as something that "women and children do when they see something multicolored" (557c). Contemporary readers would have to be able to muster a remarkable degree of moral blindness not to see a diversity of political *incorrectness* in Plato's assessment here! But don't worry, Plato also has some lovely things to say about people like me trying to do philosophy, which he compares to the circumstance of some "bald-headed tinker" seeking to "marry his boss's daughter" (*Republic* 495e). You may wish to bear this in mind as I now proceed with my argument.

You will be relieved to hear that in the remainder of my discussion I do not at all intend to defend Plato or his views on liberty and tyranny. Rather, I will do what we professional scholars are supposed to be able to do, which is to try to explain *why* Plato has such a shockingly negative view of liberty and diversity. The best way to do this, I think, is to focus mainly on what Plato has to say about tyranny and the tyrant, because it is in his remarks about the worst ruler and the worst political regime that we can see most clearly why Plato's own view diverge so far from our own intuitions.

The Powerless Tyrant

One of the aspects of Plato's writing that most intrigued me when I first started reading his works was in passages where Plato quite purposefully presents arguments that he recognizes will seem extremely heterodox to his readers. In some cases, he actually has Socrates' interlocutors gawp with incredulity at what Socrates says—only to find themselves eventually having to agree with what they had initially found so very implausible. An especially good example of this sort of moment in Plato occurs when Socrates argues with Polus about tyrants in the *Gorgias*. The passage is far too long to quote, beginning at 466b and going through 481b, so I will need mostly just to summarize it here.

The argument is first engaged when Polus reacts defensively when Socrates categorizes the rhetoric and oratory Polus so greatly admires as a kind of flattery—the sort of enterprise that Socrates contemptuously describes as "mischievous, deceptive, disgraceful, and ill-bred" (465b). Polus nearly chokes with shock, but then shows why he admires great orators in the way he does: Polus believes that they are comparable to tyrants in the power that they wield. Speaking of the orators, Polus presses Socrates:

> Polus: Don't they have the greatest power in their cities?
>
> Socrates: No, if by "having power" you mean something that's good for the one who has the power.
>
> Polus: That's just what I do mean.
>
> Socrates: In that case I think that orators have the least power of any in the city.
>
> Polus: Really? Don't they, like tyrants, put to death anyone they want, and confiscate the property and banish from their cities anyone they see fit? (*Gorgias* 466b–c[1])

The context of this argument, as it is represented in the *Gorgias*, is democratic Athens, and Polus' point is one that is readily applicable in any democratic regime: those who command the widest support from the citizens of a democracy end up having the kind of power in that regime that we would in the most extreme cases associate with tyrants. The examples Polus gives here—putting adversaries to death, confiscating their property, and banishing them—are obviously excellent examples of not just taking liberty away from other citizens, but, if you will permit me, actually taking liberties *with* other citizens: doing whatever the tyrant feels like doing to them or with them. So I think Polus here expresses a view that most of us—at least those of us who haven't read Plato yet—would

---

[1] All translations included herein are those in J. M. Cooper, ed. *Plato: Complete Works* (Indianapolis: Hackett Publishing Co, 1997).

enthusiastically agree to: tyrants, or anyone else who is given what might be called "the greatest political power" in a country, are those within that country who also have the greatest liberty. They can do whatever they feel like doing, and are the most free in both negative and positive senses: they are the most unrestricted by others in the state, and are also the most able to pursue whatever they feel like pursuing. Like Polus, I think most people would at least envy that condition, and with envy often goes admiration, as in Polus' case.

But in these first lines of the argument, Socrates has also gestured at *why* his own position is the exact opposite of Polus'. Polus envies and admires tyrants and political bigshots because of the *power* they wield; Socrates astonishingly asserts that these are the *least* powerful people in their states. And the reason he has already indicated for saying such a thing is that—without yet explaining why he believes this—he counts someone as powerful only if what constitutes their putative power is something that is *good* for them. Socrates, accordingly, has already indicated that he does not regard the things that constitute the kind of alleged "power" that is wielded by tyrants as something that is good for them. He has said that they have the "least power of any in the city" because, it seems, that what constitutes their alleged power is actually *bad* for them.

Now, again, the argument in which Socrates explains all of this to Polus, which then continues when Callicles takes up the argument from a flummoxed Polus, is long and complicated. But the argument itself is based on some things that Socrates and Polus actually agree on, which I suspect may be more controversial for us. The first of their agreements is that what should count as good for an agent is something that is objective, and not just a matter of the agent's subjectivity. What I mean by this is what made me speak earlier about doing whatever one *feels* like doing. Neither Socrates nor Polus, it turns out, is a subjectivist about value or benefit for an agent. In other words, what an agent might *feel like doing* or experiencing might also actually be *bad* for the agent.

Now, I am not going to presume to say that all of us actually accept this "objectivist" view of value. I think that some people today might think of goodness for agents in terms of what is sometimes called "desire satisfaction," where any particular kind of desire will count as relevant to the calculation of goodness. If I desire to use addictive drugs, and am provided with a lifetime supply of the ones I like best, then I might well live a life that is very full of "desire satisfaction" and very little *dissatisfaction* since I will always be able to get access to what my addiction makes me desire most of all. So for what may be called a "value subjectivist," such a life would count as an enviable and highly successful one.

Of course, I use this example because at least some of us might think that such a life would be extremely unenviable and not in the least admirable. If so, that might be taken as an indication of what is called "value objectivism," which holds that what is good for an agent is something that is objectively true about the agent, even if the agent's own subjectivity does not accept the objective good *as good*. You might now associate this position with the way parents often try to manage their children—parents often tell their children that some of the things the children might desire are not good for them. Children resist such an idea because it violates their own subjective sense of what is good for them.

At any rate, this is how Socrates can make the point he gestured at in the beginning of the argument: he says tyrants lack power because what they do have—which Polus counts as power—is not necessarily good for them. As Polus had put the point, tyrants are able to do whatever they see fit to do, that is, whatever they think is best for them. But if what is to count as really good for someone—objectively good, that is—it could come apart from, indeed even turn out to be the opposite of, whatever some agents might *think* is best for them. Polus admires tyrants because they can do whatever they see fit to do. Socrates finds nothing to admire in that, at least as long as what tyrants tend to see fit to do is not really good for them.

I hope the point under review is clear enough now: if we imagine someone who seemed to have a greatly expanded range of capacity to pursue and acquire things that were really *bad* for him or her, we might be inclined to agree with Socrates that such "power" is nothing to envy. We might actually suppose that we would be better off *not* having such capacity. We might not agree with Socrates that such capacity does not qualify as power of a sort; but recall, he only stipulated that because he and Polus only wanted to talk about power that would be *good* for an agent to have. As I say, at least some of us would rather not have power if it were only something that enabled us to harm ourselves more often or more extensively and would do us no good in its exercise.

Another premise in Socrates' argument with Polus that they both accepted, but which at least some of us might not accept, and that comes out a bit later in the argument (467c–468e). Socrates and Polus agree that all of us want what is good for us, so that if we do something that is bad for us, we actually act in a way that qualifies as not doing what we want (5.468d). Again, this reflects the value objectivity on which they agree, but now there is an additional element in the picture, which has to do with human psychology. According to Socrates and Polus, we all desire only what is good and never what is bad. If we do act as if we desire what is bad, that is only because we have made a mistake about it: we have taken the bad thing to be good for us, when in fact it is bad for us.

Now here may be found a view that many people find implausible. Just think about it this way: haven't many of us experienced desires for things we recognize are bad for us? To just give an example from my own past: I was a cigarette smoker until I was thirty. It may be the case when I first started smoking that I was just ignorant about how bad smoking is for smokers. But by the time I was thirty, I knew well enough that smoking was bad for me. As anyone who has tried to quit smoking knows, it is one thing to recognize the badness of smoking and quite another not to desire to smoke. So doesn't this sort of example show that we *don't* as a matter of fact desire only what is good for us and never what is bad for us?

Now it turns out that on this issue, the differences between Greek and English somewhat occlude the point that Polus and Socrates agree on. When we talk about *wanting* something, we can mean it in several different ways. Any desire of any kind will count as an instance of "wanting" its object(s). Greek has different words that might all equally be translated as "desire," however, and while what I am about to say is controversial among scholars, I think

Socrates and Polus are in agreement here only because it is a certain *kind* of what we call "desire" that they have in mind. The Greek word used throughout this argument is *boulêsis*, which is often translated as "wish" or "want." But as I say, there are other kinds of desires, which might be translated as "appetitive desires" or "appetites" (*epithumiai*). I suggest that when Socrates and Polus agree about what we *wish* or *want*, they are talking about the attitude that at least most people take towards what is objectively good for them. There may be a kind of desire that couldn't care less about what is good for me, but it does seem that at least most of us feel some pull within us towards those things that we regard as good for us. So if the struggling dieter gives in to temptation and eats that exquisitely well-crafted piece of German chocolate cake, he will also feel a pang inside—that pang will be the whisper of something else the dieter wishes or wants but in this case does not fulfill: his desire to do what is really good for him and not to do what he realizes is bad for him. His appetitive desire for the cake in this case wins out against his other sort of desire, which is interested in a different kind of goal: the attainment of (only) what is good for him. In yet another dialogue, Plato has Socrates say that there are at least three different kinds of psychological processes within us that we might all call by the single word, "desire": *boulêsis* which aims at what is actually good for us; *epithumia* which aims at pleasure, and *erôs*, which aims at what is beautiful (*Charmides* 167e).

So perhaps there are people who have become so depressed or otherwise disordered that they actually lose all interest in what is actually good for them. But it is maybe not so strange that Socrates and Polus seem to agree that at least as a generality about people that we do all desire what is good for us in some way—even if that kind of desire can at times be overpowered by other kinds of desire.

If so, however, then we have learned something very important about tyrants, which is that the great license they enjoy to pursue any and all sorts of desires may not be good for them: if they pursue kinds of desire that are not at all focused on what is good for them (appetites, for example, or what we might call "cravings"), such pursuits may result in much greater frustration of the will to achieve what is really good for themselves, even as they can satiate other sorts of desire—whose satiation is not good for them.

This brings me to the further point. The way that Plato has Socrates finally win the argument—even as his interlocutors balk—is by showing that the threat of "appetitive desires" is not just that they do not necessarily aim at what is really good for us. The greatest threat comes from the way in which these appetites respond to satiation: the more we focus on these appetites and the more success we have in satiating them, the more demanding they become—to the point where they begin to control our behavior in ways that increasingly interfere with and defeat our will for only what is actually best for us. As Socrates explains to Callicles, when it comes to dealing with these sorts of desires, the best one can hope to achieve is to keep them in a disciplined condition so they will not interfere with what a person needs to do to pursue what is really good, instead. Socrates compares this process to what doctors do with people who have become sick:

> Socrates: Now isn't it true that doctors generally allow a person to fill up his appetites, to eat when he's hungry, for example, or drink when he's thirsty as much as he wants to [again *bouletai*] when he's in good health, but when he's sick they practically never allow him to fill himself with what he has an appetite for? [...]
>
> Callicles: Yes.
>
> Socrates: And isn't it the same way with the soul, my excellent friend? As long as it's corrupt, in that it's foolish, undisciplined, unjust and impious, it should be kept away from its appetites and not be permitted to do anything other than what will make it better. (505a–b)

The way Plato has Socrates put this is to compare what is good and bad for our bodies with what is good and bad for our *souls*. But I think the point can be made without a Socratic or Platonic conception of souls. The point is that once we accept that there are things that are really good for us, whereas there may be other things that we desire in other ways, which are not good for us, then we have to accept the challenge of resisting the kinds of desires that will harm us and promoting our interest in what is actually good for us, instead. And this is why Socrates said to Polus that what Polus had thought was a kind of power that was good to have was actually nothing we should envy and something we would reasonably prefer not to have. Tyrants have the liberty to pursue and acquire maximally the kinds of pleasures and activities that are not really good for them, but this sort of "power" actually affords them no advantage at all in terms of what is really good for them. But not just this: in exercising their enhanced capacity to serve and satisfy their appetitive desires, they actually damage themselves in the most important and intimate way. As Plato has Socrates put it in the *Gorgias*, they damage their souls, and the more successful they are in this self-destructive path, the more likely it is that they will actually become *ruined* souls—so badly damaged that even the gods in the afterlife cannot fix what they have broken in themselves (*Gorgias* 525c).

In addition to this theory of desire—or perhaps I should say "desires," since it now seems that there can be different kinds with different aims—Plato has Socrates complete his disparagement of the putative power and liberty of the tyrant by attaching this theory of moral psychology to a theory of *agency*. That is, Socrates associates this picture of psychology with a theory about how people act and why they act in the ways they do. This theory is sometimes called "intellectualist," which is the jargon term for the view that Socrates expresses at *Gorgias* 467e to 468c, where he and Polus agree that it is not just that we always *want* what is good for us, as a matter of fact, we always do whatever we do because we think that acting in that way will be good for us. To put the point in a slightly different way, a theory of agency is "intellectualist" if it maintains that one's actions as an agent *always reflect one's beliefs*—in this case, beliefs the agent has regarding what is best for the agent, among the options of which the agent is aware, at the moment of action. Now, as I said, Polus agrees with this claim, but it is worth pointing out that from this claim it follows that no one ever acts in a way they believe is actually *contrary* to their best interests—at least at the moment they act. Of course, it certainly *seems* like people do this sort of thing—recall my example of smoking when I was already well aware that it wasn't good for me.

We might accordingly simply dismiss this theory as just a mistake that Socrates and Polus have made, but before we do that, we should take a closer look at how that theory must work. So, first, let us remind ourselves that Plato thinks there are different kinds of desires, with different aims. Only the kind of desire that he calls "*boulêsis*" has the real good as its aim. But now we have learned that whenever we act, we act as if it is this sort of desire that is in control—we act as if we are aiming to achieve the goal of *boulêsis*, and not just some other sort of desire, such as appetite. As I just said, that seems, when we consider how we act sometimes, to be simply false. But one way to make it more plausible is to consider how these other sorts of desire represent their objects to us.

To go back to my case of the struggling dieter confronted with an obviously well-crafted German chocolate cake. He reminds himself that eating this cake is a violation of his diet. On the other hand, he does feel very much as if he wants to eat that cake. But why? Well, Socrates might reasonably insist that he wants to eat that cake because it really *looks good* to him. If it didn't look good, he wouldn't feel so tempted. To put it the way Plato has Socrates put it in a different dialogue (the *Protagoras*) the cake presents an *appearance* of goodness. It does so, I claim, in virtue of being the aim of a certain kind of desire—in this case, an appetitive desire. So I understand what Socrates has in mind as something like this: appetitive desires aim at what is pleasurable, but not just that—they also represent what is pleasurable as something *good*, something good for the agent to pursue. And because they are represented to the agent's judgment as something good for the agent to pursue, then the agent will be disposed to *believe* that what the appetite presents as good actually *is good* for the agent. So if the dieter finds himself struggling with the desire to eat the German chocolate cake, it is not necessarily correct to think that he does not at all believe that eating the cake will be good for him. Rather, his struggle is not just in terms of conflicting *desires*, it is in terms of conflicting inclinations about what he should *believe* about eating the cake—he has reasons to think that it would be good (as satisfying an appetitive desire, which he is inclined to think is good because that is how appetitive desires work); but he also has reasons to think it would not be good, but bad for him (because he has reasons to think that eating the cake will violate a diet that he has committed himself to). So whether he eats the cake or not will depend on which of these processes—each of which inclines him to believe different things about the value of eating the cake—actually gets him to the belief that will trigger and underpin whatever he ends up doing.

If this is right, then we can see very clearly why Socrates thinks we need to keep our appetitive desires in check: if we don't keep them in check, they can grow in power, which means that they can increase their ability to influence our evaluative judgments of things. The problem is that they do not, in fact, aim at what is good for us, and so they are very unreliable guides for us to follow in judging what is really good for us. But in representing their aims as goods, and thus inclining us to judge that their aims are actually goods, they end up misleading us about what we all really want for ourselves, which is to be benefited and not harmed. The more the influence over our decision-making grows, the less able we are to pursue intelligently our own true benefit.

Socrates thinks that this shows that tyrants are, in fact, not to be envied, but actually deserve our pity and contempt. Their alleged "power" is simply an expanded access to the kinds of things for which they feel appetitive desires, and in taking advantage of this greater access, they increasingly damage their own judgment of what is really good for them. In the end, they are left in the very unenviable condition of being the most unreliable, extremely poor judges of what is really best for them. Always acting, as all of us do, in such a way as to do what they think is best for them, their judgments of what is really best for them is less and less accurate, more and more errant, with the result that they actually end up in conditions we should do everything in our power to avoid. So much for the tyrants' allegedly enviable power.

The Self-Enslaved Tyrant

I began by making some observations about the way in which Plato makes democracy, with its concern for individual liberty, really just one step away from tyranny, where all the liberty craved by the democrat ends up in the hands of the tyrant. I believe that what I have discussed from the *Gorgias* helps us to understand why Plato feels such contempt for tyranny—it is because the sort of liberty tyrants tend to be associated with, the kind they assign to themselves and deny to others, is not a kind of liberty that conduces to what is really good for the tyrant (or for that matter, to anyone else).

For various reasons, I do not believe that the psychological theory or the theory of agency that Plato has Socrates provide in the *Republic* is precisely the same as the one I have reviewed in the *Gorgias*. But for my purposes herein, the differences do not matter. Rather, I believe we can take the basic picture Plato has Socrates offer in the *Gorgias* and extend it fruitfully to what he says about liberty and tyranny in the *Republic*.

In the *Republic*, the factor that Plato identifies as the root of all evil is the desire for wealth—he says that a city becomes a democracy "because of its insatiable desire to attain what it has set before itself as the good, namely, the need to become as rich as possible" (*Republic* 555b). The problem here should by now be familiar: from the fact that people desire wealth, it does not automatically follow that wealth is really good for a city or for the people who have it. As Aristotle later puts it so well in Book 1 of his *Nicomachean Ethics*, where he rightly says that wealth "is merely useful and [is sought] for the sake of something else" (*Nicomachean Ethics* 1096a6–7).[2] The problem, as far as Plato is concerned in the *Republic*, is that the desire for money is inevitably appetitive—the "something else" that Aristotle says makes money useful is that it can make more available to the one who becomes wealthy the very things craved by the appetites (so see *Republic* 553c). Moreover, as Plato makes clear,

---

[2] Trans. W. D. Ross in J. Barnes, ed. *The Complete Works of Aristotle* vol. 2 (Princeton: Princeton University Press, 1984).

democracy sets wealth "before itself as the good." But, of course, wealth is not the good, and tends only to have the effect of making the objects of appetites more accessible. The achievement of this sort of goal, as Plato has Socrates put it with obvious contempt, is that those who so treasure wealth have the effect of making "their young fond of luxury, incapable of effort either mental or physical, too soft to stand up to pleasures and pains, and idle besides" (*Republic* 556b–c). Rather than keeping their appetites in disciplined conditions, Plato thinks that democracies tend to celebrate appetitive desire as if the satiation of such desires was objectively good. As we have now seen, however, Plato regards the path of reckless empowerment of appetitive desire as the most unreliable way to improve our judgment of what is good for us—but that is what the great liberty provided in democracies makes more possible. In a democracy, we all get to do as we please, to do what we think is best for us, much more than in regimes where our autonomy is more limited. That might be good for us if we were already good judges of what really is good for us. But Plato thinks we cannot and will not ever be able to be good judges of what is good for us as long as we valorize—as we saw Polus did—expanding our capacities to pursue appetitive desires.

Now Plato does understand that appetitive desires are not always or necessarily bad for one, nor do they always or necessarily mislead us as to what is good for us. In the *Republic*, he has Socrates carefully distinguish between the kinds of appetitive desires that he calls "necessary," which are "those whose satisfaction benefits us […] for we are by nature compelled to satisfy them" (8.558d–e). The problem is that so many of our desires are not these necessary ones—there are many others that are unnecessary, ones "that someone could get rid of if he practiced from youth on, those whose presence leads to no good or even the opposite" (559a). Plato has Socrates give as examples of the former the desire to eat wholesome foods; the latter would presumably include such things as the desire to eat German chocolate cake.

The effect of surrendering our judgment to the mere appearances of good provided by unnecessary appetitive desires is that our entire conception of value becomes distorted, leading to such corruption of judgment that we end up "calling insolence good breeding, anarchy freedom, extravagance magnificence, and shameless-ness courage" (8.560e). But within us, the effect is not at all the freedom or liberty that we might suppose is good; instead, exercising the liberty to pursue unnecessary pleasures actually destroys not only our evaluative judgment but, paradoxically, even our autonomy. The truly democratic man lives

> always surrendering rule over himself to whichever desire comes along, as if it were chosen by lot. And when that is satisfied, he surrenders the rule to another, not disdaining any but satisfying them all equally. (561b)

In the end, allowing one's judgment of what is actually good for one to be so controlled by the whims of each new unnecessary desire, "democracy's insatiable desire for what it defines as the good [is] also what destroys it" (562b). Earlier, Plato has Socrates say that democracy arises from counting wealth as the good; but as I said earlier, what makes wealth seem valuable to the democrat is that it adds to one's ability to pursue any and all of his or her appetitive desires. That is why he now says that what democracies define as the good is freedom, and this is what causes their destruction (8.562b–c). The city becomes so addicted to the freedom that licenses any whim they may wish to pursue to the point that it becomes lawless and anarchic (8.563d–e). As Thomas Hobbes so aptly puts it much later, in cities like this, human life becomes "nasty, poor, brutish, and short" (*Leviathan* 13.9). And, much as Hobbes later imagines it, in order to gain protection from such conditions, democracy will ultimately give itself over to the autocracy of an absolute monarch—what the Greek call a tyrant: one who is initially regarded as a leader of the people, but who collects all of the liberties excessively bestowed in democracies to himself. While I certainly do not agree with much of what Plato has to say about democracy more generally, I must admit that on this point what he says has begun to seem distressingly familiar in recent days.

It comes as no surprise, at any rate, that Plato regards the tyrant as the most wretched of human beings. For the freedoms he has monopolized are the same ones that had poisoned democracy: they are freedoms to pursue and enjoy the aims of blind appetites which crave unnecessary pleasures and thereby destroy one's own ability to judge what is in one's own best interest. In the life of the tyrant, "many terrible desires grow up day and night [...] needing many things to satisfy them" (9.573d). But without any discipline to control them, the tyrant spends all the wealth he has in the vain attempt to bring the good they so falsely promise. Having exhausted his own resources, he must prey on others' in order to continue his frenzy (9.574a). The effect of such a life is that the tyrant is a friend to none, and never knows true freedom, for he has become the slave of appetites for what is neither necessary nor good for him (576a). Just as the city under tyrannical rule is the least free of cities, so is the soul of the tyrant the least free, with what Plato calls the "maddest and most vicious" elements within him as his master (577d). And so in Book 9 of the *Republic*, we find that the tyrant, just as he was said to be in the *Gorgias* is the least likely of all human beings to do what he wants (577d), having ceded all decision making to the part of himself that is the least concerned with his real benefit. He thus lives the most wretched life possible for a human being (578b–c).

Summary and Conclusion

So, let us review what got us to this point, which, stated bluntly and without all this explanation, might seem simply absurd: Plato accepts that the tyrant is a person with effectively limitless capacity to pursue any and all of his or her whims. But he also argues that such a person would be most likely the most pitiable wretch possible. How, again, does he get there?

First, I argued that an important assumption of Plato's view is that it is an objective matter whether something is or is not good for us. Because this is so, we are not infallible judges of what is good for us. We are well supplied with subjective views on the matter, but Plato thinks that what we subjectively judge as good for us may in fact not be good for us, and so the fact that something *seems* to be good for us is an inadequate reason to accepting it as such. The result is that being given vastly increased capacity to pursue whatever seems to be good for us may be no benefit, and may even be disadvantaging—to the degree that we are not good judges of our own benefit.

Second, I claimed that Plato recognized different kinds of desire. He says we all desire what is genuinely good for us, though we may not always be reliable judges of what that actually consists in. But we also have other sorts of desires that do not aim at our benefit, but at other things—most important among these sorts of desires are those Plato calls "appetitive," which aim at satiations we experience as pleasures. Many of these—indeed most of them, it seems, are desires for things that we do not actually need, and that are not always or even usually good for us.

Third, I claimed that Plato supposed that our desires are responsive to habituation through our responses to them. The more we allow a certain kind of desire to be satiated, the more that desire will strengthen within us. Recognizing this as a fact of human psychology, Plato recommended retraining our appetitive desires in such a way as to keep them in what he called a "disciplined condition," to prevent them from growing too strong and unruly.

Fourth, I noted that Plato has an intellectualist view of agency: he thinks that whatever we do as agents, we do for the sake of what we take to be good for us. I sought to explain this feature of his view by saying that he must suppose that appetites work in us by representing their objects as good things for us, things that if we were to do as our appetites bid us to do with respect to these things, we would be better off for it. The way this works with the point about habituation and disciplining appetitive desires is that it indicates that Plato supposes that one who is too indulgent with respect to appetitive desires will suffer damage to his or her ability to make sound evaluative judgments. The reason for this is that appetitive desires incline us to believe that their targets are actually good for us, but such beliefs are not veridically reliable. Since the appetites aren't really aiming at what is truly good for us, they cannot be relied upon as indicators of our good. But even so, they work in such a way as to influence what we believe about our own good.

These points, then, are what inform Plato's peculiar views about liberty and tyranny. He views increases of liberty in societies with great skepticism, because he thinks that such increases are inevitably aimed not at what is really good for us, but at the very unreliable and misleading indicators of benefit that have their basis in our appetites for unnecessary and even deleterious pleasures. But we also find that in the end, he characterizes what most of us take to be true liberty to be the very opposite—to be, in fact, the chains that would enslave and ruin us. It is this false sense of liberty that turns the tyrant into the most slavish of all human beings, and the least powerful in terms of what is good for him.

If we attempt to read between these lines into what Plato thinks true liberty might consist in, we can see that it, too, will have a paradoxical character: real freedom, for Plato, derives from self-*restraint*. We might find very odd the idea that the right conception of freedom relies on a condition of restraint. But that is Plato's view: it requires making ourselves as *unfree* as we can possibly make ourselves, with respect to the kinds of liberty we typically pursue with the greatest avidity. Not only should we not pursue unnecessary pleasures—we should live our lives in such a way as to feel as little desire for such things as is humanly possible. If we can just be free of our own propensity for slavish cravings of what is not good for us, then at last might we achieve the only kind of autonomy that is worth having. But that is not what the tyrant achieves. The tyrant does not do what he wants or do himself any good at all. Pity the tyrant!

Bibliography of Sources Cited

Aristotle, *The Complete Works of Aristotle* in 2 vols., ed. J. Barnes. Princeton: Princeton University Press, 1984.

Hobbes, Thomas. *Leviathan or the Matter, Forme, & Power of a Commonwealth Ecclesiasticall and Civill.* https://socialsciences.mcmaster.ca/econ/ugcm/3ll3/hobbes/Leviathan.pdf

Plato, *Plato: Complete Works*, ed. J. M. Cooper, Indianapolis: Hackett Publishing Company, 1997.

PLATO ON THE TYRANNICAL TEMPTATION

Richard S. Ruderman

If the most memorable political teaching in Plato's *Republic* is that of the philosopher-king, a close second would seem to be his seemingly comprehensive and devastating attack on tyranny and the life of the tyrant. In Book 1 of the *Republic*, Socrates so firmly rebukes Thrasymachus (a mere teacher of tyranny) that many scholars treat the two as polar opposites. Asked by Glaucon and Adeimantus in Book 2 to compare the lives of the just and the unjust individuals, Socrates responds by elaborating a city-in-speech, the discussion of which practically culminates in a comparison of the philosopher and the tyrant, presented as though they were exemplars of the two opposed ways of life. And the comparison, of course, is very much to the tyrant's disadvantage.[1] If we are to judge by their respective enjoyments of happiness, Socrates offers the perhaps mock quantitative analysis that the philosopher's life is "729 times" more pleasant than that of the tyrant (*Republic*, 587e).[2] And when ranking those inferior but more likely-to-exist regimes that fall short in various ways of his model "noble city," Socrates places tyranny dead last (Book 8). So prominent, in fact, is Plato's opposition to tyranny that Machiavelli, writing two millennia later, makes one lone reference to Plato in his magisterial *Discourses on Livy*: Plato is there referred to, not as the teacher of the Ideas, or of the disembodied soul, or of the mysteries of eros, but as the teacher of two conspirators who fail

---

[1] Newell, summing up the standard view, characterizes Book 9 as a "contest between philosophy and tyranny" in which Socrates "defend[s] justice against the tyrannical extremes of injustice" (Waller R. Newell, *Ruling Passion: The Erotics of Statecraft in Platonic Political Philosophy*, [Lanham: Rowman & Littlefield 2000], 175).

[2] All parenthetical references, unless otherwise indicated, are to Stephanus pages in the *Republic*. I rely on Bloom (1968) for the translation, but make several alterations for the sake of greater accuracy.

to kill a tyrant.[3] However ineffective Plato's political teaching may be, its core has long seemed to be an unforgiving opposition to tyranny.

The Tyrannical Temptation

Given the massive impression left by the *Republic* that Plato was utterly—if apparently somewhat impotently—opposed to tyranny, it is all the more surprising to find, both in the *Republic* and in other dialogues, an array of remarks that seem to qualify and undercut that blanket opposition. There are, in fact, three types of such observations. First, Plato suggests, most prominently in the *Laws* and the *Letters* recounting Plato's own efforts with Dionysius,[4] that tyranny can sometimes be productive of some political good. In the *Laws*, the Athenian Stranger encourages his sober and therefore shocked interlocutors to consider the possibility that tyranny—in partnership with a wise ruler—could be an element of a good or even the best regime (*Laws* 709e–710e). Second, the tyrannical individual (at least before he is corrupted by actually becoming a tyrant) seems to understand something important about life that people of ordinary decency do not. In the *Hipparchus*, for example, Socrates recounts several sayings of the tyrant Hipparchus in an almost wholly positive light.[5] And third, his Socrates gently raises the possibility that the tyrant does in deed (while "awake") what all non-philosophers dream of doing (576b).[6]

---

[3] Machiavelli, *Discourses on Livy*, 3.6.16.

[4] See especially *Second Letter*, 310e–311b.

[5] See *Hipparchus* 229a–b. Consider the general thesis of the *Hipparchus*: though "everyone wants the good things always," the "decent" impose limits on their quest for gain (227d). Socrates calls Hipparchus a "good and wise man" who sought to "educate his citizens [to be] the best possible" (228b1, c3–4). Like Socrates, Hipparchus wishes to remove the "wonder" observers might feel at the Delphic pronouncement "Know Thyself," so as to accomplish it (228e2–3).

[6] Nietzsche, both limiting and intensifying this view, writes: "The whole of history teaches that every oligarchy conceals the lust for *tyranny*; every oligarchy constantly trembles with the tension each member feels in maintaining control over this lust. (So it was in *Greece*, for instance: Plato bears witness to it in a

Perhaps most important for our purposes in understanding the *Republic*'s teaching on tyranny, Socrates is less wholly opposed to Thrasymachus than it first seems. If we reconsider his criticism of Thrasymachus in light of his later claim that he was "never an enemy" to him, we discover on closer examination that Socrates had limited himself to saying that he could "in no way agree" only with one specific claim of Thrasymachus: that "the just was the advantage of the stronger" (498c–d, 1.347d). And Socrates then indicated something the reader may have initially overlooked: he and Thrasymachus are in fact in agreement on the most fundamental question that "he who knows would rather be benefited by another than go to the trouble of benefiting another" (347e). That is, while Thrasymachus may mistake *what* one's advantage is, he correctly teaches—from the point of view of the philosopher—that one *ought* to pursue one's own advantage.

Finally, in assessing human nature broadly, Socrates seems to detect a rather widespread, if often buried, temptation to tyranny in many—in fact the vast majority of—human beings. When introducing his discussion of the tyrant, Socrates pauses to observe that "there are...some [unnecessary pleasures and desires] that are hostile to law and that probably come to be in *everyone*" (571b; emphasis added). At the conclusion of the *Republic*, Socrates recounts the Myth of Er, which reveals that the deceased man who gets to choose first (by lot) whichever life he would like to lead when sent back to earth chooses nothing other than the life of the tyrant (619a–b). That is, even the average human being, unexposed to the sophisticated or sophistic arguments of a Thrasymachus (or "countless others"; 358c), harbors tyrannical longings. In fact, Thrasymachus half-justifies his own promotion of tyranny on the grounds that the tyrant "is called happy and blessed, not only by the citizens [over whom he tyrannizes!] but also by whomever else has heard he has done injustice entire" (344b–c). And Glaucon claims that the apparent condemnation of tyranny by most people is ironic or hypocritical: they

---

hundred passages—and he knew his own kind—*and* himself...)" (*Genealogy of Morals* 3.18, emphasis in original).

praise those who abstain from injustice (where they could get away with it) to "each others' faces," so as to shore up the public law-abidingness that protects them, while secretly thinking anyone who turns down a tyranny is a "fool" (360d5). Finally, Socrates himself, precisely when demonstrating that the life of the tyrant is the "most wretched," is careful to distinguish the actual tyrant from those who are "tyrannic [but] live out a private life" (578c). While Plato's Socrates does condemn the (acting) tyrant, then, he also wishes to examine what about tyranny invokes the envy of "everyone" and, in particular, wishes to identify and acknowledge the key insight into the human condition possessed by the rare, self-aware tyrannically inclined person.

It seems, then, we can begin to account for both the intensity and the strangely co-mingled sympathy with which Socrates criticizes tyranny in the *Republic*: it may be the most widespread, if typically deeply suppressed, of human temptations. Even if it is left only to those with the cleverness, tenacity of vision, and simple toughness to *act* on this impulse, almost all of their less capable fellow citizens appear at least to suspect that tyranny is somehow the best way of life. Moreover, Socrates emphasizes that tyranny "emerges out of" democracy (562a). Here, he follows the model according to which each of the previous regimes discussed "emerged out of" the prior one. In each case, a hidden desire of some sort, held to be illegitimate by the prior regime, comes out into the light and overturns the regime from which it emerged. In the honor-loving timocracy, that is, the hidden desire for wealth emerges, creating an oligarchy, while in the money-loving oligarchy, the hidden desire for freedom emerges. In the case of democracy, however, where seemingly every desire (both "necessary" and "unnecessary") is permitted, it would seem that there are *no* suppressed desires. Socrates in fact exaggerates this unrestrained aspect of democracy to such an extent (even the animals show no respect! [563c]) that, I suspect, he is trying to draw our attention to the one desire that is in fact still suppressed. That desire, ignored or rejected as unjust by freedom-loving (in the sense of self-legislating) human beings, turns out to be the desire to rule over—in the sense of imposing necessities on—human beings.

While the tyrant, then, agrees with the philosopher that the best rule dispenses with the rule of law, he disagrees with the philosopher over the desirability of ruling even so understood. That disagreement (regarding the best way of life) seems to turn on the different critiques of the rule of law that tyrant and the philosopher undertake. Let us first consider the tyrant's critique of the rule of law.

According to Socrates' interpretation, the tyrannical individual arises on the basis of having indulged in and then found wanting the extensive freedom of the democratic regime. He seems in particular to be struck by "the absence of any compulsion to rule" in a democratic city (557e). Why should the absence of a "compulsion" to rule, however, amount to the suppression of rule? Insofar as the democratic city is not, after all, anarchic, it must employ something as a substitute for ruling. That substitute appears to be "serving" the city or asking some of its citizens to be public servants. And the prospective tyrant, as though educated by Thrasymachus, seems to recognize that the democratic leader, far from ruling, is thereby ruled in a hidden fashion by the people. The absence of a compulsion to rule issues in a kind of moratorium on rule.

Now, in his effort to escape the easy-going, unfocussed life of the democrat, the nascent tyrant begins by submitting to the "tyrant Eros" (573d3). As we shall see, he does so, not out of some masochistic pleasure that he will later convert into the sadistic one of tyrannizing, but for the liberation from the Law that Eros's demands provoke. (As more than one enraptured lover has said: "I'd do anything for the person I love."[7]) Like the philosopher—or the student of dialectic discussed at the end of Book 7—the tyrant has seen through the merely apparent necessity that the Law, in its august appearance, wishes to impose. But unlike the philosopher (or the student of dialectic), the tyrant considers overcoming the Law to be itself somehow noble. And while the philosopher seeks to discover the natural necessities with which he cannot but comply, the tyrant

---

[7] The first person in literature to turn to Socrates for help—Aristophanes' Strepsiades—agrees to worship Socrates' gods, the Clouds, largely in order to escape "necessity" by successfully breaking the law (*Clouds*, 437).

seeks to recapitulate for others, through his sheer willfulness, the tyranny of Eros that he credits with liberating him from the Law.

None of this is to say that all or most members of a democracy have a barely hidden desire for tyranny. As Socrates suggested earlier in the *Republic*, most people are simply lukewarm, unambitious, and incapable of achieving much that is either great or evil (491e). Their dedication to virtue is too weak; they are merely decent. We now see, however, that Socrates has deferred discussion of the tyrant to this late moment in the dialogue because of a twofold concern: (1) the very ambitiousness of the tyrant's soul places him closer to the philosopher than Socrates wants us initially to see and (2) inflaming the ambitiousness of Glaucon and Adeimantus (the motor that drives the entire construction of the city-in-speech) must succeed entirely, so to speak, convincing both boys to become or to admire philosophers unqualifiedly, or it runs the considerable risk of making them admire or wish to become tyrants.

On the Origins of Tyranny

How then does Socrates himself understand the origin and nature of tyranny and the tyrannical individual? For he is not simply seeking to talk his listeners out of becoming a tyrant or of teaching tyranny to others. Rather, he seeks to understand how and why the tyrannical impulse comes to be. Taking a cue from Glaucon and Thrasymachus, he seems to offer two distinct analyses: one that we might label a "moral" case for tyranny and the other that we might label an "intellectual" case for it. The first and far more prominent route is found in Books 8–9 (Socrates' analysis of all regime types and the human types that exist in them—with a disproportionate amount of attention paid to tyranny and the tyrant). It arises in the transition between democracy and tyranny, for "tyranny…is transformed out of democracy" (562a). This account is presented primarily to Adeimantus, himself the rather moralistic brother of Glaucon. According to this account, the tyrant is driven by a moral revulsion (shared by Adeimantus) at the "anything-goes," charmingly self-indulgent ethos of democracy to re-apply order and the lash of necessity with a vengeance. That is, this kind of tyrant not only co-opts the moral revulsion and shame of the citizens over the loss of law and order, he seems to share them (see 563a–b: the worst disorders in a democracy arise from a fear in teachers and elders to appear "unpleasant or despotic").

Despite giving the massive impression that the tyrant is the unjust man incarnate, Socrates actually shows—a trick he got away with in refuting Thrasymachus in Book 1[8]—that the tyrant is merely "akin," but not simply equivalent, to the unjust man. For what Socrates actually determines is that we can merely "agree to assert" (as opposed to classify correctly) the tyrants are "as unjust as they can be" (576a) and that while the tyrant is the most "wretched" or "unhappy" being, he is not precisely the most unjust. And the specific difference between the tyrant and the unjust man lies in the tyrant's being moved, at some level, by justice itself to become a tyrant. The people, moved by a widespread disgust with various aspects of "late" or "ripe" democracy (such as the outsize influence of a demagogic or chattering class, inequalities of wealth, and an alienated but vast lower class; see 564d–565a), eventually "set up some one man as their special leader" (565c). This tyrant (who "grows naturally" [563e]), then, is chosen by the people in good democratic fashion—a fashion he seems to respect. Now, as this "leader" transforms into an actual tyrant, he utterly abandons justice, behaving in the typically savage, unjust, and demagogic ways of one overseeing a tyranny. And Socrates continues his thoroughly realistic account of the tyrant as he achieves perfection: his cynical affectation of a gracious manner, his demagogic and vague promises of "redistribution of wealth," his engaging in foreign wars in order to cement the greater need for him at home, his domestic war on freedom of thought, and so on. Socrates' unflinching realism here even ends up exposing the

---

[8] There, Socrates tricked Thrasymachus into conceding that the just man was "wise and good" on the less than solid grounds that the just man is "akin" to the wise and good (350c). While the wise and good man, then, may not exactly be just, neither is the unjust man (presumably the tyrant) simply "bad and unlearned" (ibid.).

bogus character of the earlier "realism" of Thrasymachus, with which the latter had justified tyranny.[9] For Socrates mockingly says this tyrant ends up "so happy" and "blessed" that he must purge his regime of any who are "manliest...great-minded [and] prudent" (567b–c, e; cf. 344b). Thrasymachus was wrong to think (if he ever did) the tyrant happy—and seems to have missed the fact that the only people who "call" the tyrant happy are the "worst" types who do so out of sycophantic fear, not envy.

Dialectic and the Threat of Tyranny

But there is a second, rather more obscured account by which a tyrannical individual might arise. Plato obscures this account by placing it prior to any discussion of tyranny or the other regimes. Before turning to his account of the regimes, Socrates explains the path to philosophy, culminating (at the end of Book 7) in a discussion of dialectic (532a–540c). There, he warns of the dangerous, liberating "power of dialectic" (532d8). In the discussion, he notes that when "a question" is asked—namely "What is the noble?"—the dialectical response will refute, "many times and in many ways," the one asking until, convinced that nothing is noble, he becomes an "outlaw," seemingly on his way toward tyranny (538d-539a). It seems that the question "What is the noble?" is not simply "a" question in the sense of one question out of several possibilities, but "the" question that lies at the heart of dialectic. And while Socrates does not offer an example here of a dialectical consideration of the question, he reports—apparently based on long experience of having undertaken such considerations—that "the argument" *always* refutes the questioner. And he reports the effects—at least the initial effects—of the dialectic as well: to the inquisitive young person who, with Socrates' help, raises the question, neither the *law* nor *justice* will appear any

---

[9] That Thrasymachus entertained a relatively "idealistic" view of the tyrant is suggested by his use of terms like "tyrannical laws" (as though a tyrant would be expected to employ them) and his insistence that the true tyrant relies on intelligent deceptions and not only or chiefly on brute force (1.338e).

longer to be any more "noble" than their opposites (538e1–2).[10] As Socrates later demonstrates, a life no longer capable of devoting itself to the noble will have to pursue some type of pleasure, chief among which are the pleasures of tyranny and the pleasures of philosophy (580d–583a). In the passage on the student of dialectic, however, Socrates is silent on which of these two fates awaits him. This, especially in the context, leaves open the possibility that the student of dialectic will reconsider the possibility of tyranny, at least until he can (with the help Socrates offers in Book 9) distinguish its lesser pleasures from the greater pleasures of philosophy.

From these facts, we might deduce (with the help of remarks Socrates makes earlier in the *Republic* and throughout the Platonic corpus) a very crude sketch of how the dialectic—or the initial stages of the dialectic—might proceed. If the noble attracts us with its promise to offer something that transcends our mere self-concern— that appeals to our desire to act for others or the common good, even at a cost to ourselves—then the law and justice would seem to be the paramount exemplars of the noble. And if—as seemed to be the result of the conversations in Book One—we can be shown that we also (always) expect the law and Justice to *serve* our own interests, then the noble stands refuted as self-contradictory. Consider Cephalus' conflicting claims—which cause Socrates to be "filled with wonder"—that he both benefits from old age as a time of "great peace and freedom" (a good in itself) and, through nobly transcending its sufferings, finds it only "moderately troublesome" (329c–d). Or Polemarchus' conflicting desires to do justice for the good of others (unlike his father) but, as Socrates reveals to him, only to others who are themselves just, and who therefore can be presumed to reciprocate (thereby serving his interests after all) (334c–335d). Even Thrasymachus, the great promoter of tyranny, seeks to teach

---

[10] There is an ambiguity in this result. If *every* form of the question "what is the noble?" leaves the questioner refuted, we might expect the student of dialectic to conclude that nothing is noble. In specifying that neither the law nor justice will any longer appear noble, however, Socrates leaves open the possibility of coming to understand, presumably through philosophy, "the noble by nature" (*Laws*, 10.889e7).

others how to achieve the greatest good possible, not only rejecting it for himself but even quasi-knowingly putting himself at risk of being the first person the newly-installed tyrant would kill.[11]

The lure of the noble, then, is powerful, subtle, and surprisingly widespread: even those who believe they have dispensed with justice are moved by it. It is also, as presented in the *Republic*, deeply paradoxical. For those, like Polemarchus, who consciously seek it, are troubled when they are led dialectically to see that its pursuit cannot quite overcome self-concern in the end. And those, like Thrasymachus, who believe they see through it, can be made by Socrates to be ashamed to see that their conscious pursuit of the greatest self-interest was in fact dogged by an underlying and unconfronted longing for the noble. Hence, returning to the focus on the dialectical analysis of the noble in Book 7, we begin to see why such dialectic is both necessary and necessarily dangerous.[12] For the discovery that the case for the noble will be refuted "many times and in many ways" constitutes a fork in the road, one branch of which leads ultimately to philosophy—presented as the most just life—and the other to the life of tyranny—presented as the most unjust life.[13] Of course, standing at the fork in the road, one has lost all conviction in the nobility of justice and so, if one is unaware of the Socratic argument presented in the *Republic* for a less than purely noble justice,[14] one runs

---

[11] Thrasymachus, that is, is one of the "shepherds" in his political tale, believing that he "cares" for the "sheep" (the people) for "their masters' good and their own" (1.343b2). He fails to register, that is, how the "master" (the tyrant he has educated) exploits him no less than the sheep, and would surely put him to death the moment the master suspected him. Thrasymachus further reveals his hidden admiration for the noble in referring to "aristocrats" precisely where we would expect him to refer to "oligarchs" (338d6–7).

[12] Aristotle notes and explains the dangerous character of dialectics at *Topics*, 160b17–24.

[13] It is worth noting here that Polemarchus is the sole interlocutor in the *Republic* who is expressly said to have gone on to partake of philosophy (*Phaedrus* 257b3–4). It seems one cannot grasp the meaning of the refutation of the noble without having first been captivated by it.

[14] Consider the road not taken at 358a, where Socrates suggests justice is good "both for itself and for what comes out of it."

the risk of not even being aware of—or trusting in the existence of—the non-tyrannical path that lies ahead. Teaching, as Socrates does, through dialectic runs the considerable risk that the student will, so to speak, drop the class before the final exam and emerge with a belief in a dangerous half-truth.[15]

Plato foresaw that dialectic would be perhaps the most controversial if not hated aspect of Socratism—and that it would be hated precisely for its apparent and dangerous association with tyranny. Socrates himself introduces the topic by asking Glaucon if he has noticed "how great the harm coming from the practice of dialectic [is] these days…[for] its students are filled with lawlessness" (537e). When Socrates provided an account of his life at his trial, he reveals that most people "hated" undergoing the supposedly benign and enlightening Socratic method (*Apology* 21d1, e2, e4, 22e6, 28a4, 37d2). And in every case, the hatred arose on account of some aspect of Socrates' questioning of the noble or of the interlocutor's genuine dedication to it. The politicians were enraged to find that there was nothing both "noble and good" (to which they had dedicated their lives); the poets that they could not explain or account for the "many noble things" that they "say" (or "assert"; *Apol.* 21d4–5, 22c2–3).[16] And dialectic remained particularly controversial thereafter. In his commentary on Aristotle's *Topics* (his treatise on dialectic), Alexander of Aphrodisias compares the moral character of "dialecticians" to that of the rhetorician who also "attacks by argument on opposite sides of a question and proves the same things now noble, now

---

[15] Averroes, in his comments on this passage, characterizes such students as "pretenders to philosophy"; see Averroes 1974, 100. That is, the "pretenders to philosophy" are not chiefly (basically harmless) faux-metaphysicians but rather those who believe they have been liberated from the noble so they can pursue self-interest unrestrained.

[16] Socrates seems to have respected the genuine "knowledge of many noble things" possessed by the craftsmen (the final class he questioned) to the extent of not refuting them at all (22d2). He merely reports having learned from them that knowledge of the noble in some restricted sphere (e.g., how to make a beautiful pair of shoes) tempts its possessors to believe illegitimately they know (the noble character of?) "the greatest things" (22d7).

ignoble; now expedient, now inexpedient; now just, now unjust."[17] A millennium later, Islamic and Jewish political philosophers, attempting to make a place for Greek philosophy in their respective worlds, conceded its potentially pernicious aspects. Ibn Khaldun warns: "One knows what harm [logic] can do. Therefore, the student of it should be aware of its pernicious aspects as much as he can. Whoever studies it should do so (only) after he is saturated with the religious law and has studied the interpretation of the Qur'an and jurisprudence."[18] And Judah Halevi's Jewish scholar (speaking in the *Kuzari*) avers that even and especially "people of perfect wisdom, such as prophets...cannot refute those who argue with dialectics....[D]ialectic knowledge will cause harm to the true faith" (*Kuzari* 5.16.2). This of course implies that when dialectic is turned against the noble directly (the aspect of the religious law Ibn Khaldun and Halevi champion), there is no remedy at all. In the twentieth century, Karl Popper attacks (Hegelian) dialectic for being in some degree responsible for European fascism, claiming it "encouraged totalitarian modes of thought."[19] And Leo Strauss, whose interpretation of the *Republic* is premised on the notion that philosophy and "the city" may be at odds (Strauss 1964), simply passes over in silence the passage on dialectic under consideration. Such is the potential danger posed by dialectic, especially when directed to the question of the noble, that Socrates does not mention "tyranny" in his discussion of it and, instead, presents his arresting portrait of the worst regime and the human type associated with it a great distance away.

Socrates does not, to repeat, openly say that the student of dialectic, undergoing the refutation of the noble, will risk becoming a tyrant. He says only that he will become an "outlaw" or lawless. And,

---

[17] Alexander of Aphrodisius 2001, 6 (1.1.4).

[18] Ibn Khaldun 1969, 257–258.

[19] See Popper 1945, vol. 2, ch. 12 and sec. 17 of his 1961 "Addenda." Popper claims Plato restricted the usage of dialectic (to those over 50) in his city-in-speech because he is "afraid of the power of thought" to liberate people from the totalitarianism he is supposedly promoting (vol. 1, 133). Popper concedes Plato's opposition to tyranny—on the grounds that it is too democratic (vol. 1, 315n63).

thus far in the discussion, only the philosopher-king has been presented as a ruler who, on account of his wisdom, can rule "lawlessly." In his subsequent discussion of the tyrant, however, Socrates reveals that the tyrant too rules without the law. Despite Socrates' efforts to stress the opposition between the philosopher and the tyrant, he concedes they share this one important characteristic: they both proceed (when ruling) in a lawless manner. Like the tyrant (again, the real tyrant, not the idealized one of Thrasymachus' imagination), the philosopher-king rules without being restrained in any way by laws (which would only interfere with the wise disposition of the individual case). Not only do laws obstruct the rule of wisdom, however, they can themselves be seen as tyrannical. This was indeed a part of Thrasymachus' argument that Socrates did not express his complete opposition to, namely "each ruling group sets down laws to its own advantage" (338e1; cf. Xenophon, *Memorabilia* 1.2.40–46). It is not then chiefly by "lawlessness" that Socrates characterizes tyranny. Rather, for Socrates, tyranny seems to involve rule over "unwilling" rather than "willing" subjects (see *Statesman*, 276e4–6).

We may now be in a position to understand why Socrates described the one who underwent the dialectic's refutation of the noble as an "outlaw" but not as a tyrant. Such a one might not only, by continuing along the path of education outlined within the city-in-speech, become a philosopher and not a tyrant, but he might also, recognizing the compulsory or tyrannical nature of the law, evolve into a wise though not philosophic ruler whose lawlessness permits and even induces him to persuade his future subjects, converting them from unwilling subjects (who might well call him a tyrant) into willing ones. That is, this strange but promising character would, thanks to dialectic, be able enough to rule in an unrestricted fashion and sensitive—or rhetorically able—enough to be able to win his subjects' consent and thereby evade the opprobrium of being called a tyrant (cf. Strauss 1991, 75).[20]

---

[20] Note that, while "good men...are not lovers of honor," they merely wish not to be "*called* hirelings [or]...get called thieves" (347b5–9; emphasis added).

The Genuine Tyrant

It is thus not this figure but the genuine tyrant that Socrates analyzes in Books 8–9. The genuine tyrant is distinguished both from the philosopher and from the student of dialectic who was disabused of his love of the noble by a singular and curious characteristic: his erotic nature. Socrates, Strauss suggests, presents the tyrant as "Eros incarnate."[21] Plato, that is, presents an account of the "authoritarian personality" rather different from the one that was developed by social science in the aftermath of World War II. Where those social scientists ascribe tyrannical impulses to anger (what Plato calls *thymos* or spiritedness), Plato suggests that the true tyrant loses interest in anger (which Plato in fact connects much more closely to justice, patriotism and political life generally) and is consumed instead by *eros*. But it is far from clear how *eros* explains the genuine tyrant.

Let us first consider the related and subordinate question of why Socrates directs his criticism of the tyrant—which contains within it the troubling concession that the life of tyranny is *the* alternative to the best life, the life of philosophy—to Adeimantus. After all, it was Glaucon who had expressed an interest in becoming a tyrant in Book 2. And it was to Glaucon that Socrates directed his remarks on the refutation of the noble in Book 7. Adeimantus, more cautious and less bold, had expressed only an interest in becoming a member of an "old boys' club," a kind of secret oligarchy hidden within a regime ruled by others (365d). The answer seems to be connected with the fact, already discussed, that Socrates' critique of the tyrant is not without its grudging admission of something impressive or clear-sighted about the tyrant. It is as though Socrates must first tempt Adeimantus to think of becoming a tyrant—or to see that he has harbored a hidden desire to become a tyrant all along—before Socrates can present a truly compelling critique of tyranny to him.

It seems we have arrived at the following conclusion. Despite using an argument structured to make us think of philosophy and

---

They are, then, lovers of gain who understand the importance of not appearing to be so.

[21] Strauss 1964, 111, 133.

tyranny as the most diametrically opposed extremes (see note 1), the argument (of Books 8–9) actually indicates they have a certain kinship.[22] One of the grounds of that kinship seems to be their respective connections to democracy. For, we recall, democracy is both the only regime (other than the imaginary city-in-speech) in which a philosopher can emerge *and* is identified as the regime "out of which" the tyrant emerges. There is something incomplete about democracy, about the regime most dedicated to freedom and variety (which ought thereby to contain all human types or possibilities within it). But while philosophy seems capable of carrying on its work within a democracy, tyranny aspires to achieve or provide or enact that missing something. As suggested earlier, the chief thing missing appears to be the (beneficial) felt presence of some kind of rule or necessity. And this most immediately accounts for the emergence of the tyrant from democracy. When he—or those who promote him as their champion—becomes disgusted with the waywardness, the lack of any and all sense of complying with necessity, the tyrant is moved to re-impose it with a vengeance.

It is worth very briefly considering the career of necessity in modern political philosophy, understood as the outlook designed to liberate humanity most completely from necessity. For a surprising amount of effort was put into pursuing and justifying the Platonic tyrant's insights and path (as presented in Books 8–9) rather than the philosopher's. When Machiavelli overturned the twin pillars of classical political philosophy (with its view that nature somehow compels us to certain ends) and Judeo-Christian theology (which issues commandments, either serially or "completed" in Christ), he immediately turned to the task of discovering or imposing "new necessities" in order to keep a republic "free" (*Discourses on Livy*, 1.49).

---

[22] Note that the exchange and extended correspondence between the twentieth century's leading Socratic, Leo Strauss, and its only thoughtful or philosophic defender of tyranny, Alexandre Kojève, is initiated by Kojève's insistence that "there is no essential difference between the tyrant and the philosopher" (Strauss 1991, 158). As though attempting to win Kojève from the tyrannical path outlined in Bks. 8–9 to Socratic philosophy, Strauss proceeds through a dialectical analysis outlined in Book 7 of the implicit Kojèvian claim that tyranny is noble.

The chief political concept drafted to impose those necessities is none other than "what is called tyranny by the authors" (1.25).[23] And Machiavelli justifies this harsh teaching as follows:

> As it has been written by certain moral philosophers, the hands and the tongue of men—two very noble instruments for ennobling him—would not have worked perfectly nor led human works to the height they are seen to be led to had they not been driven by necessity (3.12.1).

That is, while Machiavelli rejects the various so-called necessities traditionally shaping and driving humanity, he re-emphasizes the need to construct new ones in order to "ennoble" humanity.

Afterward, Hobbes and Locke, both impressed by the precarious and inhumane state of perfect freedom from all necessity in the State of Nature, sought ways to freely impose legitimate legal authority over us that would function as man-made necessity. Rousseau infamously argued people must be "forced to be free," a suggestion that more than a few have linked to a kind of tyranny. Even Kant, seeking to liberate humanity from its "self-imposed tutelage," turned to imposing a self-legislated (autonomous) morality with fully compelling power to replace the heteronomous compulsions we had bowed down to in the past. And he did so precisely as the only way to elevate humans above the beasts. Finally, in response to the failure of enlightenment liberalism to effectively reimpose any "new necessities," Nietzsche, repulsed by the Last Man-character of what this teaching had wrought—namely a being whose liberation from necessity was so complete that he resembled nothing so much as the democratic man from *Republic* 8, without even a passing interest in philosophy—responded with a call for a return of effective necessity in human life. He did this in various ways, both by rehabilitating "heteronomy"[24] or by drafting the *übermensch* to the task of ruling

---

[23] Machiavelli adds, in praising ancient Rome's politics, that they "never took refuge" in the "remedy" of the dictator "unless for necessity" (1.49).

[24] "All great things first have to bestride the earth in monstrous and frightening masks in order to inscribe themselves into the hearts of humanity with eternal demands" (*Beyond Good and Evil*, Preface).

and calling on the rest of us to re-embrace the notion of obeying (see "On War and the Warrior," *Thus Spoke Zarathustra*). But Nietzsche wavered on the question of whether philosophy prepared the way for slavishness or whether it had been in competition (with religion) for rule over humanity. He too that is, saw (in his fashion) both features of *Republic* 8–9 that we have been discussing: the one that suggests philosophy and tyranny are polar opposites and the other that suggests they are in some ways alike. Accordingly, we return to Plato's consideration of the tyrant and his specific motivations.

Tyranny and Eros

The distinctive difference, Socrates stresses, between the two ways of life that share the character of being beyond the law is that the tyrant and not the philosopher is driven by *eros*. Each side of this comparison requires not a little clarification. Socrates, after all, is widely considered to be an "erotic" thinker.[25] The only exception to the ignorance from which Socrates everywhere claims to suffer seems to be his assertion that the only thing he knows is erotics (see *Symposium* 177d7–8, 198d; *Theages* 128b1–4). But to know or understand erotics does not mean to understand oneself as being inescapably in its grip but to understand it adequately so as no longer to be in its grip.[26] In stressing the tyrant's continued embroilment with *eros*, then, Socrates is surely drawing a crucial distinction between the tyrant and the philosopher.

But in what sense is the tyrant motivated by *eros*? Socrates begins this part of the discussion by suggesting the tyrant is similar to many others (perhaps all, save the philosopher): rather than tyrannizing others through erotic passion, he begins at least by being ruled over by the "tyrant" *eros* (573b6, d3). Yet, Socrates continues, a man "becomes tyrannic in the precise sense when either by nature or by his practices or both he has become drunken, erotic, and

---

[25] Nietzsche himself calls Socrates a "great erotic" (Nietzsche 1982, 477).

[26] See in particular the second speech Socrates claims to have heard from Diotima (*Symp.* 207a–212c) and the thorough and powerful analysis in Levy 2013, esp. 126–150.

melancholic" (573c5–7). Like the adult who was a childhood victim of bullying and who then grows up to be a bully himself, the tyrant suffers, apparently more than most, from having felt utterly ruled over by erotic passion and then seeking to escape it, not so much by becoming free (or of course winning freedom for others) as by becoming "Eros incarnate."[27] The pain inflicted by (apparently unsatisfied) erotic desire, having driven him to melancholy and the drunkenness that seeks to evade both the former and the latter—a pain that appears to leave others in that pathetic state—inspires or drives the tyrannical soul to become the tyrant Eros himself. The tyrant truly wishes to make those over whom he rules happy, but he does so blindly (and even self-forgettingly): he wants to turn his subjects into lovers, either of him or of the fatherland. This appears to be the deepest level of what we have called the tyrannical temptation, the curious envy that "perhaps everyone" has of the tyrant: somehow the tyrant seems to have escaped the eternal see-sawing between being either lover or beloved, by becoming Eros itself. The tyrant, that is, seems to have mastered Eros itself by somehow becoming it.

We now see the most important way that the genuine tyrant differs from the student of the dialectic whom we considered earlier. Whereas the latter learns simply to disregard the law upon undergoing the refutation of the noble, the former becomes—or has always been—a "hater" of the law (9.572d7). That is, whereas the student of the dialectic began as someone who admired the nobility of the law and law-abidingness, the tyrant begins as someone who resents or hates the compulsory nature of the law.[28] And so, whereas

---

[27] The tyrant, that is, is not in direct rebellion against a law or against his father (as the pattern in the sequence of regimes would imply) but against the chaos of feelings in his soul prior to Eros's gaining empire over him. Socrates describes that feeling as a "longing" to become the "leader" of the desires in his soul (572e6, 573a6). Cf. Socrates's earlier suggestion that *eros* is like an impoverished man who seeks to regain his wealth (552c2–4).

[28] It is striking that the tyrant comes to hate what are the most lax or indulgent laws, the democratic laws of his father. It seems only rather demanding laws inspire in us the love of the noble.

the student of the dialectic enjoys the liberation from the law and justice and moves on to seek genuine truths in a spirit of equanimity, the tyrant—who appears never to have heard the noble refuted[29]—continues to believe in the law and even in its nobility even as he hates it. He seems attracted to Eros not least because it arms him with the good conscience necessary to break the law. And yet, he soon comes to realize—or at least dimly to sense—that he has liberated himself from one tyrant (the Law) only by giving himself over to another (Eros).

In describing the tyrant as "Eros incarnate," then, Strauss does not mean the tyrant is most "in love with" his subjects and his fatherland. As Socrates says, the tyrant's "way" of "cherishing his dear old motherland...and fatherland will be to enslave them" to his supporters (575d4–6). If Eros compels individuals to be enslaved, the tyrant ultimately wishes to enable the greatest of enslavements, that of his citizens to himself or to the fatherland.

Conclusion

While the tyrant and the philosopher do then differ on the most important question—that of the best way of life—they share something of great importance: an appreciation of necessity and its somehow beneficial role in human life. They are even presented at first as sharing the same response to that human need, namely exercising rule unlimited by law. But Plato makes clear in Book 7 that the philosopher has no taste or inclination to rule (517c–d; cf. 347d: good men fight over *not* ruling) and that, according to Glaucon, it would be unjust to compel him to do so. They are then again linked, as Book 9 suggests, by a shared taste for pleasures. But this proves too much, as Book 9 suggests *all* parts of the soul and human types seek or have their respective pleasures. In fact, the elevation of pleasure as the standard only shows again how the philosopher and the tyrant

---

[29] Socrates speaks of how the *opinions* of the "noble and the base things" that the tyrant held since childhood are "mastered" by new (more savage and libertine) ones that "act as Eros's bodyguard" (574d4–6). That is, the tyrant is still moved by a certain notion of the noble.

differ: the philosopher enjoys the pure pleasures while the tyrant enjoys only false ones. What they do seem to share is a thoroughgoing immoderation, a "divine madness" (*Phaedrus* 244a–245b), a desire to possess all that is highest and best in life.[30] The tyrant wishes to rule everything (perhaps ultimately even the wills of those he rules) while the philosopher wishes to think through everything (thereby overturning every false form of rule over him). But this latter freedom—something that democracy seems able to satisfy or at least countenance—cannot be the philosopher's highest aim. It seems that the philosopher aspires to be ruled, then, only by genuine necessity—by the necessities of nature. Plato's analysis of democratic freedom and its discontents, then, suggests two possible roads to contentment: the tyrant's insane erotic desire for imposing his will or the philosopher's desire to discover and thereby to submit to and in some sense be freed by natural necessity.

Finally, we can now account for Socrates' readiness to discuss the dangerous power of dialectic. While it can lead the ambitious young to become outlaws, it is also the only tool with which to engage and dissuade those already inclined toward the tyrannical life as if to something noble. For only through a dialectical analysis of the proposition "tyranny is noble"—which unfortunately but necessarily requires first entertaining the grain of truth in that proposition—can the philosopher, in refuting that proposition, win that ambitious and intelligent youth to philosophy.

Bibliography

Alexander of Aphrodisius. 2001. *On Aristotle's Topics 1*, trans. Johannes M. Van Ophuijsen. London: Bloomsbury.

---

[30] Levy provides an excellent account of the tyrant's divine madness, culminating in his desire to rule gods and even to become one (Levy 2013, 44–49). Noting "[i]t is difficult to say in exactly what the [tyrant's] worship of eros consists," Levy goes on to stress the tyrant's desire to "adorn eros" and thereby make it "something worthy of worship" (44). This powerful insight comports well with my slightly differing emphasis on the tyrant's *submission* to eros as though to a god.

Averroes. 1974. *Averroes on Plato's Republic,* trans. Ralph Lerner. Cornell Press.

Bloom, A. (trans) 1968. *The Republic of Plato.* Basic Books

Ibn Khaldun. 1969. *An Introduction to History,* trans. F. Rosenthal. Princeton.

Levy, David. 2013. *Eros and Socratic Philosophy.* Palgrave.

The Portable Nietzsche. 1982. Trans. Walter Kaufmann. Vintage Books.

Newell, Waller R. 2000. *Ruling Passion: The Erotics of Statecraft in Platonic Political Philosophy.* Rowman & Littlefield.

Popper, Karl. 1945. *The Open Society and Its Enemies, vols. 1 & 2.* Routledge & Kegan Paul.

Strauss, Leo. 1964. *The City and Man.* The University of Chicago Press.

Strauss, Leo. 1991. *On Tyranny.* Eds. Victor Gourevitch and Michael S. Roth. The Free Press.

THE MYTH OF THE TRIPARTITE SOUL IN PLATO'S *REPUBLIC*

Devin Stauffer

The most extensive discussion of tyranny in Plato's *Republic*—in fact, in Plato's entire corpus—is in the last part of Book 8 and the whole of Book 9 of the *Republic*. In this extended discussion of tyranny, Socrates considers, among other human types and political possibilities, the extreme case of a man with a tyrannical soul who rules over his city as a tyrant. The discussion of this man is in a manner also a discussion of liberty, not only because the tyrant with the tyrannical soul destroys the freedom of his subjects, but also because he sacrifices his own freedom. To say nothing of the fears of revolution that torment him, he is a slave to his own desires, especially his *eros*, which, as a great winged drone, breaks free from the restraints of law, decent opinion, and reasonable judgment (see 572d7–575a7, 577d1–580c8).[1] The most memorable image in Book 9 of the domination of *eros* and the other passions in the soul of the tyrant comes shortly after Socrates' argument that the "kingly" man, whose soul is governed by reason, lives 729 times more pleasantly than the tyrant, who is enslaved to his own desires. In this image, three "ideas"—a many-headed beast, a lion, and a human being—are brought together and housed inside a human body (588b6–e1). The tyrant is the man who has allowed the many-headed beast of desire to dictate to the lion and to entice it to join in tyrannizing over the human being.

Now, as this image and many other passages in Book 9 indicate, the depiction and critique of tyranny in the *Republic* relies on an account of the soul that is developed much earlier in the book. That

---

[1] Unless otherwise noted, all references given in parentheses in the text are to Plato's *Republic*. I have used Burnet's Oxford text in *Platonis Opera*, Volume IV. Translations are my own.

account is the famous tripartite conception of the soul articulated in Book 4. This conception runs throughout much of the *Republic*; its use in the critique of tyranny is only one of the many places it appears (see also, e.g., 549c2–550b7, 553a8–d7, 602c4–603b1, 606d1–7). And it has come to be regarded as Plato's central psychological doctrine. Plato, as nearly everyone familiar with his thought would say, had a tripartite conception of the soul.

But did he? Or in what sense did he? If we turn from the dramatic confrontation with the tyrant in Book 9 back to the passage in Book 4 in which the tripartite conception of the soul is developed, we will find, so long as we pay close attention to the details, that the account there is full of ambiguities, hesitations, and difficulties. It is worth taking a close look at that earlier passage as a precursor to considering the use of the doctrine of the tripartite soul in more striking but less fundamental sections, such as Socrates' discussion of the tyrant in Book 9. The aim of this essay, then, is to do some of that necessary preparatory work.

I.

The occasion for the account of the soul in Book 4 arises as the conversation in the *Republic* approaches a complicated crossroads. Socrates, Glaucon, and Adeimantus are on the hunt for justice in Book 4, in keeping with a plan set early in Book 2 (see 368c4–369a3, 427c6–e5, 434d2–435a3). After they have found justice in the city and defined it as each class in the city minding its own business, Glaucon is at least momentarily satisfied that justice has been discovered, and he seems ready to be done with the matter (see 433e12–434d1). Socrates has to remind him that the plan all along was to use justice in the city as a model to be applied to the individual, to find justice there. Only once they have done that will they be done, at least if what came to sight as justice in the city also comes to sight as justice in the individual. Socrates suggests that if there is some discrepancy between the two definitions of justice, they might rub them together like two sticks such that the flame of justice itself will burst forth (434d2–435a3). Now, it would be getting ahead of things—although it is ultimately necessary—to wonder whether this rubbing of the two sticks actually occurs in Book 4, or, if it does, whether it leads to the bursting forth of a single flame of justice. More important for present purposes is the simpler point, or what appears at first to be the simpler point, that the application of the model of the city and its classes to the individual requires that the individual's soul have a structure at least roughly analogous to the structure of the city. Only if the soul resembles the city in the city's tripartite structure of guardians, auxiliaries, and money-makers can there be even a hope that the method of using the city as a model for the discovery of justice in the individual can succeed. Thus Socrates puts the crucial question to Glaucon: Does the soul have in it three parts that correspond to the three parts of the city (435b4–c6)?

Immediately upon raising this question, however, Socrates gives us our first reason to be cautious in placing too much stock in the coming account of the soul. For he tells Glaucon, who, to his credit, is struck by the difficulty of answering the question Socrates has raised, that they will not be able to answer the question with much precision by means of the approach and arguments they are about to use. Socrates says that there is a longer and better path they could follow (435c9–d5). Yet, perhaps in deference to Glaucon's limitations, or perhaps for other reasons, Socrates points to the longer path as the road not to be travelled in the present circumstances. And if Glaucon deserves some credit for sensing the difficulty of the question at hand, he can be faulted for readily expressing his willingness to accept what Socrates has indicated will be a shortcut that comes at the expense of a lost opportunity for greater precision (435d6–7).

Even before he begins his account of the soul, then, Socrates warns his listeners—and, by extension, Plato warns us as readers—not to mistake the path that will be followed for a truly adequate or precise account of the soul. This warning is the first fly in the ointment of the doctrine of the tripartite soul. The second one flutters in when Socrates turns to argue that the soul does indeed have within it the very same forms and dispositions as there are in the city. Socrates' argument in this regard gains some initial plausibility from his observation that it is hard to imagine exactly where else the forms and dispositions of the parts of the city come from, if not from the souls of its individual citizens, and from the further considera- tion that people in certain regions of the world display in greater vividness certain traits of the soul, such that the political or the cul- tural seems to be a reflection of the psychological (435e1–436a3). But the argument runs into difficulty as soon as Socrates restates the central question, the difficulty of which he twice underscores (see 436a8–9, 436b2-3): Do human beings act in the various ways we do with the same part of ourselves or, in various instances, with one of three parts? Do we learn with one part, act in a spirited way with another, and desire the pleasures of food, procreation, and other such things with some third, or do we act with the whole soul in each instance (436a8–b3)? Socrates goes on to argue, of course, that we act in different ways with three different parts of ourselves, which he will eventually identify as reason (*logismos*), desire (*epithumia*), and spiritedness (*thumos*). But not only is it striking that he indicates at the outset of his argument that it is hard to rule out the alternative that we act with the whole soul in all that we do, or at least in our most important endeavors, but the brief argument that he then mounts for the separate action of the three parts of the soul is not beyond question.

Socrates' argument rests on the premise that one and the same thing will not be willing at the same time to do or suffer opposite things with the same part of itself and in relationship to the same thing; anything found to be experiencing such simultaneous oppo- sites must therefore not be one but many, in the sense of having multiple parts (436b8–c1). This premise, or at any rate the use Soc- rates makes of it, can be challenged, as Socrates himself indicates by considering two possible counterexamples. Having suggested, as a specific instance of the general proposition in question, that it is im- possible for one and the same thing simultaneously to stand still and to move with respect to the same part of itself, Socrates introduces a nameless objector, who points to the example of a human being who stands still while moving his hands and head, and then to the example of a top that spins even as it stands fixed in place. Socrates' response is to argue that neither of these examples disproves the premise or the conclusion that he wants to build on it regarding the separate actions of the parts of the soul, because in each instance, although there seem to be simultaneous opposite actions taking place in a single being, they are not simultaneous opposite actions of the same parts of the being, but of different parts—of the various parts of the human being and of the straight, fixed peg and the spinning circumference or periphery in the case of the top (436c8–437a2). But how sound is this argument? To focus on the example that Socrates discusses at greater length, the example of the top, is there really any part of a spinning top that is not spinning? It is true that one can speak of a top's axis or its straight aspect (*to euthu*). But there is no part, at least none any with any extension, that is not in motion. And insofar as the top, as a whole, is doing two apparently opposite things—standing erect and spinning—those are features of one and the same action and, even if they differ, they depend on one another. That the axis of the top begins to tilt and wiggle as the motion slows (see 436e4–7) confirms the interdependence of the spinning and the standing. Even if it is possible in a certain respect to regard the top as having different aspects, then, the example hardly shows the separateness or independence of the action of genuinely distinct parts.

Socrates indicates that he is well aware that his argument about the spinning top does not settle the matter regarding his key premise and the alternative it is supposed to support. He once again calls attention to the brevity and limits of the account of the soul he is sketching (see 437a4–9). Nevertheless, he plunges ahead.

That to which Socrates plunges ahead is a consideration of desire in its various forms. And his first point about desire is that it does indeed have various forms. Socrates approaches the matter by asking Glaucon whether he would set down as pairs of opposites the following experiences: accepting and refusing, aiming at the attainment of something and rejecting it, and drawing something toward oneself and pushing it away (437b1–4). Whether these experiences are actions or affections—a question to which Socrates points, but then says does not matter to the question at hand (437b4–5)—the three pairs provide a framework in which Socrates then sets the desires, and not just simple desires, such as thirst and hunger, but all desires, as well as wishing and wanting (437b7–c1). Socrates asks Glaucon whether he would not say that, in every instance of desire, "the soul of the one desiring" either aims at the attainment of that which it desires, draws toward itself that which it wants to become its own, or, insofar as it wishes that something be provided to it, accepts and then reaches out for what it desires by an internal affirmation that resembles the soul nodding to itself in response to a question (4437c1–6).

Now, Glaucon affirms everything that Socrates suggests in this dense and difficult account. But he surely understands what he is agreeing to in light of the principle of the incompatibility of opposites that Socrates has just defended, and thus he is not likely to appreciate the complexity of Socrates' account or the questions to which it points. The complexity of Socrates' account goes beyond the obvious fact that, in speaking of three pairs of opposites, Socrates suggests that desires come in different forms or fall into multiple classes. There is also the question of whether the three classes that Socrates mentions are better understood as classes of actions (*poiēmatōn*) or affections (*pathēmatōn*) of the soul. If that question truly does not matter, why did Socrates bother to point to it? Might it be the case that the desires, in their various classes, have to be understood as various blends of affections and actions, insofar as the desiring soul is both affected and active in the full experience of desire? And might the desires also have to be understood, at least in some cases, as combinations of opposites? Glaucon, we may assume, takes Socrates' suggestion here as an extension to the desires of the apparent lesson of the example of the spinning top. But the true lesson would seem to point in the other direction, such that it might indeed be possible for a desire to move the soul both toward and away from an object at the same time. To begin to understand that possibility, it is worth noting that Socrates manages, even in this brief account, to point to the role that thought plays in the experience of the desiring soul. For he indicates that the soul is not just impelled by this or that desire, but that it moves in different ways toward the objects of its desires in accordance with its wishes and wants. That this movement involves thought is clearest in the last case Socrates mentions, in which he speaks of the desiring soul accepting and then pursuing the provision of something it wishes to have, as if the soul had been asked a question to which it then nods in assent (437c4–6). That formulation indicates that the full experience of desire, at least in some cases, is a kind of composite of a primary desire and a response that can involve an internal approval of the pursuit of the object of desire. But if the soul can approve of some of its desires and act on that approval, can it not also disapprove of others, such that it then pushes away their objects or seeks to drive its desires out of itself (consider 437c8–10)? And might not the source of that disapproval and resistance in the soul be, at least in some instances, not simply a higher faculty that checks a lower one, but a conflict between or even within thought-infused desires? Although Socrates has yet to bring *thumos* into his account, we might wonder whether there is not a foundation in desire itself, especially in its multiplicity and complexity, for the apparent self-overcoming that is displayed in some manifestations of what will later be called *thumos*.

To see the character of the deeper account to which Socrates is pointing, however, one has to correct a simplification he introduces and the distortion it creates. The simplification emerges as Socrates continues his account of the desires by turning to thirst and hunger, the most manifest of all desires. No longer speaking of three classes into which the desires fall, but rather of a single class or "form" of desires (see *ti...eidos* at 437d2–3), Socrates treats thirst and hunger as desires of the soul, rather than, as would seem more accurate, of the soul and body together. But, more importantly, Socrates suggests that "thirst itself" is directed by nature only to "drink itself," and "hunger itself" only to "food itself" (437d2–e6, 439a1–7). With this suggestion, Socrates treats the relationship of each of these desires to its object as if it had an existence, as a relationship, independent of all other relationships. Thus, while he grants—what could hardly be denied altogether—that desires are relational, Socrates confines their relational character by isolating simple relationships between discrete desires and singular objects. This requires that each desire be isolated not only from the various conditions that shape particular manifestations of it—for instance, from the effect hot weather has in turning thirst toward *cold* drink—but also from the most pervasive and powerful of all conditions of our desires, namely, that they are desires of needy beings who desire good things. Do we not desire not just drink and food, but *good* drink and food, because all of us desire good things? Socrates gives voice to this as an objection "someone" might raise to his account of thirst and hunger (438a1–5). But he responds by sticking to his denial that it is in the nature of thirst itself to be related to anything other than drink itself and in the nature of hunger to be related to anything other than food itself. Thirst and hunger are, of course, just two examples of a broader suggestion that Socrates is making about the desires (see again 437d2–4). He includes even the pursuit of knowledge in his account. The pursuit of "knowledge itself" aims, not at this or that kind of learning, but at "learning itself" (438c6-e8).

But is there really such thing as thirst itself for drink itself, hunger itself for food itself, or the pursuit of knowledge itself of learning itself? Is it not the case, rather, that all of our desires are shaped by the fact that we are needy beings living in a world of complex inter-relations between things, in which nothing is one, itself by itself, not even any relationship (cf. *Theaetetus* 152d2–3)? And is not the objector whom Socrates briefly allows to speak right to insist that our concern to have good things rather than bad things enters into all of our desiring, such that is not correct to say that when we are thirsty, we desire merely drink itself and not necessarily good drink? If a thirsty man were presented with two cups of water, one putrid, the other pure, would not his thirst, understood as his desire to drink (see 439a9–b1), be stronger in one case than in the other?

The difficulty with Socrates' argument is clearest, or at any rate most interesting, as he weaves knowledge into his account of those things that are related by nature not to this or that particular kind of thing but to something in itself. Knowledge itself, Socrates contends, is of learning itself (*mathēmatos autou*). Although he acknowledges that there are particular kinds of knowledge, such as the knowledge of house building or medicine, Socrates presents these as branches of a tree whose trunk has a different character, since knowledge itself is not of any particular subject matter, but simply of "that alone to which knowledge is related," learning (see 438d1–e8). This suggestion, however, requires that Socrates create the fiction that there can be a form of knowledge that is a knowledge of no specific thing, and that such a form of knowledge, as it were, grew into existence before the specific forms of knowledge eventually branched off from it. If he manages to point to the role of human needs and desires in giving rise to specific forms of knowledge, including those of the arts, as well as the knowledge of goods and evils (consider 438e1–8), Socrates leaves unexplained what could ever have led human beings to seek knowledge of learning itself, not to mention what meaningful content such knowledge could have.

Riddled with problems as it is, Socrates' argument nevertheless serves a purpose. In fact, the purpose goes some way toward explaining the problems, especially the distortion involved in treating each desire as directed not at this or that particular kind of object but at an object "in itself." For that distortion makes it possible for Socrates to argue, with Glaucon's approval, that whenever the soul draws back from something it desires, it must be something in the soul other than desire that does the restraining. Relying on the premise that the same thing would not simultaneously do opposite things concerning the same matter with the same part of itself, Socrates takes up the case of those who are thirsty, and thus bidden by their desire to drink, yet are unwilling to drink. Must not that which holds back the would-be drinkers, that which wins the internal struggle and prevents the satisfaction at which their thirst aims, belong to a different part of the soul than the desire that impels them toward drink (439b3–c7)? Socrates gives the impression that there is only one possible answer to this question. And that enables him to argue that what does the forbidding in such cases arises from reasoning, and that the part of the soul with which the soul reasons, the rational part, is separate from the part of the soul with which it loves, hungers, thirsts, and is stirred up by the other desires. The soul is thus at least bipartite, insofar as it has a rational part, on the one hand,

and what Socrates calls here an "irrational and desiring" part, on the other (439c9–d8).

Socrates' bipartition of the soul has the effect of denigrating desire. Not only is desire said to belong to—or to *be*—the irrational part of the soul, but it is described in the course of Socrates' argument as impelling us in the same way it impels beasts (439b3–5), as arising on account of sicknesses (439d1–2), as setting the soul aflutter (439d6–7), and as aiming at mere replenishments and pleasures (439d7–8). The denigration of desire, prepared by the simplification of its character, will continue as Socrates turns to further divide the soul such that the bipartite soul becomes tripartite. Before we turn to that next stage of his argument, however, let us take stock of what has been denied without sufficient warrant in the stage we have just considered. We should focus on the experiences to which Socrates has called our attention, those instances in which the soul somehow resists its own desires. It may be true that what goes on in some of these cases is best described as reason's intervention over and against desire. But is it not possible, in other cases, that the source of the resistance to a desire is, variously, an interaction between desires, something internal to a complex desire, or our overarching desire to have good things and avoid bad things? Although Socrates seems to be denying all of these possibilities, he manages to point to the first of them by using as an illustration of the impossibility of the same thing simultaneously doing opposite things with the same part of itself the example of an archer, who uses one hand to thrust away his bow and the other to pull it toward himself (439b8–11). It may be the case that the archer is using two different parts of himself, but they are both hands, and, as with the example of the aspects of the top, their opposed motions work at once against and with each other. As for the second possibility, it is worth pondering Socrates' inclusion of *eros* in his final list of desires in this section (see 439d6–8). For in *eros* we can see vividly what is sometimes true of other desires as well, namely, the capacity of a single desire, due to its complexity, at once to draw us toward an object and to hold us back from indulging in the pleasures it makes us desire. This is an aspect of *eros* that Socrates surely knew well, since he gives a beautiful description of it in another context. The restraint that he describes there comes not from an imposition on desire by the rational part of the soul, but from the awe, fear, and hope that belong to the experience of *eros* itself (see *Phaedrus* 250c8–252c2). The inclusion of *eros* in our present passage speaks also to the third possibility. For *eros*, as Socrates acknowledges in yet another context, is the most intense expression of our concern to have the good for ourselves (see *Symposium* 204e1–206b3). And that concern, while it may be served and even refined by the rational part of our souls, is also necessary for the full development and guidance of our rationality. Our concern to have good things (see again 438a3–4) is a matter neither of desire alone nor of rationality alone. It involves both together and, in depending on their interaction, displays the problem of separating them too strictly.

II.

Having identified two "forms" (see *eidē* at 439e2) in the soul, the rational and the desiring, Socrates now asks Glaucon about a possible third. Should that in us by which we act thumotically be regarded as a third part of the soul, or does it have the same nature as one of the two already identified (439e2–4)? Glaucon answers, not without some plausibility given the complexity of desire, that perhaps it has the same nature as the desiring part of the soul (439e5). But Socrates argues that *thumos* should be regarded as a separate part, and with this argument he completes his tripartition of the soul.

But how separate from the other parts of the soul is *thumos*? Socrates gives us an example to consider, an example of *thumos* in action. It is a story that Socrates says he once heard of the internal struggle of a certain Leontius, son of Aglaion (439e6–440a3). As Socrates retells the story, Leontius was walking one day from the Piraeus back up to Athens when he came upon the corpses of some criminals who had been killed by the public executioner. After a battle within his soul between his desire to look at the corpses and his disgust at himself for that shameful desire, Leontius eventually gave in, but in a way that at once indulged the original desire and punished himself for it. Uncovering his eyes and rushing toward the corpses, he rebuked his eyes even as he gratified them: "Look, you miserable wretches, take your fill of the noble sight!"

Socrates claims that the example of Leontius' struggle shows that anger, the most obvious manifestation of *thumos*, often makes war as an ally of reason against desire (see 440a5–6 together with 440a8–b4). The example itself, however, suggests something more complicated than that. Was not Leontius' original desire to look at the corpses shaped by both thought and *thumos*? The details of the story suggest that it was not mere morbid curiosity that made Leontius want to see what he must have regarded as the deserved, if brutal, fate of the criminals. That Leontius speaks of the corpses lying near the public executioner as a "noble sight" would seem to carry a double meaning—at once serious and sarcastic—since it is a vision of justice done, even if it is also shameful to delight in it (compare *Laws* 859c6–860c2). And if Leontius' original desire to look depended on a certain fusion of thought, desire, and *thumos*, what about his resistance to it and then his punishment of himself for it, a punishment that paradoxically but not absurdly consists precisely in indulging in it? Does it suffice to characterize all of this as an example of *thumos* allying itself with reason against desire? Again, it is more complicated. For Leontius' reaction to his own desire depends on the conviction that it was not just a bad idea, but a shameful transgression to look at the corpses. He regards his desire to look as belonging to a low and wretched aspect of himself, which he associates with his eyes, rebuking them as if they were possessed by evil spirits (see *kakodaimones* at 440a3). And in turning against his own desire, even as he indulges it, or precisely *by* indulging it, he is also acting out of what can plausibly be described as another desire to purge himself of impurity, a desire that has been intensified by his struggle with his own thought-infused passions and passion-infused thoughts. What is really happening in this story is that one thumotic desire is doing battle with another thumotic desire—and in the case of neither desire is reason or thought simply absent or acting in a merely supervisory role.

Let us consider further the relationship between *thumos* and thought in particular. Despite Socrates' suggestion, accepted by Glaucon, that *thumos* always allies itself with reason against irrational desires (440a8–b8), reflection on the Leontius story and on what Socrates goes on to argue in its wake indicates that *thumos* tends to ally itself, rather, with moral convictions or with "what seems just" (see *tōi dokounti dikaiōi* at 440c8). Of course, moral convictions may be correct; what seems just may be truly so. But there is no guarantee of that in every case. Socrates acknowledges elsewhere in the *Republic* that the convictions to which *thumos* attaches itself are sometimes false, and, in such cases, *thumos* is more an enemy of reason than an ally (see, e.g., 378b8–e3, 410c8–d9, 411c4–e2, 586c7–d2, 588e3–589a4). Even in our present passage, Socrates indicates that *thumos* tends to flare up or subside as thoughts of justice rouse or relax it. This tendency of *thumos* displays itself in experiences such as the willingness to submit to punishment when one believes one has done wrong, boiling anger at perceived injustice, long endurance for the sake of vengeance, and even the fortitude of some to die for what they believe is a just cause (440c7–d3). If *thumos* is a dogged tenacity in the face of obstacles—a tenacity visible even in beasts and children, as simple struggles call it forth (see 441a7–b3), but more pronounced in fully formed human beings, when it is strengthened by thoughts of justice—then it is certainly a powerful force in the soul, but it is neither wholly separate from thought and desire nor always a reliable ally of reason. If *thumos* never strayed beyond the dictates of reason, there be no need for reason ever to call it back and calm it down like an angry dog (see 440d2–3, 441e4–442a2).

Socrates gives another example of *thumos* in action. Invoking the testimony of Homer, he reminds Glaucon of a striking moment in the *Odyssey*, the night before Odysseus' destruction of the suitors. As he was lying on a bed of sheepskins plotting his attack, Odysseus, still disguised as a beggar, saw some of the women of his house cheerfully going off to the beds of the suitors. Furious at the sight of their infidelity, Odysseus had to restrain his desire to slaughter them on the spot lest he ruin his plan to kill the suitors and reclaim his house the next day. It was difficult for him to restrain his anger. To do it, he "struck his breast and reproached his heart with a speech," reminding himself that he had suffered worse when he was forced to watch the Cyclops devour some of his companions (441b3–6; see *Odyssey* 20.17–21). When Socrates alluded to this moment of the *Odyssey* earlier in the *Republic*, it was as an example of praiseworthy endurance (see 390d1–5; see also *Phaedo* 94d6–e6). It is that here too, but in a way that shows the ambiguity of *thumos* in relation to reason. Odysseus, according to Socrates, used his reasoning about what was better and worse in the circumstances to rebuke and restrain his irrational *thumos* (441b7–c2).[2] It is striking that *thumos* in this example is not a reliable ally of reason, even by Socrates' explicit account. And in speaking of Odysseus' desire to slaughter the women as belonging to "the irrationally thumotic" part of his soul, Socrates may mean more than that Odysseus' anger was threatening to lead him down a dangerous path. He may mean also that the belief on which Odysseus' anger rested was unreasonable. Were the women, who were, after all, slaves who had been compelled for many years to endure the troubles of a house without a master, really so culpable for seeking the only outlet for *eros* available to them? Odysseus' heart may have been growling inside of him like a mother dog whose puppies were threatened by a stranger (see *Odyssey* 20.14–16). But was it reasonable of him to be so possessive and vindictive, especially when he had been gone for so long and had not himself remained unfailingly loyal to his house? There is also the question of what restrains Odysseus in this instance. Is it not likely that his reasoning about what was better and worse in the circumstances was shaped by his desire, not just to reclaim his house, but to unleash an even greater vengeance on the suitors, with whom he was even more angry (see *Odyssey* 20.5–6, 20.25–30, 20.36–40)? If Odysseus tapped into that deeper anger as he struck his breast and exhorted his heart to endure its bitter raging, then he was using a thumotic desire to restrain a thumotic desire. Once again, as with the example of

---

[2] Homer himself speaks of the surge of *thumos* Odysseus experienced and of the battle between his *thumos* and his "mind" (*phrena*). See *Odyssey* 20.9–10.

Leontius, it would seem that the true story here is too complicated to be best understood in light of a simple picture of the soul as having three separate parts.

III.

There is an obvious question raised by my argument to this point, and I will conclude by briefly considering it. If the doctrine of the tripartite soul is such an oversimplification as to amount to a myth, why this myth? The answer cannot be only that Glaucon would not have been capable of following Socrates down the longer road to a more precise account of the soul, nor that it would simply have taken too long under the circumstances to travel down that road (see again 4.435c9–d8). Those considerations, true as they might be, do not explain why Socrates takes the particular shortcut he takes and simplifies things in the way that he does. What, then, are the further reasons for Socrates'—or Plato's—creation of the myth of the tripartite soul?

Two further reasons suggest themselves, one more obvious than the other. The more obvious reason is indicated by the context in which the doctrine is developed. The doctrine of the tripartite soul is essential to Socrates' suggestion in Book 4 that justice in the soul, understood as the proper order of the soul's three parts, is analogous to justice in the city, understood as the proper order of the city's classes, in which the three classes stick to their assigned tasks (see 441c4–e2, 442d4–9, 443b1–444a6). Now, it is true that a comparison of these two notions of justice—a rubbing together of the two sticks (see again 434e4–435a3)—raises as many questions as it answers. For instance, what does Socrates mean when he says that justice in the city is a mere image or phantom (*eidōlon*) of justice (443c4–7)? If that formulation gives pride of place, as true justice, to justice in the soul (see 443c9–d1), does justice in the soul, as it is described in Book 4, really merit the name "justice," directed as it seems to be to preserving an internal condition in an individual's soul without any necessary connection to the city (see 443c9–444a2)? It might be possible to rub together Socrates' two definitions of justice so that a unified justice would burst into flame by arguing either that a man with a well-ordered soul will never fail to perform his task in the city or that performing one's task in the city is necessary to achieving a well-ordered soul. But any efforts Socrates makes in such directions in Book 4 are limited. He argues that a man with a well-ordered soul will conform to the "vulgar standards" (*ta phortika*) of justice in the sense that he will refrain from ordinary crimes, such as temple robbery, theft, and adultery. But this claim is offered as hardly more than an assertion (see 442d10–443b3). And even if one grants its plausibility, the claim goes only so far: Socrates speaks of refraining from crimes, not of any positive contributions to the common good that such a man would make. Does it not also matter, even with regard to his restraint, whether the source of the man's actions (or non-actions) would be a sense of devotion and duty or merely a concern not to disturb his own inner harmony (consider 443e2–444a2, 444c1–6)? As for the possible argument that performing one's task in the city is essential to the internal harmony of one's soul, that is the argument one most expects to find at the end of Book 4. But it is not there. Why does Socrates not make it?

These are difficult questions—each in its own right and all of them together, as aspects of Plato's articulation of the problem of justice in the *Republic*. Yet, although they are not easily resolved, the questions could not even *arise* if it were not for the doctrine of the tripartite soul. Or to put the point more cautiously—since Plato in his ingenuity probably could have found another way of presenting the problem of justice—the doctrine of the tripartite soul is essential to the presentation of the problem that, judging by his decisions, Plato deemed best.

The less obvious reason for Plato's creation of the myth of the tripartite soul has to do with desire and the war that Plato has Socrates wage against it in the *Republic*. The doctrine of the tripartite soul, of course, demotes desire. Not only is it presented as the lowest part of the soul, but desire, as we saw, was denigrated in the course of Socrates' development of the doctrine (see pages 88-89). It is denigrated again when Socrates uses the doctrine to develop his account of justice in the soul. According to that account, reason and spirit-edness, once they have been well trained and educated, should establish their rule over the desiring part of the soul, lest its insatiable yearning for money and the pleasures of the body becomes so powerful that this lowest part of the soul comes to dominate the higher parts and, by enslaving them, overturns the whole of life (4.442a4–b3). Socrates' attack on desire in Book 4 is only one of the battles he fights against it in the *Republic*. There are others, such as the austere education given to the guardians, the emphasis on economics and occupations rather than love and private attachments in the city-in-speech, and the infamous communism of women and children. The most striking example of all is the one mentioned at the outset of this essay and most directly relevant to the theme of our volume: the depiction of the tyrant as a slave to his own desires and as dominated especially by his *eros*. In Book 9, Socrates brings together his critique of tyranny and his attack on desire. Even there, however, his target is more the tyrant that is desire itself than it is tyranny in the most obvious and political sense.

Why is desire in all of its forms, but especially as *eros*, the target of attack in the *Republic*? That is another simple question without a simple answer that lies at the heart of the *Republic*. The answer in this case is hard to know because there may be both practical and theoretical reasons for Socrates' attack on desire. After all, desire can produce both unruly citizens and clouded minds, and Socrates in the *Republic* is both a proto-philosopher king of his city-in-speech, laying out the preconditions of the rule of men like himself, and a philosopher simply, examining the political and psychological foundations of his own way of life. To make matters even more complicated, Socrates' two roles, though they overlap in certain ways, may be in some tension with one another, since it is one thing to create citizens who could tolerate philosophy at the helm of the city and another to fertilize the soil from which philosophy grows. A confrontation with desire may be necessary in each case. But does not *eros* have an important part to play in the cultivation of philosophy? If *eros* is not just an obstacle but also an impetus to philosophy, as the *Symposium* and the *Phaedrus* suggest, then the attack on desire in the *Republic* should be taken with a grain of salt or at least re-garded as only one part of Plato's complex teaching about the soul and its needs.

THE FREEDOM OF THE MIND AND THE TYRANNY OF THE PASSIONS: SOCRATES' CRITIQUE OF HOMER'S EDUCATION IN THE *REPUBLIC*

Peter J. Ahrensdorf

In the most famous passage in Plato's *Republic*—Socrates' account of the image of the cave—Socrates virtually identifies philosophy with freedom. It is the philosophers whose minds are released from imprisonment in the cave so that they may enjoy the happiness of contemplating the world as it truly is.[1] It is those with philosophic natures, "the best natures," who are liberated from darkness and falsehood so that they may become truly educated and "experienced in the truth" and may live by the light of the truth (517b7–c5, 519b7–c6). And yet, the foundation of the philosophic education set forth by Socrates in the *Republic*—an education that culminates in the freedom of the mind—entails a severe curtailment of the freedom of the mind. For, as Socrates explains, the education of philosophic natures requires the suppression of certain truths lest they provoke passions that will overwhelm and enslave their reason.

Socrates' account of the proper education of the philosophic guardians of his imaginary just city[2] consists in large measure of a remarkably harsh critique of Homer, the poet singled out in the *Republic* as the educator of the Greeks.[3] Socrates does express "a certain love [*philia*]" for Homer as well as a certain "shame" before the poet that has possessed him "since childhood" (595b9–10; see 599d2). Nevertheless, Socrates emphatically attacks Homer for undermining the sway of reason in the souls of those shaped by his poems. This

---

[1] *Republic* 515c1–516c7, 517a8–d3, 518c4-d2.

[2] 376b11–c2; see also 410b10–412a2, 415b3–c6, 424a4–b1, 497b1–d2, 519c8–520c1, 525b3–9.

[3] 606e1–607a5; see also 376e2–377e4.

attack, moreover, is distinctive to Plato's Socrates, since Xenophon, who also wrote Socratic dialogues, and who presents his dialogues as historical,[4] never presents Socrates criticizing Homer.[5] Plato's Socrates attacks Homer for telling harmful lies and also harmful truths about gods and humans; attacks Achilles, the hero presented by Homer as the best of humans,[6] as wholly unworthy of imitation; and attacks the Homeric education as a whole for empowering the passions over reason and hence for setting up as "ruling in us" what "ought to be ruled" (606d1–7). Socrates therefore insists that Homer be expelled from the most just city imaginable—the city that is to be ruled by philosophers.[7] If Homer is the educator of the Greeks, that education is, according to Plato, profoundly defective.

Plato's Socrates does not criticize Homer for being intentionally hostile to philosophy. Indeed, Socrates presents Homer as friendly to philosophy and even as a philosophic thinker himself. In the *Republic* he speaks of Homer as a wise man comparable to such philosophers and sophists as Thales, Pythagoras, Protagoras, and Prodicus (1600a4–d4). In the *Theatetus*, Socrates identifies Homer as the forerunner, "general [*stratēgos*]," and apparent inspiration for such Greek philosophers and sophists as Protagoras, Heraclitus, and Empedocles, indeed, for "all…the wise ones" except the philosopher Parmenides.[8] Socrates suggests there as well that, by stating, through the mouth of Hera, that Oceanus was the "origin [*genesis*] of the gods," Homer covertly set forth his own thesis that "all

---

[4] See, for example, Xenophon *Memorabilia* 1.3.1.

[5] See *Memorabilia* 1.2.58–59, 1.4.3, 2.6.11, 3.1.4, 3.2.1–2, 4.2.10, 4.2.33, 4.6.15; *Apology of Socrates to the Jury* 26, 30; *Symposium* 3.5, 4.6–7, 4.45, 8.23, 8.30–31.

[6] *Iliad* 2.768–769, 17.279–280, 22.158–159.

[7] *Republic* 377b11–392b6, 392e2–393b4, 398a1–b4, 473c11–e5, 595a1–c3, 606e1–607a8.

[8] *Theatetus* 152c8–153a2; see 153c6–d7, 160d5–e2; *Cratylus* 401e1–402c3. See also Aristotle *Metaphysics* 983b7–34, 1009a39–1010a15. Christopher Bruell notes that Aristotle includes Homer "among the natural scientists" and that Aristotle "regarded it as possible that a natural scientist might choose, on occasion, to speak as a theologian" (*Aristotle As Teacher* [South Bend, IN: St. Augustine's Press, 2014] 73–74, 117).

things...are offspring of flowing and motion"—that is, that all things are products of natural forces and hence that supernatural beings do not exist—and thereby founded the philosophic tradition of skepticism concerning the gods exemplified later by Heraclitus, Empedocles, Protagoras, and others.[9] One may wonder why, if Homer is as philosophic as Plato's Socrates intimates, Homer does not present explicitly philosophic characters in his poems, who speak of philosophy, argue for the philosophic life, and live that life. Plato offers a possible answer to this question through the mouth of his Protagoras. As his Protagoras observes, Homer was the first of a long line of cautious wise men or "sophists"—of men who both possessed and taught wisdom, but who sought "to make a disguise for themselves and to cover themselves with it, some in poetry, as in the case of Homer and Hesiod and Simonides"—in order to avoid popular hostility (*Protagoras* 316d3–9).[10] In this way, Plato suggests, Homer himself lived the life of the mind and deliberately hid it.[11]

Homer's poems provide considerable evidence for the Platonic suggestion that Homer was a philosophic thinker. As Leo Strauss noted, it is in Homer's poems that the foundational philosophical term "nature" [*phusis*] first appears in extant Greek literature, in the *Odyssey*, where the god Hermes reveals to Odysseus that there is a certain fixed order of the world—a natural order—that limits the

---

[9] *Theatetus* 152e5–9; see as a whole 152e1–153a7 and 160d5–e2; *Cratylus* 401e1–402c3; Homer *Iliad* 14.201, 302; see also 3.5, 16.40, 19.1, 14.246. For the religious skepticism of Protagoras, see fragments 1, 4 (Diels 5th edition); Cicero *De Natura Deorum* 1.2, 63, 117–119; Sextus Empiricus *Against the Physicists* 1.55–57; Diogenes Laertius 9.51–52. For that of Heraclitus, see fragments 5, 14–15, 27, 30, 32, 40–42, 80, 96, 102, 132. For that of Empedocles, see fragments 17, 21, 28, 13–134D.

[10] See also *Republic* 378d3–e1, *Alcibiades II* 147b1–d8; Xenophon *Symposium* 3.5–6; *Memorabilia* 1.2.58–59.

[11] Montaigne too identifies Homer as the man who "laid the foundations equally for all schools of philosophy" (*The Complete Essays of Montaigne*, trans. Donald M. Frame [Stanford: Stanford University Press, 1976], 377). According to Vico, all philosophers up to his own time viewed Homer as "the source of all Greek philosophies" (*The New Science*, trans. David Marsh [London: Penguin Books, 1999], 386; see 355–356).

power of the gods.[12] Moreover, Homer's first and more fundamental poem, the *Iliad*, indicates that Homer's education of the Greeks is one that points to the contemplative life of the mind as the best way of life.[13] To be sure, the leading model of human excellence in Homer is Achilles.[14] But what does it mean to imitate Achilles? Achilles is not only the most formidable warrior in Homer's poems, but is also the hero who speaks most effectively in the assembly to save the army from disaster (1.53ff.); the hero with the widest and the deepest friendships;[15] the only hero in the *Iliad* who loves and performs music (185-191); and, as he shows at the end of the *Iliad* when he freely grants the Trojan King Priam and his people a twelve day truce to bury their beloved Hector in peace, the most compassionate hero in the poem (24.650–672). Most importantly, Achilles is the only hero in the poem who questions the life of the hero, who questions the value of honor and the goodness of virtue. He is the hero who comes closest both to accepting the finality of death and to recognizing the truth that the carefree gods neither care for humans nor understand them.[16] And yet Achilles is also the most criticized character in the poem. The *Iliad* opens with a devastating criticism of Achilles, whose "destructive" anger led to the deaths of "countless" numbers of his fellow soldiers, and he is repeatedly criticized over the course of the poem, by his king;[17] by his beloved companions;[18] by Apollo (24.33–54); by Homer;[19] and by Achilles

---

[12] Leo Strauss, Introduction, in *The History of Political Philosophy*, 3rd edition, ed. with Joseph Cropsey (Chicago: Rand McNally, 1987), 2–3; Homer *Odyssey* 10:303. See Leo Strauss to Jacob Klein, October 10, 1939, in Leo Strauss, *Gesammelte Schriften*, Band 3, ed. Heinrich Meier (Stuttgart und Weimar: J. B. Metzler Verlag, 2001; 2nd rev. ed., 2008), 582.

[13] See Peter J. Ahrensdorf, *Homer on the Gods and Human Virtue: Creating the Foundations of Classical Civilization* (Cambridge: Cambridge University Press, 2014).

[14] *Iliad* 2.768–769, 17.279–280, 22.158–159.

[15] 9.192–204, 9.606–616, 18.80–82, 23.555–557, 24.572–575, 24.650.

[16] 9.314–409, 21.99–113, 24.517–551.

[17] 1.174–177, 11.663–667.

[18] 9.496–523, 9.624–632, 9.9.677–9, 11.652–653, 16.21–35.

[19] 15.598–599, 22.395, 23.24, 23.174–177.

himself.[20] Furthermore, Achilles is a character who suffers terribly in the poem, more terribly than any other character. Accordingly, Homer presents Achilles as weeping more than any other character of the poem.[21] Homer, then, centers his education in human excellence on a complex hero, a great but evidently and admittedly flawed and sorrowful model of human excellence, a human being who questions the life that he leads, and hence a model who points beyond himself. To imitate Achilles is to imitate a tragic figure, whose flaws and sorrows—upon reflection—lead one to consider another, less visible, but superior model of human excellence, that of the contemplative and humane singer, Homer himself.

The happiest we ever see Achilles—the happiest we ever see any human being in the *Iliad*—is the moment when he is singing, "delighting his mind with his lyre": "with it he delighted his spirit and sang of the glories of men" (9.186–189). The fact that Homer says that Achilles delighted his *mind* by singing of the "glories of men" suggests that Achilles has found pleasure and satisfaction in reflecting on men like himself, who have performed deeds that are worthy of glory and who may or may not have received the glory they deserved (see 9.524–525). Thinking about honor, rather than seeking it or even possessing it, has, for the moment at least, supplied Achilles with some portion of the happiness that has eluded him. In his contemplative singing, Achilles points to the example of the contemplative singer, Homer.

Now, Plato's Socrates does not deny that Homer intends, through his education, to celebrate the contemplative life of the mind.[22] He does not criticize Homer for being opposed to the cultivation of reason. Socrates rather criticizes Homer for being ineffective in his efforts to cultivate reason, above all because he

---

[20] 18.82, 18.98–110, 18.324–327, 19.56–64; see also 18.32–34.

[21] See 1.348–361, 18.22–35, 19.4–6, 19.338, 23.12–18, 23.108–110, 23.152–155, 23.222–225, 24.3–13, 24.507–512. For other characters who weep much, but less than Achilles, see especially Thetis (1.413, 18.35–49, 18.66, 18.71, 18.94, 18.428), Andromache (6.405, 6.484, 22.515, 24.746), Priam (22.90, 22.429, 24.510–511), and Antilochus (17.695–701, 18.17, 18.32).

[22] Consider *Republic* 378d3–e1.

underestimates the threat posed to reason by the passions. Homer assumes, not that reason naturally rules over human beings, but that humans have a certain natural openness to reason and a certain general capacity to develop it, especially through experiencing, as his great hero Achilles does, the tragic conflicts of political and military life and the painful questions those conflicts give rise to. But, in the *Republic*, Socrates suggests that reason always has a precarious position in the human soul of even philosophic natures, that even such souls do not possess a nature that simply supports reason, and that the passions in particular always threaten to overwhelm and dominate reason. Therefore, for Socrates, the proper nurture of even philosophic natures is crucial in order to strengthen their reason and that nurture must begin from early childhood (376c4–8). For humans' souls can be molded in radically different ways. As Socrates remarks, "Don't you know that the beginning is the greatest part of every work, especially with whatever is young and tender? For at that time it is especially molded and takes on the impression that someone might wish to stamp on each" (377a12–b3). Philosophy—the love of wisdom—does not naturally tend to rise to lead the soul as a result of challenging, thought-provoking experiences in politics and war, as Homer suggests. Philosophy requires a soul that has been properly educated, properly prepared and molded by appropriate tales—by salutary lies—in order to predominate in the soul (377b5–d9).

Socrates' critique of Homer's education in human excellence takes the form of a ferocious attack on Achilles, the hero Homer identifies as the greatest by far, but whom Socrates criticizes each of the five times he names him.[23] Socrates explicitly attacks Achilles by name for wailing and grieving like an unserious woman and for possessing the "diseases" of "illiberality together with a love of money" and "arrogance toward gods and human beings."[24] And when citing Achilles' words without mentioning his name, Socrates implicitly

---

[23] *Iliad* 2.768–769, 17.279–280, 22.158–159; *Republic* 388a5–6, 390e4, 390e7, 391a4, 391c1.
[24] 387e9–388b4; 390d7–391c6.

attacks him for lacking courage in the face of death, and lacking moderation inasmuch as he is disobedient toward his ruler Agamemnon.[25] What renders these attacks on Achilles especially scathing is their singular and unremitting character. No other hero is criticized as severely or as comprehensively as is Achilles. Socrates criticizes Priam, Achilles' tutor Phoenix, Theseus, and Perithous by name, but only once each.[26] Socrates praises Diomedes by name for his moderation insofar as he enthusiastically obeys his ruler Agamemnon and never criticizes him.[27] And while Socrates implicitly criticizes Odysseus for immoderately praising food and drink, he also implicitly praises him for being "the wisest man" and for his endurance.[28] But Socrates never praises Achilles at all, explicitly or implicitly.[29] He criticizes Achilles more than any other hero for lacking courage in the face of death and for lamenting the death of a loved one, and he criticizes Achilles and Achilles alone, among all the heroes, for immoderate disobedience of his ruler, love of money, and arrogance toward gods and humans.

Socrates' attack on Achilles is clearly polemical, an evident attempt to dethrone Achilles as the model of human excellence for the Greeks. Socrates singles out Achilles for lacking courage, even though he is far more courageous than any other Homeric hero.[30] Socrates singles out Achilles for immoderate disobedience to Agamemnon, even though Diomedes, Nestor, and—as Megillus points out in the *Laws* (706d4–7)—Odysseus also rebukes Agamemnon, even though Agamemnon later rebukes himself, and even though

---

[25] 386a1–c7, 386d4–5, 387b1–c5, 389d7–e2, 389e12–390a3.

[26] 388b4–7, 390e4–7, 391c8–d1.

[27] 389e4–11.

[28] 390a8–b1, 390d1–6. See 620c3–d2.

[29] Socrates does praise Achilles' father Peleus as "most moderate" and his teacher Chiron as "most wise," but only in the context of lamenting that Achilles, who enjoyed such parentage and instruction, and also a lineage from Zeus, should be so vicious (391b7–c6). Socrates also suggests that Homer's account of Achilles is unworthy of Achilles, but he never cites any other account of Achilles (390e7–391a1; see 391a3–b5, 388a5–6).

[30] 3.386a6–387c5; see *Iliad* 1.53–196, 1.165–166, 9.328–329, 9.411–420, 22.358–360.

Achilles saves the Achaians from disaster by taking it upon himself to defy Agamemnon.[31] Socrates singles out Achilles for loving money, even though he refuses the extravagant treasures Agamemnon offers to him and even though other Achaians, most notably Odysseus, love money more.[32] Socrates condemns Achilles for slaughtering (twelve) captured prisoners and praises Odysseus for his endurance, even though Odysseus practices endurance specifically so that he may later slaughter twelve captured maidservants as well as eight male servants, all one hundred and eight of the largely unarmed suitors of his wife—including Leiodes who rightly protests his innocence—and, Odysseus hopes, "all" of the dead suitors' relatives.[33] Perhaps most remarkably, Socrates never praises Achilles at all, for example, for his hatred of lying, even though Socrates declares that the citizens should not lie to their rulers and even though, as Socrates himself notes in the *Hippias Minor*, Achilles, in contrast to the frequently mendacious Odysseus, denounces lying most emphatically.[34] Homer himself criticizes Achilles sharply in the course of the poem, but he also praises his hero.[35] Socrates, however, has nothing but criticism for the best of the Achaians.

Socrates does, however, offer a serious, non-rhetorical criticism of Achilles as well, one that forms the basis of and justifies the desire to dislodge him from his position as the hero of the Greeks. In Socrates' view, Achilles is not only a flawed character, as Homer himself acknowledges, but one whose example risks harming those who

---

[31] *Republic* 389d9–390a5; *Iliad* 9.32–49, 9.102–111, 14.83–102, 19.181–183, 9.115–120, 19.85–138, 1.8–147.

[32] *Republic* 390d7–391c6; *Iliad* 9.378–387 (see also 19.146–150, 19.199–202, 22.348–354); *Odyssey* 9.218–229, 13.215–219, 18.281–283.

[33] *Republic* 391b5–7, 390d1–5; *Iliad* 21.26–33, 23.174–177; *Odyssey* 20.1–30, 22.417–445, 16.245–246, 22.61–64, 22.310–329 (cf. 21.146–147), 22.381–389, 24.526–528.

[34] *Republic* 389b2–d5, *Hippias Minor* 364d7–365c4 (but see 369a7–371e5); *Iliad* 9.312–313, 10.382–502; *Odyssey* 4.240–258, 8.492–520, 9.280–286, 13.250–286, 13.293–295, 14.192–259, 14.468–503, 17.415–444, 18.138–140, 19.165–202, 19.269–307, 24.258–314.

[35] Compare *Iliad* 1.1–7 and 15.598–599 with 1.407–412, 16.233–238. See 22.395–436 and 23.174–177. But see also 2.768–769, 17.279–280, 22.158–159.

model themselves on him. And even though Homer may intend that admirers of Achilles be led, upon reflection, to recognize the superiority of the contemplative life to the life of the dutiful warrior, Socrates suggests that Achilles is presented as such a brilliant, if flawed, hero, that he inevitably overshadows the hidden figure of the wise, humane singer who composed the *Iliad*.

The broad focus of Socrates' criticism of Achilles concerns his passionate character: his fear of death,[36] his weeping over the death of his beloved friend,[37] his anger,[38] his (alleged) love of money,[39] and his love of honor.[40] A consideration of the passionate character of Achilles helps to clarify, in a general way, both Homer's understanding of the relation between the passions and reason and Socrates' critique of that understanding. For Achilles is the most passionate character in the *Iliad*—the angriest and the one who weeps the most—and also the most thoughtful character—the one who questions most the dutiful life of the warrior and the providence of the gods and the one who comes closest to accepting the finality of death.[41] Moreover, in Homer's account, Achilles is thoughtful, not despite his passionate character but, in some measure, because of it. It is Achilles' intense anger at Agamemnon and the Achaians that leads him to question the life of the dutiful warrior that he has led for nine years and it is his intense grief over the death of his beloved Patroclus that leads him to contemplate the finality of death and to call into question the providence of the gods.[42] Through the example of Achilles, Homer suggests that it is the passions that give humans the motive and also the strength to question their most cherished convictions and their deepest hopes. But Socrates suggests—especially by highlighting the degree to which Achilles remains in the

---

[36] *Republic* 386a6–387b7.

[37] 387d1–388b4.

[38] 389e12–390a4, 391a3–c6.

[39] 390d7–391a1, 391c4–6.

[40] 390e9–391a1.

[41] *Iliad* 9.314–327, 9.400–409, 21.106–113, 24.524–526, 24.549–551.

[42] *Iliad* 9.314–345, 9.378–420, 24.511–526.

grip of sorrow and anger even at the end of the *Iliad*[43]—that Achilles does not pursue the questions he raises further than he does because the very passions that inspire his questions overwhelm his reason and therefore arrest his questioning. Socrates might concede that Achilles has moments of genuine questioning, moments—in conversation with his friends in Book 9 and with Priam in Book 24—in which he appears to transcend his passions and achieve a considerable measure of clarity concerning the problem of the life of duty, the gulf between humans and gods, and the finality of death. Nevertheless, Socrates suggests that each of Achilles' moments of lucidity is overwhelmed by his unbridled passions of grief, anger, and hope.[44] Homer's overall presentation of Achilles as a model of human excellence, then, vividly reflects Homer's dangerous underestimation of the power of the passions and of their abiding opposition to reason.

The specific focus of Socrates' criticism of Achilles concerns his posture toward death: his fear of death, his lamentation at the death of his beloved companion, and his refusal to accept the finality of death, as his treatment of the corpses of Patroclus and Hector as though they were alive reveals.[45] Socrates begins his critique of Achilles as a model of human excellence by arguing, first, that the poets must praise death in order to inspire the guardians to be "courageous" (386a6), that is, to "fear death least" (386a7) or even to be "fearless toward death" (386b5). He then suggests that those who embrace Achilles' view of death and Hades as bad will fear death

---

[43] Of the twenty-five passages Socrates cites from Homer in his critique of Homer in Books II and III, nine focus specifically on Achilles (379d2–8, 386c5–7, 386d4–5, 387a2–3, 388a4–8, 388c1, 389e8–9, 391a6–7, 391b3–4—six are spoken by Achilles (*Iliad* 24.527–532; *Odyssey* 489–491; *Iliad* 23.103–104, 1.225, 22.15–20, 23.140–151), two are spoken by Homer (23.100–101, 24.10–12) and one by Thetis (18.54) about Achilles—and, of those nine, six are taken from the final three books of the *Iliad*.

[44] See *Republic* 386d4–5, 387a2–3, 388a5–b4, 391a3–b7 and also 379d3–e2. Compare *Iliad* 9.314–327 and 9.401–420 with 9.369–392 and 9.611–614; 21.106–113 with 21.120–135; and 24.525–526 and 24.549–551 with 24.527–530, 24.559–572, and 24.582–595.

[45] *Republic* 386a6–388e4, 391b2–5.

107

more than slavery and that they will be "hotter and softer than they ought" (387c4–5). Yet, as Socrates certainly knew, Achilles evidently did not fear death more than slavery, for he continued to fight bravely at Troy up through his death, and he did so even though, unlike all the other warriors, he knew that his death at Troy was certain if he remained there to fight.[46] What then is Socrates' serious criticism of Achilles with respect to courage?

Homer suggests that true courage entails the recognition that death is an evil and the willingness to face it nonetheless. The Achaians are more courageous than the Trojans because, while the latter must whip themselves into a frenzy and hence suppress their reason in order to go into battle—like screaming birds and cranes and bleating sheep, says Homer—the Achaians "went in silence, breathing spirit" and hence do not simply suppress their rational awareness of the evil of death that they are facing.[47] Now, Achilles is the most courageous of the Achaians, not only because he is always at the forefront of every battle, but also because, while all the other warriors know that they risk death at Troy, he alone knows with certainty that he will die at Troy should he remain and fight.[48] Moreover, Achilles alone has the courage to stand up to the mighty Agamemnon when that king foolishly and selfishly imperils the survival of all the Achaians by defying the priest of Apollo.[49] To be sure, Achilles fears death and wrestles with that fear throughout, and he even wonders whether a long quiet life of peace is not superior to a short life as a dutiful warrior.[50] Nevertheless, the fact that Achilles persists in fighting on, even though burdened with such anguish and such (reasonable) doubts, demonstrates, in Homer's account, the superior quality, the strength and reasonableness, of his courage.

In the context of his critique of Homer, Socrates affirms that, in reviling rather than praising death and Hades, the poets "say what

---

[46] *Iliad* 9.411–416.

[47] 3.1–9, 4.429–436.

[48] 1.165–166, 9.328–329, 9.411–420, 22.358–360.

[49] 1.22–25, 1.53–91, 1.225–232, 1.293–303.

[50] 9.314–345, 9.393–409.

is neither true nor beneficial for the ones who are to be fighters" (386b8–c1). But Socrates omits here any argument whatsoever that death and Hades are in truth good and praiseworthy but instead explains why it is harmful for poets to portray death as an evil for the spirited and philosophic guardians, that is, for men who are to be "both warrior and philosopher" (7.529b8–9):[51] "If they are to be courageous, must one not tell them these things and of a sort that will make them fear death least? Or do you believe that anyone will ever come to be courageous having this terror in him?" (3.386a6–b2); "Do you suppose that anyone who believes the things in Hades exist and are terrible will be fearless toward death and will choose death in battles before defeat and slavery?" (3.386b4–6); "so much less must they [these passages from Homer] be heard by boys and men who must be free, having feared slavery more than death" (3.387b4–6). Socrates evidently does not argue here that death is not truly an evil or that the fear of death is unreasonable. He argues, instead, that, if one believes, even reasonably, that death is an evil, one will be enslaved to one's fear of death. And such enslavement to the fear of death, Socrates suggests, is harmful in two respects. First, as Socrates stresses, it is harmful because it leads humans to sacrifice the freedom of their political community in order to stay alive at all costs. But secondly, as Socrates indicates, such enslavement to the fear of death is harmful to human reason because it precludes the freedom from the sway of the passions necessary to think clearly and soundly. Accordingly, as Socrates later affirms, one who has a "philosophic nature" "will believe that death is not something terrible" (486a1–b5).

Now, reason would seem to suggest that death is indeed evil, for, as a wise woman, Diotima, reportedly taught Socrates, we humans naturally long to possess the good "always,"[52] and, insofar as it marks the term of our existence, death necessarily thwarts that

---

[51] As this citation indicates, Socrates continues to describe the guardians as both philosophic and spirited or warlike later in the dialogue as well. See 410b10–412a7, 521d4–7, 543a1–5.

[52] *Symposium* 201d1–5, 205e7–2016a13, 206e8–207a4.

longing. On the other hand, since death is inevitable to human beings, it would seem to be unreasonable to devote one's life to fleeing it in the hope that one can fully escape it.[53] Reason, then, would seem to counsel at once a recognition that death is evil and an acceptance of its inevitability. But what Socrates suggests in the *Republic* is that, even though the fear of death may well be reasonable inasmuch as death is evil, the fear of death is so powerful that it threatens to overwhelm both the love of freedom and reason itself and hence threatens to undermine the courage either to risk one's life or to accept the inevitability and finality of one's death. Paradoxically, the rational fear of death undermines reason. Therefore, Socrates argues, the fear of death can only be properly controlled by instilling in human beings, from childhood, the firm conviction that death is not evil but good and hence that it is unreasonable to fear death (see also 387d6). In this way, the menacing fear of death can be, as Socrates puts it in the *Phaedo*, "charmed away" (77e8–9) by the soothing belief in the goodness of death, and the human mind can be freed to contemplate with balance and calm. Even if, then, it is false to believe that death is good, Socrates suggests that this falsehood is necessary for the empowerment of reason.

Here again, Socrates points to a fundamental theoretical disagreement with Homer, a disagreement over the relative strength of human reason. Homer believes that humans as a whole can recognize the evil of death without being enslaved to the fear of death. But, Socrates contends, human reason is weak. It is vulnerable to the passions, perhaps especially to the fear of death that always threatens to overwhelm and enslave it. Therefore, in order for reason to prevail in its struggle with the always potentially enslaving passions, reason stands in need of lies, a bodyguard of lies, that, from childhood on, protect reason from the passions by calming the passions.

In order to understand Socrates' contention in the *Republic* concerning the enslaving power of the passions and the relative weakness of reason, it is helpful to consider the opinions and the example of the character in whose son's home the dialogue takes place,

---

[53] *Apology of Socrates* 35a4–7.

Cephalus. The "very old" (328b9) Cephalus virtually opens the conversation by affirming the enslaving power of the passions but he then suggests that what liberates reason and virtue from such tyranny is not education but old age: "as the other pleasures connected to the body waste away, so do the desires and pleasures concerning speeches increase" (328d2–4). Then, mentioning "freedom" for the first time in the dialogue, Cephalus declares, "For in every way, there comes to be much peace and freedom from such things in old age. Once the desires cease to strain and become slack...it is possible to be released from very many mad masters" (329c5–d1). When Socrates invokes Homer (for the first time in the dialogue)—citing the phrase spoken twice by Priam on the evils of old age—to suggest that the time of life when one approaches death may be "hard," Cephalus emphatically denies the suggestion.[54] And yet, under Socrates' questioning, Cephalus quickly acknowledges that

> when someone is near to supposing that he will come to an end, fear and care enter him...for the tales told about the things in Hades, that the one who has done injustice here must pay a penalty there, which were laughed at until then, at that time twist his soul lest they be true...then he comes to be full of suspicion and terror...frequently waking up from sleep, just as children do, he is terrified and lives with evil expectation. (330d5–331a1)

In Cephalus' account the fear of death, triggered not simply by old age but by the awareness that one is to reach the end of one's life, dominates one's mind, awake and asleep, and hence dominates one's very soul, completely. Cephalus does suggest, through his speeches and through his example, that the passions as a whole always tend to dominate reason: the young tend to be dominated by their sexual desire and the old tend to be dominated by their fear of death. But in his account the domination of the fear of death seems more complete, for it alone fills the soul, rules it day and night, and torments it. It is true that Cephalus speaks in the third person when speaking of the old man who, mindful of past misdeeds, wakes up

---

[54] 1.328d7–329d6; *Iliad* 22.60, 24.487; see also *Odyssey* 15.246.

in a fright from sleep. But the facts that Cephalus speaks of having been dominated by his passions when young—by "very many masters" who are "mad";[55] that he speaks on his own authority when describing the old man troubled by his past misdeeds—as though he speaks from personal experience—but cites the authority of Pindar in describing the one "conscious in himself of nothing unjust";[56] and that he devotes himself so assiduously and eagerly to making sacrifices to the gods, as he suggests the fearful unjust man would,[57] all indicate that Cephalus is himself the man he describes who is frightened of death and the hereafter. Through the example of Cephalus, Plato illustrates the enslaving power of the fear of death and also suggests that poets such as Homer, with their frightening tales of Hades,[58] intensify the despotic hold that the fear of death may come to have on a man like Cephalus, who has evidently heard such tales from youth.

But what about the example of Achilles, who is clearly courageous, clearly capable of risking death and even, at times, of recognizing and seeming to accept the finality of death,[59] while still believing that death is an evil? Is he not, as Socrates says the courageous guardians must be, "free" (387b5), that is, free from the

---

[55] 329d1; cf. 329c4–5; see also 328d2–4, 330d7–e1.

[56] Compare 330d4–331a1 with 331a1–9.

[57] Compare 330e2–331a1 and 331a10–b7 with 328b8–c3 and 331d2–9.

[58] One may wonder why Homer presents the afterlife, Hades, as terrible, as Socrates suggests he does, rather than simply present death as the end of human existence, as Homer's own detailed accounts of death suggest. Perhaps he simply articulates the beliefs and fears that humans naturally tend to have about what occurs after death. But Homer's account of Hades is, notwithstanding Socrates' claims, not simply terrible. For instance, Achilles consorts and converses with his friends there (*Odyssey* 11.466–540, 24.15–98). One might say that Homer's is a relatively moderate portrayal of the afterlife when compared, for example, with the accounts that, in some measure, terrify Cephalus (*Republic* 330d4–331b7): there is some punishment (*Odyssey* 11.568–600) and there are some who, like Menelaus, go to the Elysian Field or, like Heracles, go to Olympus (4.561–568, 11.601–604), but in general humans seem to live in a twilight existence which is neither simply terrible nor simply attractive.

[59] See *Iliad* 9.320, 9.400–409, 19.23–27, 21.106–113, 24.549–551.

tyranny of the passions? Socrates suggests in two ways that Achilles is not truly free from the sway of passion. First, by referring twice to Achilles' dream of the dead Patroclus, Socrates indicates that Achilles continues to be frightened of death, of what death might hold in store for his friend but also for himself, and this fear haunts his dreams, as the fear of death evidently haunts the dreams of Cephalus.[60] Secondly, Socrates seems to have Achilles in mind when he suggests that those who believe that death and Hades are evil will be overwhelmed by fear and as a result of such fear, they will be "hotter and softer than they ought" (387c4-5). For Socrates suggests here, not only that a powerful fear of death may lead humans to be "soft" in the sense of being cowardly, but that it may lead humans to be "hot" in the sense of giving themselves to passion, perhaps especially the passion of anger, to overcome their fear of death.[61] As Homer himself highlights in the first line of the *Iliad*, Achilles is possessed by wrath, and is especially moved by wrath when risking his life on the battlefield.[62] Moreover, as Socrates later notes, Achilles continues to speak to Patroclus, and of him, as though he were alive, even though he is dead, and continues to punish Hector even though he is dead, and thereby indicates that he does not truly face death and accept its finality, notwithstanding his battlefield courage.[63]

Socrates suggests, then, that, the principal defect of the Homeric education is that, in the first place, insofar as it instructs humans to follow the example of Achilles, it does not truly liberate humans from the sway of the passions but attempts to counteract

---

[60] *Republic* 386d4–5, 387a2–3; *Iliad* 23.59–107.

[61] See David Bolotin, "The Critique of Homer and the Homeric Heroes in Plato's *Republic*," in *Political Philosophy and the Human Soul: Essays in Memory of Allan Bloom*, eds. Michael Palmer and Thomas L. Pangle (Lanham, MD: Rowman and Littlefield, 1995), 85.

[62] *Iliad* 1.1; see, for example, 20.1–2, 20.75–78, 20.163–175, 20.261–263, 20.381–503.

[63] *Republic* 386d4–5, 387a2–3, 391b2–6. Achilles addresses the dead Patroclus six times (*Iliad* 18.333–42, 19.315–337, 23.19–23, 23.94–98, 23.179–183, 24.592–595), as many times as he addresses the living Patroclus (1.337–344, 9.202–204, 11.607–614, 16.6–19, 16.49–100, 16.126–129).

the power of the fear of death with the power of anger and other passions and, in the second place, it does not overcome the enslaving power of that fear in an effective and lasting way. Socrates suggests that the wiser way to free humans from the enslaving power of the fear of death is to defuse that fear from childhood by instilling the calming and reassuring, albeit false, opinion that death is not to be feared. For in this way, humans can fight to defend their freedom from conquest by others but can also free their minds from the enslaving fear of death. By rearing humans to be calm and collected, by stilling their fear of death, Socrates hopes to free reason from the rule of the passions, and habituate humans to think calmly and clearly. In his view, reason is such a fragile flower that it requires untruth. The truth, especially about death, threatens reason; the freedom of the rational mind therefore requires the aid of lies, especially about death, to protect it from the enslaving passions that the truth will inevitably stir up.

A defender of Homer might argue that Homer himself exhibits a rational acceptance of the finality of death, one that is rendered far more impressive than that Socrates advocates, by its rootedness in a clear-eyed account of human mortality and in a humane sympathy for the suffering it entails. For example, over the course of the *Iliad*, Homer offers remarkably detailed and vivid descriptions of one hundred and thirty-four battlefield deaths. These accounts reveal Homer to be a keen observer of how death occurs, a careful student of the anatomy of death, and acutely interested in the causes, the experience, and the human significance of death.[64] One overpowering, inescapable conclusion driven home by Homer's medically accurate accounts of death is that human life depends for its very existence on the physical integrity of certain vital parts of the body.[65]

---

[64] As Jasper Griffin puts it, "Homer describes hundreds of killings in battle, many of them in pitiless detail, without sliding either into sadism or into sentimentality" (*Homer: Iliad IX* [Oxford: Clarendon Press, 1995], 36).

[65] As Donald Lateiner notes, "Most of the pathophysiological causes of death are precisely recorded and medically sound" ("*The Iliad*: An Unpredictable Classic," in *The Cambridge Companion to Homer*, ed. Robert Fowler [Cambridge:

As Homer highlights over and over again, once one's head is stabbed, lopped off, or broken, or once one's belly, chest, liver, throat, or heart is pierced, one's existence comes to an end: "he took the spirit out of him;"[66] "And his soul and fury were there released;"[67] "he drew out at once both his soul and the spear" (16.505); "He breathed away his spirit, like an earthworm that lies stretched out on the ground. Out flowed the black blood and it wet the earth;"[68] "Idomeneus pierced Erymantas in the mouth with pitiless bronze. The bronze spear passed straight through beneath the brain and shattered the white bones. His teeth were shaken out and both eyes filled with blood, and, gaping, he blew it [blood] out through his mouth and nostrils. And a black cloud of death covered him" (16.345–350). Through such accounts, Homer sternly impresses upon his audience the finality of death. He reveals himself to be free of the belief in immortality cherished by all of his heroes, even the lion-hearted Achilles.[69] In this way, Homer comes to sight as the true model of human excellence in the *Iliad*.

Socrates, however, suggests that this crucial, culminating aspect of the Homeric education suffers from a paradoxical defect: it is insufficiently poetic. Homer's heroes, above all Achilles, are grand but flawed heroes, tragic heroes, and as such they point beyond themselves. But the figure these vivid heroes point to, the figure of the wise, humane singer, is not only hidden behind the Muses[70] but remarkably abstract, not graspable by our imagination and hence imperceptible, one might say, to our mind's eye. The figure of Homer

---

Cambridge University Press, 2004], 13). For an apparent exception, consider 10.454–457.

[66] *Iliad* 4.531; see also 6.17, 10.495, 16.828, 20.459, 21.179, 21.201.

[67] 5.296; see 8.123, 13.444, 17.298.

[68] 13.654; see also 4.524, 16.468–469.

[69] For example, on thirteen occasions, Homer's human characters address corpses, as though they were still somehow alive: Idomeneus (13.370–382), Hector (16.858–861), Briseis (19.282–300), Hecuba (24.747–759), Helen (24.761–775); Andromache (22.477–514, 24.719–745), and Achilles (18.333–342, 19.314–337, 21.115–135, 21.179–204, 22.364–366, 23.17–23).

[70] 1.1–7, 2.761–762, 2.484–487, 11.218–220, 14.508–510, 16.112.

in his poems lacks flesh and blood, lacks human details, lacks even a name. We know Homer only through his mind.[71] We have to think our way through his characters, his judgments, his descriptions of death, and also his magnificent similes, to apprehend Homer himself. But Socrates suggests that, in this critical aspect of his education, Homer again overestimates the strength of reason. Homer does not recognize that reason requires the support of habituation, a habitual practice in the virtues and the freedom from passion that are necessary for living a life guided by reason.[72] But such habitual practice must be inspired by the desire to imitate an exemplary human being, who vividly displays in his own person such virtues and such freedom, who indeed embodies the life of reason. Plato's Socrates contends, then, that Homer does not recognize that poetry, a poetry that brings the philosopher to the fore as a hero to be imitated, is needed to strengthen and support philosophy. Homer does not recognize the need for an imitative, philosophic poetry such as Plato's.

It is true that Plato hides himself as Homer hides himself. But, unlike Homer, Plato does not hide the way of life he admires, the philosophic life, his own way of life. Rather, for the first time in history, with unsurpassed vividness and charm, Plato openly presents a model of genuine human excellence, the philosopher Socrates.

This is the revolution brought about by Plato, a revolution explained and justified by Plato's Socrates' critique of Homer in the *Republic*. Unlike Homer and unlike also the tragic poets (and Thucydides) who follow Homer, Plato presents the philosopher in the full light of day, as a model for imitation. Accordingly, Plato offers a dramatic portrait of the philosopher, especially in the three dialogues in which Plato himself appears or is mentioned, and in which his brothers, Glaucon and Adeimantus, appear prominently: in the

---

[71] See *Republic* 393a3–394b1 (cf. *Iliad* 1.1); 599b3–600e2. Consider as well *Protagoras* 316d3–317c6.

[72] See *Republic* 395b8–c5, 395d1–3, 396c5–e1, 424a5–b1, 606e1–607a5; see also 401b1–402a6.

Apology, where we see Socrates on trial for his life; in the *Phaedo*, on the day of his death and at the moment of his death; and in the *Republic*,[73] in which Socrates presents an extensive, edifying, and, as Glaucon says, a "wholly noble" (7.540c3), depiction of the philosophic life.[74] In all the dialogues, but in these three in particular, Plato offers the philosopher Socrates as a model for imitation for philosophic natures and thereby completes the education of philosophic natures that Plato's Socrates sketches in his critique of Homer in the *Republic*. In all the dialogues, but in these three in particular, Plato founds the Platonic education—the Platonism—intended to replace the Homeric education.

The Platonic education focuses on the imitation of Socrates. How does such imitation reflect Socrates' critique of the Homeric education? As we have seen, Socrates' critique of Achilles focuses on his stance toward death: his passionate fear of his own death and of the deaths of his loved ones, a fear that can only be overcome by such passions as anger. In his *Apology* and *Phaedo*, Plato presents Socrates as apparently fearless in the face of death. In his defense speech before the Athenian jurors, Socrates denounces the fear of death as unreasonable and declares that what may well set him apart from most human beings is that he does not fear death (29b2–9). And Socrates seems to match these words with his deeds: rather than beg for his life in any way, Socrates is remarkably defiant throughout his defense speech. By asserting that death is not an evil and by backing his words with his emphatically fearless behavior toward the jury, Socrates evidently seeks to inspire his companions to master their own fear of death, as Socrates argues that poets should do in the *Republic*.[75] Even more notably, in the *Phaedo*, his companion Phaedo bears witness to Socrates' remarkable serenity in the face of his actual death (58e1–59a3). The *Phaedo* also bears witness to Socrates' remarkable self-sufficiency, a self-sufficiency that Socrates in the *Republic* calls on the poets to celebrate and criticizes Homer's

---

[73] See also *Symposium* 172c3; *Parmenides* 126a1–4.

[74] 474b4–540c4.

[75] *Apology of Socrates* 28b3–31a7, 34b7–35d8, 36b3–37a1, 38b1–9.

heroes and gods for lacking. Not only does Socrates refuse to lament his own death, but he apparently feels no sorrow at leaving behind his family and friends.[76] As Phaedo explains to his philosophic audience, Socrates convinced his friends, through his demeanor in the face of death and his arguments for the immortality of the soul, that death is not evil and thereby calmed their pity, sorrow, and especially their fear of death.[77] The culmination of Socrates' efforts to free the mind by assuaging the fear of death is his promulgation in the *Phaedo* and also at the end of the *Republic*,[78] of the Doctrine of the Immortality of the Soul, a doctrine which, along with the Doctrine of the Forms, was to constitute the doctrinal core of Platonism.[79] Through his powerful poetic portrayal of Socrates' apparent fearlessness in the face of death in the *Apology* and the *Phaedo*, and through his presentation of Socrates' arguments for immortality in the *Phaedo* and the *Republic*, Plato seeks to promote a Platonic education that strengthens the rule of reason over the potentially enslaving fear of death more effectively than does the old Homeric education.

To be sure, in the *Apology*, the *Phaedo*, and the *Republic*, Plato's Socrates indicates that there may be reasons for wondering whether death is truly not an evil and hence whether it is truly unreasonable to fear death.[80] Furthermore, as modern, contemporary, and even ancient commentators have noted, Socrates falls short of demonstrating the immortality of the soul in either the *Phaedo* or the *Republic*.[81] Nevertheless, the powerful example that Plato presents on

---

[76] *Phaedo* 59e8–60a8, 63a4–9, 115b1–c1, 116a7–b2.

[77] See 88e4–89a7, 117c5–d1, 118a15–17.

[78] *Republic* 608d3–621d3.

[79] These are "the twin pillars of Platonism," according to F. M. Cornford, *Plato's Theory of Knowledge* (London: Routledge, 1935) 2.

[80] See *Apology of Socrates* 29d1–31a1, 40c9–e4, 42a2–5; *Phaedo* 63b5–c4, 69e6–70b5, 77a8–c5, 80b8–10, 84c5–7, 84d4–88e3, 91a1–c5, 106c9–e7, 107a8–b9. See also *Republic* 10.611a10–612a6.

[81] See, for example, G. W. F. Hegel, *Lectures on the History of Philosophy*, trans. E. S. Haldane and F. Simson (New Jersey: Humanities Press, 1955), 2:43; Paul Friedlander, *Plato*, trans. H. Meyerhoff (Princeton: Princeton University Press, 1969), 3:45–49, 54, 57–60, 474; David Gallop, *Plato's Phaedo* (Oxford: Clarendon Press, 1975), 104–113, 134–136, 140–142, 216–222; David Bostock

the surface of both the *Apology* and the *Phaedo* is that of a philosopher serene and fearless in the face of death and the surface impression that Plato conveys in both the *Republic* and the *Phaedo* is that a follower of Socrates should embrace the Doctrine of the Immortality of the Soul. Ultimately those who strive to follow Socrates and Plato most attentively and most faithfully must, in their maturity, critically examine both Socrates' arguments for immortality and his demeanor. Such an examination would ultimately free their minds from the prejudices of their Platonic education. But those followers will be better able to carry out such an examination in a dispassionate and self-possessed manner thanks to their habitual imitation of the dispassionate and self-possessed Socrates and thanks to their longstanding adherence to the calming and reassuring Doctrine of Immortality.[82]

Through all of his dialogues but especially through the *Apology*, *Phaedo*, and *Republic*, Plato offers a new Platonic education as a replacement for the Homeric education that encourages admiration first for the tragic warrior hero—the virtuous, pious, passionate, sorrowing, and questioning Achilles—but ultimately for the enigmatic, humane, philosophic poet, Homer himself. For that education, as Plato's Socrates explains in the *Republic*, gravely underestimates the weakness of reason and the potentially enslaving power of the passions, and consequently ends up romanticizing and strengthening, at the expense of reason, the passions of anger, honor, pity, sorrow, love, and, especially the fear of death. Through his vivid presentation of Socrates, the fearless, dispassionate, self-sufficient philosopher who promulgates the reassuring Doctrines of the Immortality

---

(Oxford: Clarendon Press, 1986), 38–41, 52–59, 116–121, 187–193; Cicero *Tusculan Disputations* 1.49. See also Peter J. Ahrensdorf, *The Death of Socrates and the Life of Philosophy: An Interpretation of Plato's Phaedo* (Albany: SUNY Press, 1995).

[82] In the *Republic*, Socrates does compare the philosopher to an erotic lover and thereby suggests, to the erotic Glaucon, that the philosopher is, or at least resembles, an erotic human being (474b4–475c5; 485a10–c9). But even there, Socrates goes on to explain that the philosophers' passion for the truth effectively renders them dispassionate since that passion is so all-consuming that it leaves all their other passions considerably "weaker" (6.485d3–e2).

of the Soul and the Forms, as an explicit object of admiration and model for imitation, Plato offers an education that seeks to calm the passions, to strengthen reason among philosophic natures, and to enhance the status of reason and philosophy in the world as a whole. In this way, even though Plato certainly does not expect all to become philosophers,[83] he does, as Plutarch says, seek effectively to open a "path" to philosophy for "all" (*Nicias* 23).

---

[83] See 428e3–429a3, 490e2–491b2, 503b4–10.

SOPHISTRY, RHETORIC, AND THE CRIMES OF WOMEN: PLATO'S *GORGIAS* AND *PROTAGORAS* ON FEMALE INJUSTICE

Mary Townsend

In the *Gorgias*, Socrates remarks that men and women who are beautiful and good are happy, and those who are unjust and wicked (ἄδικον καὶ πουερὸν) are miserable (470e). Only half of this statement ends up being explored: much of the remainder of the *Gorgias* is dedicated to proving, with many impressive rhetorical flourishes, that the unjust *man* is miserable, and that real men chose a life of justice (512e). But readers do not receive a separate argument or rhetorical image for the unjust and wicked women to whom Socrates so briefly alludes; and in this dialogue, at least, we're left in ignorance of just what their crimes might be, or what kind of rhetoric, if any, might persuade them out of their life of crime.

By contrast, in the *Republic*, Socrates attributes many crimes and injustices to women: trading their husband's life for a necklace (590a), robbing corpses on the battlefield (469d), being immoderate in sickness and impiously wrangling with the gods (395e), and, crucially, being immoderate in *eros* (395e).[1] On occasion, it is their

---

[1] The interesting question of the imitation of women's *eros* occurs at *Republic* 395e, in the context of Socrates' general statement that if the guardians must imitate something, they should restrict themselves to imitating men who are brave, temperate, pious, free, and all such things (395c); he embarks on a long series of parallel things women do that the guardians, at that point being men, will not be allowed to imitate; he contrasts young women and old, those who reproach husbands versus those who reproach gods, those who believe themselves happy either in both (τε καὶ) good or bad fortune versus those who take up laments (καὶ θρήνοις ἐχομένην), and finishing it off with a colon followed by a triple parallelism: "and those who are wearied, in love, or in the pains of labor, we will keep them well away from." Socrates' penchant for altering the structure of his sentence

complaints to their sons about the shortcomings of the father with respect to money and power that help bring down a regime, as in the case of the mother, who along with her slaves, helps form the timocratic son (549d–e). Like the tyrant, Socrates notices, housewives sit sunk in the recesses of their home full of envy and greed (578b). In the *Theages*, Socrates makes the connection between women and the "most perfect injustice" of tyranny explicit:[2] he asks the youth Theages, himself desirous of a godlike state, whether he's looking for a teacher who has the same skill as Callicrite, daughter of Cyane, who "knows the tyrannic art" (*Theages* 125e).

We are familiar with Socrates' positive plans for women in the *Republic*, that the best of them should share in the philosophical education and rule of the city as members of the guardian class (457a, 466d, 540c). If Socrates is not simply playing around when he mentions in Book 6 that the best-souled natures turn out exceptionally badly when they get bad schooling (6.491e), it might be rather a qualification than a disqualification for women's rule that they also possess the capacity for the worst sort of injustices as well. In any case, for Socrates, a large amount of crime is an indicator of an imbalance in a regime that will inevitably lead to revolution (553d); and one does not have to look far outside of Plato to see Socrates' worries about the injustice of women confirmed. In the messy court cases we read about in the speeches of the orators such as Lysias, Antiphon, and Demosthenes, women lie, cheat, steal, poison husbands, substitute one man's baby for another's—you do not even need to turn to comic poets to document their misdoings, although Aristophanes certainly makes hay out of these circumstances. But it is Socrates who proposes to do something about it on the order of regime, and even if his plans lack perfection, to the extent that they

---

halfway through is on display here, since the example of Niobe unites the examples of boasting and believing oneself happy which are otherwise split grammatically and logically; but his examples seem to roughly correspond to the antitheses of freedom, piety, bravery, and temperance respectively.

[2] For tyranny as the perfection of injustice, see *Republic* 580e. My thanks to Hayden Brockett for his legal help in preparing this essay.

represent a positive zoo of impossibilities, one can sort of see why he, as well as the Athenian Stranger, might be tempted to try.[3]

Philosophers and legislators aren't the only ones who speak of the justice and injustice of women in Plato's corpus, however: the sophists and rhetoricians, in the form of Protagoras and Gorgias respectively, have own their competing thoughts. Now, Socrates is known for considering the words and motives of sophists and rhetoricians as deeply suspect, and on the whole we tend to believe him, even if we likewise suspect his own accounts to be less than perfect. If Socrates is correct to say in the *Gorgias* that sophistry and rhetoric are pale imitations of law-giving and law-adjudicating respectively (465c), it stands to reason that Gorgias' and Protagoras' accounts of women's injustice would be broken in a way that would illuminate their own shortcomings as political thinkers. Protagoras' and Gorgias' allusions to the crimes of women show that while they acknowledge the problem they do not recognize its depth, and their political solutions are likewise incomplete. First I will examine Protagoras' inconsistencies on whether political virtue is a human possession or the possession of men alone; then I will turn to Gorgias' famous speech where the virtue of a man and the virtue of a woman are separate, distinct, and do not overlap. Finally, I'll address the nature of these shortcomings based on Socrates' contention that the rhetorician and the sophist flatter us about what is pleasant in the absence of what is good (465a). Both claims fall short because they are meant to please, rather than present the truth of human nature or work towards the political good.

---

[3] The Athenian Stranger, who is also interested in altering the position of women in a regime, makes this danger explicit at *Laws* 780e–781d, and especially 781a: "Through a slackness towards [the female sex] many things have flown past you, which might have been better by far than things are at present, if they had fallen in with laws." It is worth noting that in Aristophanes' female-led regimes, the women take the reins to correct male misdeeds; while in Plato, Socrates and the Athenian Stranger take women up as citizens in order to correct women's own injustices.

A. Protagoras and Manliness

The story of the *Protagoras* follows this tried and true formula: Socrates confronts Protagoras on the imperfection of his account of virtue, and refutes him in the end. Protagoras, publicly owning his status as a sophist (317b), agrees with Socrates that what he as a sophist teaches may be called the political art; his teaching makes men good citizens (319a). Protagoras therefore argues, as he must do in order to remain consistent, that virtue *can* in fact be taught—since after all, he claims to teach it for pay. In his attempts to refute Socrates' opposite claim—echoed by a much older Socrates in the *Meno*, that virtue *cannot* be taught at all—Protagoras makes a long speech which contains both a myth and an argument.

In his myth, Protagoras describes the process by which political virtue was given to us by Zeus.[4] Since human beings (*anthropoi*) initially lacked the political art, they were set to destroy themselves from the injustices they committed against each other (322b). Zeus sent Hermes with justice (δίκη) and reverence (αιδώς) to correct this. But Hermes asks a clarifying question: should he distribute them to a few or to all human beings? Zeus is clear: unlike the way other heaven-sent arts are distributed, where one doctor's skill

---

[4] The relationship between Protagoras' art-and/or-virtue terms is confused; as always, his goal is lengthy enumeration without attempt at consistency. A list of his terms, in order: the political wisdom of Zeus (321d), humans lack political art (322b), justice and reverence to all (322d), men advise about political virtue (322e), all humans believe all men share in justice and the rest of political virtue (323a), relatives advise one to lie and say one possesses justice and the rest of political virtue (323b), injustice, impiety, and all that opposes political virtue (323e), punishment of the unjust (323e–324c), justice and moderation and piety as the virtue of a man (325a), justice, beauty, and piety taught by all (325d) and many references simply to "virtue." My guess is that "political virtue," where virtue is nearly enough synonymous with art, is Protagoras' best name for the rough category he's attempting to explain throughout his speech, since that's roughly what he agreed with Socrates he teaches (319a). Exactly what this virtue entails, and which individual virtues it contains, he is quite protean about; this is part of what inspires Socrates' response to his speech, asking whether virtue is one or many (329c). Socrates correctly identifies a weak spot in the pattern of his thinking that Protagoras will be unable to publicly defend.

suffices for the rest of the crowd, Zeus orders that justice and reverence be distributed "to all," saying: "let all have a share. For cities would not come into being if few should share in these as in the other arts (322d)." This excellence shared by all is "the principle of order in cities and its unifying bonds of friendship (322c)," and all believe that everyone should have a share of it, or else the exceptional human would "cease to be among human beings" (323b).[5] Indeed, Zeus requests that it be set as a law from him that anyone incapable of sharing in shame and justice is to be killed as "an illness to the city (322d)."

After his myth, Protagoras takes a similar approach in his *logos*, but with several crucial differences. He asks: "Is there or is there not some one thing that all citizens necessarily share in, if in fact there is to be a city?...if there is, and it is not the art of building or smithing or pottery, but justice and moderation and being pious, collecting it together as one, I pronounce this thing to be the virtue of a man (ἀνδρὸς ἀρετήν, 325a)."[6] It is worth noting that the phrase "virtue

---

[5] While Protagoras claims he officially ends his myth at 324d, his style becomes argumentative immediately after Zeus' statement is related, as Catherine Zuckert notes (*Plato's Philosophers: Coherence of the Dialogues* [Chicago: University of Chicago, 2009], 221). The *logos* seems to start as Gorgias begins explicitly justifying his myth ("as I assert," 447–527). The shift to "men" rather than "humans" takes place as the mythic style, sustained from 320c to 322d, ends.

[6] While Robert Bartlett argues that Protagoras teaches injustice, which involves the ability to exploit the many, and that the only two real virtues are wisdom and courage ("On the Protagoras," in *Plato's "Protagoras" and "Meno"* [Ithaca, NY: Cornell University Press, 2004], 74), this does not quite make sense of Protagoras' embarrassment at his inability to deal with courage. As Zuckert notes, courage is the exception to Protagoras' otherwise utilitarian rule, since courage often requires self-sacrifice that does not seem to accrue future pleasure to oneself (*Coherence*, 226–28). Protagoras' belief that one must maximize pleasure does rely on the baseline of societal order he argues is present in humans, since he needs a functioning society in order to avoid death and not have his goods confiscated (see 325b), and his goal is pleasure, not power over other men, which clearly often leads to unpleasantness; his subterfuge consists in the extent to which the many possess political wisdom, since they usually only do what the ruler tells them (317a), which will hardly allow them to maximize their pleasure for themselves as independent actors.

of a man" is not *andreia*, courage/manliness, but *arête andros*: something still definitely manful, but more generally so than as in the specificity of courage; and it is this that Protagoras now says is the thing that guarantees the existence of cities.[7]

What does this shift mean, between first arguing all humans possess political virtue, and then that only all *citizens* possess it? In the second case, we have narrowed the field from all humanity down to the Greek citizen, who is free, native-born, and a gentle*man*, specifically. Nor is this the only time that Protagoras insists on the man-part in his speech: at one point he claims that all human beings believe *men* to share in justice and the rest of political virtue (323a5), and that we listen to advice on this from *men* (323a2). It is a big shift, and a lot rests on it: can manly virtue alone perform the function that political virtue is supposed to perform in cities, that is, be the bond of unity and friendship within a city, and stop the injustices that break it apart? Is the virtue of Athenian free-born men sufficient to provide unity and friendship to all of Athens? This point becomes the more difficult as Protagoras hints that despite Zeus' best efforts, plenty of *un*just men still abound, who lie when they say they are just, at the advice of their whole household (323b). We should wonder whether Protagoras ultimately thinks that real men are just or unjust; or just how many real men are needed to give order to cities, however they do it. But on either plan, we are still arguing about, and picturing, *andres*, men, as the linchpin of cities. And if manly virtue, just or unjust, *could* be sufficient to hold a city together, why does Protagoras' Zeus initially make such a point about sending political virtue to all *anthropoi*, stressing that even a single one without it is to be considered as an illness, and as immanently worthy of death?[8] Protagoras' argumentative response to Socrates, that virtue

---

[7] Protagoras anticipates this explicit move before he announces his change to argument, when he notes that all humans believe all men share in justice in the rest of political virtue (323a).

[8] In implying that all humans consider men as having a share in political justice, it sounds like Protagoras is asserting, however briefly, that women would be part of the great crowd of humanity that agree that manly virtue is sufficient bond for cities; likewise, the whole household comes to recommend that the

can be taught because everyone teaches it, depends on the universality of such virtue; but he does not make precise what this universal stretches over.[9]

In its next sentence, Protagoras' *logos*-argument becomes still stranger: "and if there's one man (τὸν μὴ μετέχοντα) not sharing in [political virtue], it's necessary to teach and to chastise him, both child and man and woman, until the chastised man should become better; and the one who does not hearken after having been chastised and taught, should be thrown out of the city or killed, as one incurable (324a6–325b1)."[10] The sentence begins with a single person,

---

outlying male transgressor lie and say he is just (323b). But this makes the universality of Protagoras' myth unnecessary and incoherent: it would have been easy enough to make the myth manly as well, if the women were set to agree with it. In his initial turn to myth, Protagoras works within a genre that by necessity attempts to describe the *natural* whole, and so includes the female principle as a matter of course. In his move to argument, he drops the bid for wholeness, and so drops women as well; Protagoras fails to bridge the gap between nature and politics coherently. As a sophist, he lives within the *logoi* of city dwellers, where even the gods are man-made (*Coherence*, 220), and has no real commitment to articulating the natural; the genre he takes up is part of why it occurs to him to allude to the problem that women pose in the polity, without enough interest in solving it.

[9] For instance, Protagoras could have argued that Zeus gives virtue to a lot of people but not to all; but this would not be a sufficient response to Socrates, since then Protagoras would have to explain what qualifies an individual as virtuous, which he avoids above all. As Nicholas Denyer points out, arguing only that many possess virtue means the city still possesses a noticeable number of unjust people, and then "the cooperative will come to feel that they are being taken advantage of, and soon there will no longer be enough cooperation for there to be any kind of city (*Plato: Protagoras* [Cambridge: Cambridge University Press, 2008], 108).

[10] It is somewhat ambiguous what Protagoras means by "chastisement" here, the more so as one of the justifications for translating "κολάζειν" as related to punishment is given by Liddell-Scott in reference to this precise passage in the Protagoras (LSJ, s.v. "κολάζω"). Theophrastus, biologist and student of Aristotle, provides an interesting instance with regards to difficult plants: the almond tree, a "bad neighbor" (*De Causis Planatarum*, 3.10.6), due to its strength and profusion of roots, has an iron peg driven into the trunk in order to make a permanent hole in order to check the tree's growth; Theophrastus notes that some call this

grammatically male, who does not share in masculine virtue; this single subject splits into a strange triple both/and/and: both child and man...*and* woman, with woman tacked on as the awkward final third. Then all three unite as a single masculine subject again in the phrase "the chastised one" who had better get better; and the single male subject who does not hearken after his education and punishment is to face exile or death.[11] Why does Protagoras make this criminal addendum to his image of male virtue as the foundation of the city? Here he acknowledges directly what's implied in his myth, even though he cloaks it in the grammar of male misdoing, that not only men but women and even children, apparently, commit injustice; and they commit the kind of injustice that would require corrective attention, since otherwise it would threaten the city's stability and existence. What sorts of injustices is Protagoras talking about that women would commit? Is he thinking of the same kind of things that Socrates is, or about different sorts of crimes? And do their crimes act as a challenge to manly virtue, or can manly virtue reach beyond itself enough to correct the crimes that stand outside of it, in Protagoras' thinking?

The first possibility is that Protagoras is thinking of something relatively anodyne; not regime change or poisons or putting your enemies' heads in wine skins full of blood like Tomyris did to the Persian king Cyrus (Herodotus, *Histories* 1.214); but something more like the most familiar crime involving women we read of in the poets, namely adultery. Now, this could well be the sort of female

---

"chastising" the tree, since its "hubris" is punished in this way (*Enquiry into Plants*, 2.7.6). It seems chosen, perhaps, by Protagoras for its sense of correcting that does actually alter an erring person for the better, to the extent that the person becomes less capable of harm. Joe Sachs notes that *kolasis*, which he glosses as discipline, corrective restraint, and punishment, forms a contrast in the *Gorgias* with Socrates' emphasis on flattery, *kolakeia* ("Introduction," *Plato Gorgias and Aristotle Rhetoric*, trans. Joe Sachs [Indianapolis: Focus Philosophical Library, 2009], 7).

[11] Denyer argues the addition of women here simply solves the problem Protagoras raised by naming political virtue as the virtue of a man (*Plato: Protagoras*, 114); but this is helping Protagoras to a consistency he does not achieve, and doesn't even desire.

injustice Protagoras imagines to be solved, as indeed Greek law believes it is solved, by manly justice punishing male transgression.[12] In Athenian law, famously, if caught in the act, the adulterer may be killed by the husband; and in this sentence, we should note, to say "the adulterer" is to be speaking of a man, with the wife in the background, only ambiguously party to the act.[13] This is a legitimate flaw in a legal code that seeks to chastise injustice, since the problem of adultery, and the problem it poses, at the very least for the production of legitimate future citizens and heirs, does not involve the *eros* of men alone; and here Socrates' emphasis on the immoderation of women's *eros* as a real political problem in the *Republic* starts to make more sense. If women's *eros* reaches to injustice as well, then more than male moderation and virtue is desirable in a regime, just as punishment for female crime would also be necessary.

---

[12] See Eva Cantarella, "Gender, Sexuality, and Law" in *The Cambridge Companion to Ancient Greek Law*, David Cohen and Michael Gagarin, eds. (Cambridge: Cambridge University Press, 2005), 242–245. While, as I will discuss in a moment below, Athenian law did more than Spartan or Cretan law, given what records we have left, to address the crimes of women in adultery, Cantarella argues this basic pattern remains in force; this is particularly clear in the case of rape law, where women's consent was not considered relevant for punishment or acquittal (Ibid., 244ff). Of course, women were not full legal entities in Athens, as Danielle Allen discusses: "women, just like the non-elite male citizens, could participate in the penal system both in trivial dealings with magistrates and as witnesses at arbitrations and as active participants in private arbitrations. They were not, however, allowed in jury trials except as defendants or as material proof, and if a woman were to wind up as a defendant in a court case, a male citizen would have to speak on her behalf." "Punishment in Ancient Athens," in A. Lanni, ed., "Athenian Law in its Democratic Context" (Center for Hellenic Studies On-Line Discussion Series), 12. Republished with permission in C. Blackwell, ed., *Dēmos: Classical Athenian Democracy* (A. Mahoney and R. Scaife, eds., The Stoa: a consortium for electronic publication in the humanities [www.stoa.org], 2003).

[13] Cantarella emphasizes with italics the one-sidedness of Lysias' language in *On the Murder of Eratosthenes*: "Eratosthenes committed adultery *on* my wife and *corrupted* her ("Gender, Sexuality, and Law," 242); the "*moichos*" is simply male (Ibid., 244). Of course, it goes without saying that polities who via law consider the female actor as the primary or even sole force behind the business have hardly found a practicable solution either.

Now, in Athens, in contrast to Spartan or Cretan *nomoi*, there were punishments that directly affected the women involved with an adulterer.[14] But in Protagoras' list of penalties for child, man, and woman, this is exactly what he does not do: in his plan the one who fails to respond to chastisement is to receive exile or death, which along with confiscation of property are the strongest penalties the ancient *polis* can well impose, even in cases of treason.[15] In the case of adultery in Athens, death could only be a penalty for the male actor in the crime, and it was not a necessary legal consequence; in Spartan and Cretan law, death was not on the table for anyone.[16] But for the female adulterer in Athens death was specifically prohibited: "she is to refrain from attendance at public religious festivals, and if caught at them, is to suffer any suffering short of death" (Demosthenes 59.85–6). The logic of this is, perhaps, to provide some protection for wombs that make the necessary future citizens; but Protagoras' punishments do not allow for these eventualities. The limitations of his grammar seem to preclude anyone but men receiving punishment; and the nature of the punishments he

---

[14] In the law code of the Cretan city of Gortyn, adultery was punishable by a fine, levied against the man, and the amount varied with circumstances; see Isias Arnaoutoglou, *Ancient Greek Laws: A Sourcebook* (London: Routledge, 1998), 22–25; unlike in Athens, it seems that divorce was not compulsory there. For a discussion of the relation of Gortyn's law code to Cretan and Greek law generally, see John Davies, "The Gortyn Laws," *The Cambridge Companion to Ancient Greek Law*, 305–327. It is worth noting that in Sparta, there was no legal punishment for adultery at all, save occasional ribaldry (Sarah Pomeroy, *Spartan Women* [Oxford: Oxford University Press, 2002], 75). Athens' penalty of divorce and prohibiting the woman from religious participation seem to go further than other polities in its attempt to acknowledge and correct transgressing female desire; nevertheless, it still places the grammatical and active burden on male transgression.

[15] See Robert Parker, "Law and Religion," in *The Cambridge Companion to Ancient Greek Law*, 65; Parker also discusses the extreme measures of prohibitions against burial in Attica and the razing of one's house. For a recent and thorough discussion of death and exile penalties for homicide, and a keen sense of the distance between how the orators describe the crime and what we can determine as fact, see Christine Plastow, *Homicide in the Attic Orators: Rhetoric, Ideology, and Context* (Abingdon, UK: Routledge, 2020).

[16] See Cantarella for the range of possible Athenian penalties, 244.

recommends are of this sort as well. Indeed, Protagoras argues, against Socrates, that we can safely conclude that fathers *do* all teach their sons virtue, since no father would omit the sort of cultivation that, if lacking, would incur the death penalty, banishment, and confiscation of property (325b–c); here too the emphasis is on sons, not daughters, incurring the punishments of adult men.[17]

Of course, Protagoras is originally from Thrace, which for Athenians was canonically barbarous, its legal code obscure.[18] But Protagoras makes it clear he has Athenian law in mind: he remarks that like the rest of the Greeks, Athenians believe that legal punishment is for the purposes of education (324c), and he points out specifics of this that Athenian law shares with other cities (326e).[19]

---

[17] If Protagoras is seriously considering the possibility that citizen women might be guilty of worse crimes such as homicide or treason, taking this to trial might well be a thorny test of the practicability of the Athenian law codes: again, a male family member would have to speak for them in court even when the woman was the defendant, as in Antiphon's *Prosecuting the Stepmother for Poisoning*; the wrinkle being that if you prosecute your own stepmother, your own brother might be your adversary in court (Antiphon 1.6); in this case at least, however, death is called for by the prosecution. Other penalties such as exile or loss of property seem even more awkward: as Allen puts it: "Women could not, of course, be subject to a loss of political rights but they could lose their rights to participate in religious spaces and events" ("Punishment in Ancient Athens," 16). It is worth noting, however, that the laws allowing torture and execution of slaves seem to make no distinction with respect to gender (Allen, ibid.; see also Antiphon 1.20). In the case of Neaera, a woman accused of posing as an Athenian citizen wife, if convicted she would have been sold into slavery, but this penalty was not lawful for Athenian citizens, male or female (see Cynthia Patterson, "Ancient Citizenship Law," in *The Cambridge Companion to Ancient Greek Law*, 288).

[18] Herodotus is still one of our best sources for Thracian *nomos*; he reports that while maidens are not watched, the conduct of wives is strictly observed (*Histories* 5.6); he also claims that Thracians sell their children into slavery, and certainly Athenians considered Thracian slaves desirable (See Despoina Tsiafakis, "The Allure and Repulsion of Thracians in the Art of Classical Athens," in *Not the Classical Ideal: Athens and the Construction of the Other in Greek Art*, Beth Cohen, ed. (Leiden: Brill, 2000), 364–389. This latter fact contrasts oddly with Protagoras' sentimental account of childhood education.

[19] As W. R. M. Lamb notes, Protagoras seems to be referring to "correction" (εὐθῦναι) as a general Athenian ordinance where magistrates are examined after

Indeed, Protagoras' wisdom necessarily must have pan-Hellenic appeal, and his bid for cosmopolitan cleverness rests on his success in this regard. But his teachings must also have applicability and power in Athens' legal world, since otherwise Protagoras' wisdom would hardly be useful to the Athenian student. In this question of universal execution, he makes a slip that Athenians present might consider as imperfectly cosmopolitan, perhaps even barbarous.[20] As the Athenian Stranger in the *Laws* makes clear, to avoid spelling out the women's law is a perennial oversight on the part of any lawgiver (781a), and Protagoras is not free from this common mistake.[21]

One last oddity: in his long disquisition on the education of the young son (ὁ παῖς), Protagoras notes that the whole household vies amongst themselves (περὶ τούτου διαμάχονται) to teach the boy what is just, beautiful, and pious, and what is not. The household described consists of two pairs of men and women, one pair of slaves and the other free, the pedagogue and the nurse on the one hand, and the mother and "the father himself" (325d).[22] All participate in

---

their term of office (*Plato in Twelve Volumes*, Vol. 3, W. R. M. Lamb trans., (Cambridge, MA, Harvard University Press; London, William Heinemann Ltd. 1967), 147n1).

[20] As Zuckert argues, Socrates shows by his refutations that Protagoras does not understand the nature of politics in a democracy (*Coherence*, 220). It seems that either Protagoras is consciously arguing for steeper penalties than customary, which no one would find convincing, or he is primarily thinking of male misdoing while throwing in a casual nod to women and children (leaving out slaves) and then moving on. Given that Protagoras hints, as he must, that he is an expert on injustice as well we justice, this vagueness betrays a certain weakness in his bid for universal enumeration.

[21] For more on the Stranger's rare wisdom in this regard, see Mary Townsend, *The Woman Question in Plato's* Republic (Lanham, MD: Lexington Books, 2017), 78, 114ff.

[22] See Lesley Beaumont, *Childhood in Ancient Athens: Iconography and Social History* (Abingdon, UK: Routledge, 2012), 56, 118. Both nurses and pedagogues could be free or enslaved, while the latter seems more common, particularly in the case of the pedagogue, if only because the breaking of a leg could transform a slave into a pedagogue, while mother's milk is harder to come by (Mark Golden, *Children and Childhood in Classical Athens* [Baltimore: Johns Hopkins Press, 2015, 2nd ed.], 123–5, see also 33).

the boy's education in virtue, and again, Protagoras' argument that virtue can be taught depends on this universal participation; he notes that to see this, all one has to do is consider the lack of justice among savages to notice how even a little justice is universal amongst the civilized.[23] But how, we might wonder, can mothers and nurses teach virtue, without themselves possessing it? Protagoras seems to want it both ways, that manly virtue is sufficient to itself, and yet depends on the virtue of women; women help contribute to manly virtue, but themselves receive no such education.[24] Indeed, should women as a body lack any political virtue at all, by Zeus' ordinance they ought all to be put to death or exiled, as a body; which would in turn destroy any city. Needless to say, these contradictions are not resolved: Protagoras' brief asides on women and children provides a veneer or cloak of universality to his *logos,* much like his later enumeration on the manifold uses of olive oil distracts the audience from the contradictions in his arguments on whether bad things can be advantageous (334a).[25] Everyone is virtuous; Protagoras is just a little bit better at leading others towards virtue, and if he fails one does not even have to pay full fare (328b–c).

If sophistry, as Socrates argues in the *Gorgias,* is an inadequate version of the lawmaking art, it seems that Protagoras as a lawmaker falls short of being able to adequately deal with either the virtue or the injustice of women, human beings who nevertheless inhabit the human community. Just as he seems to posit that male virtue alone

---

[23] Protagoras is perhaps referring to a burlesque of so-called savagery as seen in Pherecrates' comic play *The Savages* (see Bartlett, 24n81); and yet Aristotle makes a similar argument with respect to virtue, at any rate, in *Politics*: no one would call a man happy who was so cowardly as to be afraid of every insect that fluttered by him, or who would commit any crime to satisfy thirst or hunger (VII.1). Indeed, many of Protagoras' and Gorgias' arguments find an echo in the *Politics*; but the complexities of Aristotle's project with respect to them require separate treatment.

[24] This is part of why Socrates insists in the *Republic* that the way nurses tell stories must be looked into, and action taken to regulate them (2.377c).

[25] The good legislator, like the Athenian Stranger perhaps, is also tempted to endless enumeration of possibilities; but Protagoras' enumerations are specious, manifold without enough detail to really have legislative purchase.

can be the bond of the city, he also seems to consider that punishments suited for men are sufficient correctives for all humans within the city; his argument for why he is qualified to teach virtue depends on even women possessing a share of it, but he has no plans to educate women such that they would be qualified to teach it. Protagoras' speech seems to be an attempt to show Socrates that he knows much better what the political art entails, and while there are other reasons to be suspicious that he possesses it, we should add to our suspicions the way he deals with the women's law. The legislator must consider all the forces at work within his polity, just and unjust, but while Protagoras seems to recognize the need for this, his laws have failed to be sufficiently architectonic.

B. Gorgias and the Swarm of Virtues

The dialogue *Gorgias* begins just after the famous rhetorician of that name has finished his lengthy speech on virtue. Such a speech would have been the precise parallel to Protagoras', if we readers had been able to witness it. Fortunately, we do have an example of the sort of speech Gorgias gives about virtue from the *Meno*, and we likewise have Aristotle's authority that the views attested to Gorgias in the *Meno* really are Gorgias' (*Politics* I.13). As it turns out, the relation between male and female virtue is at issue for Gorgias' views no less than for Protagoras'.

At first, Gorgias' account seems to be a direct attack on the problem in Protagoras' speech: if male virtue is not sufficient for all human beings, it might be necessary to turn virtue into a swarm, where men and women each have their own sort of virtue peculiar to them. As Meno recounts the argument of Gorgias: "In the first place, if you want the virtue of a man, that's easy. This is the virtue of a man: to be capable of carrying out the affairs of the city and in doing so, benefit friends, harm enemies, and take care that he himself not suffer any such thing. And if you want the virtue of a woman, it isn't difficult to define: she must manage the household well (τὴν οἰκίαν εὖ οἰκεῖν) both by preserving its contents and by hearkening (κατήκοον) to the man" (71e). The man has his public task, and the woman her private one; and their separate tasks are supposed to make for separate excellences, which ought to make their excellences not conflict. The bonds that unite the city, one might say, are preserved by everyone minding their own business. To be sure, however, despite this brief similarity to Socrates' account of justice in the *Republic* (433b), there's a problem with Meno's version since it seems to hint more directly, and also more directly than Protagoras', that male virtue might also involve harming others (other men?), and so involve injustice.

Indeed, Gorgias' account of male virtue is strikingly similar to Protagoras' description of what he as sophist promises to teach, but there is a crucial difference. Back up to how Protagoras puts it: "good counsel concerning one's own affairs—how he might best manage (διοικοῖ) his household—and, concerning the affairs of the city, how he might be the most powerful in carrying out and speaking about the city's affairs" (*Protagoras* 318e–319a). While Protagoras is advertising to his ambitious male students that he will teach the ability to manage one's household *in addition to* the city, on Gorgias' account, that same household management has been split off, and forms the separate and distinct virtue of a woman.

Whose job it really is to run the household is an absolutely crucial question for the possibility of women's political virtue. If it is a man's job to manage the house absolutely, then we fall back on Protagoras' unified manly virtue that encompasses both house and city, and there cannot be a distinct virtue or realm for women. But if there *is* a distinct virtue for women involved in managing the house, we need to know what it entails, and unfortunately for Gorgias' account, there seems to be trouble involved given that this management is named only as preservation and hearkening. Is preserving goods and hearkening to the husband *enough* moral material to provide a separate sphere of excellence that the argument needs? For instance, is the wife's moderation ruled and made active by her husband's work, or is it the wife's own self-rule that provides it? When pressed by Socrates on what the underlying essence of Gorgian virtue is in the light of the swarm he has presented, Meno responds, "what else but to rule human beings?" (73c). But if virtue *is* rule, then it is not clear how being subordinate to someone else's rule could ever be virtue.

Meno concludes his Gorgian speech by noting that for any activity and age, there is a virtue, "and the same, I take it, goes for vice" (72a).[26] Now, if there is a vice for every activity, age, and even sex as well, what would the vice of the wife be? If the vice is opposed to the wife's virtue, then one would assume it would have to be something like, *not* preserving the things of the house, to waste them perhaps, or to give them to others, as the women in Aristophanes give meat away to go-betweens, or open wine for themselves at all hours (*Thesmophoriazusae* 557–9). Likewise, one could imagine the wife *not* hearkening to the husband, presumably, but to go her own way, and follow her own judgment instead; possibly even to allow her judgement to rule the household, and even the husband himself, as Zeus is always claiming that Hera is attempting to do (Homer, *Iliad* I.517–523), and her attempts are not always unsuccessful (Homer, *Iliad* XIV.154ff).[27] But then the vice of the wife (rule) would collapse

---

[26] Meno's Gorgian account contains a few other awkward ambiguities when he extends the pattern onward past husband and wife: "And there is one virtue of a child, both female and male, and another of an older man, whether free, or, if you like, slave" (71e–72a). Here he seems to admit, against his enumerative pattern, that there is a single virtue of a child, for both male and female; the master of the swarm collapses childish virtue into one for this single case, even though of course, education for male versus female children in Athens was quite different. But then the categories get even more jumbled. While we might expect, in a full enumeration, is that we would see the virtue of an old man versus and old woman, either as the same or different, and then the virtue of a male or female slave, most likely as the same. By editing out everything but the virtue of an old man, slave or free (72a), what Gorgias' account edits out of the full description would be enumerating other female virtues. Why? Possibly because that there would be a virtue as such of female slaves, and of free women who are not wives, is scandalous in itself, and not very flattering to wives; but more than this, their existence seems to contradict the reason for the rationale for a separate wifely virtue, namely, that the cause of their subordination is from being female simply, and based in nature alone.

[27] Seemee Ali argues that it is only after Hera successfully tricks Zeus that the latter is able to envision "godhood beyond autocratic rule," where the two

into the virtue of the husband (rule), and to be vicious as woman would be to practice virtue as man—the kind of paradox that always sets Socrates' teeth on edge, since how can virtue ever be bad, or badness be virtue? Socrates' conclusion, that virtue does not differ at all for the man or woman, whatever their political activity turns out to be, is very tempting at this point.

Of course, Gorgias is a rhetorician; and perhaps it is more fair to judge how successful his account is as rhetoric, in its most basic sense of speech that persuades. Consider the story of Callias' second wife, the same Callias at whose house the dialogue *Protagoras* is set, "the greatest and most prosperous house" in Athens (*Protagoras* 337d); both Callias and his wife achieved a certain fame. Callias' second wife was named Chrysilla, the very young bride described in Xenophon's *Oeconomicus*—the bride who was instructed by Ischomachus on how to maintain the separate virtues of the wife, which sound a lot like Gorgias'.[28] After Ischomachus died, Chrysilla went to live with her daughter, who was at that time married to our Callias. The story goes that before long, Chrysilla was sleeping with Callias too, at which circumstance, the daughter was so ashamed she first attempted suicide, and then ran away. Although Callias at first denied Chrysilla's son as his own, eventually she managed to persuade him to marry her, making her and her son respectable once more; this very son is mentioned by Socrates in the *Apology* (20a).[29] It seems like Ischomachus failed to understand just what was going

---

might think together and share one mind; the injustice leads to better justice ("Seeing Hera in the Iliad," Center for Hellenic Studies Research Bulletin 3, no. 2 [2015], http://nrs.harvard.edu/urn-3:hlnc.essay:AliS.Seeing_Hera_in_the_Iliad.2015; Accessed September 10, 2019).

[28] Ischomachus also makes a scheme based on complementary virtues: "the law declares those tasks to be honorable for each of them wherein God has made the one to excel the other. Thus, to be woman it is more honorable to stay indoors than to abide in the fields, but to the man it is unseemly rather to stay indoors than to attend to the work outside" (7.30); he also, in fine rhetorical fashion, claims that the god has given a larger share of fear to women, for the one specific purpose that she will be a better preserver of goods (7.25).

[29] Debra Nails, *The People of Plato* (Indianapolis: Hackett Publishing Company, 2002), s.v. Chrysilla, 94ff.

on in the soul of his innocent-looking child bride as he lectured her on wifely virtue, despite Socrates' repeated questions if she was really taking in what he said (Xenophon *Oeconomicus* 7–11); what Ischomachus thought, perhaps, was excellent rhetoric towards wifely justice and moderation seems to have had the opposite effect, and the wealthy husband Callias ended up being ruled indeed.[30] When virtue of the husband is to rule, simply, without justice, it is hard to explain to the wife that rule is not desirable of itself; and this state of affairs is not conducive to justice for anyone.

Ultimately, Gorgias' claim that there is a separate subordinate wifely virtue is specious on the Gorgian grounds that virtue is rule. As Socrates points out in the *Meno*, to manage either a household or a city you need justice and moderation, and whether you are male or female, these virtues stay the same with themselves, and they do not alter. When Socrates is actually in a room with Gorgias, Socrates brings up the subject of women no less than five times, including the claim I noted at the beginning of this essay, that the just and moderate woman is beautiful and good (*Gorgias* 470e). To me, Socrates' addition of such happy women to the dialogue, which otherwise is quite a manly tale, seem to be an implicit response to Gorgias' speeches about virtue that would seek to divide virtue in order to explain it, and to Callicles' doomed belief in what constitutes real

---

[30] Nails puts the date of the *Protagoras* at 433/2 BCE, while also remarking that the date of the birth of Chrysilla and Callias' son cannot be earlier than 412 BCE (*People of Plato*, ibid.). Indeed, given Socrates' very pointed references to unsatisfactory sons, it would hardly be in good taste for him to be alluding to this particular son of Callias, although these considerations certainly do not prevent him from alluding to the son at his own trial (*Apology* 20a); likewise, Protagoras can hardly make a reference to wayward women in good taste, since he would be working harder than Socrates not to offend his wealthy host. There is however no small piece of dramatic irony in the contrast between Protagoras' assurances that mediocre sons, since still young, can yet come to good (328d), and Socrates' statements at his trial for corrupting the youth that finish off the story by reporting Callias' failure to transmit virtue to his sons via the sophists. Intriguingly, as Nails reports, Aeschines' Socrates recommended that Callias send his sons to the courtesan Aspasia, perhaps in the hope if anyone could straighten out this messy family, she could (*People of Plato*, s.v. Callias, 73).

manliness. Likewise, Socrates' attempts in the *Protagoras* to praise the education of Lacedaemonian women (342d) seek to correct the precise omissions of Protagoras' lawgiving. Gorgias' account cannot explain women's vice or virtue coherently, and it can't correct women's vice any more than Protagoras' account could. Neither account, it would seem, represents full political wisdom.

C. Cosmetology and Pastry-making

In the *Gorgias*, Socrates gives an uncharacteristically lengthy speech of his own, sketching out a handful of tantalizing proportions that display the relation between real politics and the false versions sophistry and rhetoric present. Socrates chooses two ordinary but odd professions that treat with the body to articulate what he finds wrong with the soul-oriented, political versions. Sophistry, he argues, is like cosmetology, which exists to cover the unhealthy body with rouge, paint, and cloth, while rhetoric is like pastry-making, which offers strawberry shortcake in the guise of the medicine necessary to heal what ails (465b–d). All four of these professions, for bodies and souls alike, come from a knack (τριβή) rather than art (465b), and ultimately they are a kind of flattery, substituting a flattering, pleasing version of what ought to be good laws (sophistry), or a flattering, pleasing version of fair and right decisions about who is guilty and what punishment they deserve (rhetoric). Ultimately, both "make guesses about what's pleasant in the absence of what's best" (465a), and like the pastry chef's creations, their images are usually so very pleasant that if put to the test in a contest with the artful doctor or the one with political truth in hand, those with knowledge of the best are more likely than anything to starve to death (464e). Therefore, when we turn to the question of laws and justice for women, we have to be on the look out for what is flattering, pleasing, and unhealthy in Protagoras' and Gorgias' views; and as Socrates implies, the extreme likelihood is that we will be overwhelmingly tempted to consider the unhealthy to be health itself.

When Protagoras covers over the manifold phenomena of human excellence by painting over the whole with the image of masculine virtue, to me it seems that he, like Socrates' cosmetologist, presents a flattering portrait, well draped and rouged, of what political virtue looks like—but it is a seeming without a being. Who is he flattering? Possibly the roomful of young men who surround him at the wealthy Callias' house, from whom he wishes to obtain honor, money, and further rivers of admiring young men as students.[31] The sophist Hippias, attempting to soothe the waters between Socrates and Protagoras, remarks that since those gathered are the wisest of the Greeks, it would be a shame to be at odds with each other in the manner of the paltriest human beings (337d); and yet the conversation remains a contest rather than a dialectical conversation, as Socrates' adoption of the premise that pleasure is the good displays.[32] Male virtue is not enough to secure the city; it is like the unhealthy body that can look like complete human health and wisdom only with flattering tricks. Ultimately, Protagoras offers a cloak of justice designed to make the male actor as self-sufficient, secure, honored, and wealthy as possible, rather than comprehensive laws for a working polity.[33]

Gorgias, by contrast, necessarily has to spread his flattery over a wider audience. Like the tragic poet who must in the theaters flatter children, women, and men all together, slaves as well as free (*Gorgias* 502d), the rhetorician must have a speech saved up that flatters any age and position, and if one speech will work for all, so much the better. On Gorgias' terms, virtue is for all; yet each, to be virtuous, only has to continue to do what they were already doing, regardless of justice or moderation; this is appealing pastry, sweet

---

[31] See *Sophist* 222a for the rivers of youth and wealth that the sophist fishes in.

[32] For the refutational reasons why Socrates adopts this deeply un-Socratic thesis, see *Coherence*, 228n21.

[33] Protagoras tells us he actively practices such concealment at 317b. Notably, Protagoras does not have the sort of admiring love for the seeming natural strength of the unjust that Thrasymachus or Callicles flirt with; if he had really thought through the reality of women's injustice, as Socrates seems to, he might well have considered such natural injustice worthy of educational attention, but of course he does not.

without the sustenance real excellence gives.[34] Commentators often gloss the problem with Gorgias' account of female virtue as a mere description of "social role," rather than proper internal virtue.[35] But when his speech is seen as political art *manqué*, it becomes clear that this appeal to political hierarchy is made on purpose: it describes a regime, a regime where men are at leisure and in charge, the better to make war on each other, for the sake of gold and silver (*Meno* 78d) and the hope of power over each other (*Meno* 73d), the rest of everyone falling into haphazard order underneath.

Now, we might question whether Protagoras' sophistical emphasis on punishment, and Gorgias' rhetorical flourishes that seem to deal with law-making fit perfectly with Socrates' schematic; Socrates notes that while his proportions represent what is the case for both professions by nature, the two often "get mixed together in the same place dealing with the same subject, and they themselves have no more notion of what use they are than others do" (465c). Nevertheless, as Plato writes them, Protagoras and Gorgias show themselves to be exemplary enough of their kind, resembling Socrates' account to the best of their ability. For instance, Socrates points out that sophistry is more beautiful than rhetoric to the same degree that lawmaking is more beautiful than judging (*Gorgias* 520b); and it is certainly true that Protagoras' account is the more elegant, if the less persuasive, in its unifying portrayal of virtue. Gorgias' more work-a-day version, however, remains the more universally soothing alternative, even if unlovely in its tiresome iterations.

---

[34] As Devin Stauffer puts it, "Gorgian rhetoric is flattery in the sense that it convinces people that they can fulfill their desires with a good conscience; it convinces them that what they want to do coincides with what justice demands, and thus that they can be satisfied and good" (*The Unity of Plato's Gorgias* [Cambridge: Cambridge University Press, 2006], 48). It is worth noting that the later version of Socrates' descriptions of true rhetoric, which potentially satisfies real desires rather than simply desire for pleasures, which raises it to an art, is recognized by Socrates as something different from what Gorgias is practicing, and hence still open to the pastry chef critique (*Unity*, 156).

[35] See for instance Roslyn Weiss, *Virtue in the Cave: Moral Inquiry in Plato's Meno* (Oxford: Oxford University Press, 2001), 46.

To be sure, Gorgias' scattered hierarchies prove an effective device, capable of retaining an electric rhetorical power when brought to bear in court against its transgression, and are perhaps the more dangerous flattery. For instance, in Demosthenes' *Against Neaera,* a case where an allegedly foreign courtesan had been allegedly attempting to pass off her illegitimate daughter as a legitimate Athenian-born woman, the orator Apollodorus concludes with a Gorgias-like enumeration of the roles of courtesan, concubine, and wife: "Hetaerae we keep for pleasure, concubines (*pallakai*) for daily attendance upon our person, but wives for the procreation of legitimate children and to be the faithful guardians of our households."[36] Just like Gorgias, for each political role there is a specific purpose, but without any real justification of why the virtue of one accidental role becomes vice in a different context, the pleasure of the attendance of the courtesan at a drinking party the vice of the wife, or the attempt of the courtesan to become a respectable married woman.[37] The rhetorician pronounces themselves to be shocked, shocked, that such a female could be so impious as to commit a crime; but there was never any moral reason of substance why it was a crime in the first place, other than the need to maintain the specious hierarchy of the regime. Such expression of shock is pleasant because it flatters the belief there is moral justification for the pursuit of what benefits us at any cost. Gorgias' image of wifely virtue flatters us that being subordinate to the rule of the husband *regardless of justice* is a sufficiently satisfying political position such that few would dare or

---

[36] Demosthenes 59.122.

[37] Part of the flaw in Apollodorus' argument is that much of his evidence that Neaera is a foreigner is simply that she acted as a prostitute: her transgressive act rather than her actual parentage placed her outside; see Grace Macurdy, "Apollodorus and the Speech Against Neaera," *The American Journal of Philology*, Vo. 63 no.3 (1942): 267. Athens did not have strict customs for formally recognizing the birth of daughters, which made identification difficult ("Neaera's Daughter: A Case of Athenian Identity Theft?" *The Classical Quarterly*, New Series, Vol. 59, No. 2 [Dec., 2009]: 398–410). For a discussion of the difference between courtesans and *pallakai*, see Daniel Ogden, *Greek Bastardy in the Classical and Hellenistic Periods* (Oxford: Oxford University Press, 1996), 157ff.

bother to depart from it. But the problem is that this is rhetoric, and also that it is not quite true, to the extent that even a life of crime seems preferable to many Greek wives, not to mention to courtesans and enslaved women as well; and such temptation to crime is not a good political state of affairs.

Socrates is no stranger to rhetoric, and he is not above sophistry when trying to make a point; he remains an imperfect legislator. But he also offers something legitimately different in his attempts to persuade us that justice is health of the soul, and that rule over one's self is, at any rate, desirable because it is truly good. When he offers a share in just rule, education, and health of soul to women in the *Republic*, part of his point is that even if his solution would not work, the woman question writ large does really need a better solution than Athenian law, if only because crime doesn't pay. Perhaps in the *Republic*, Socrates offers us the female rhetoric—if also the sophistry—that Gorgias and Protagoras cannot muster.

Bibliography

Allen, Danielle. "Punishment in Ancient Athens." In A. Lanni, ed., "Athenian Law in its Democratic Context" (Center for Hellenic Studies On-Line Discussion Series).

Republished with permission in C. Blackwell, ed., *Dēmos: Classical Athenian Democracy*, A. Mahoney and R. Scaife, edd., The Stoa: a consortium for electronic publication in the humanities (www.stoa.org), 2003.

Antiphon 1, "Against the Stepmother for Poisoning." In *Minor Attic Orators, Volume I: Antiphon, Andocides.* Loeb Classical Library 309:

Antiphon, Andocides. *Minor Attic Orators, Volume I: Antiphon. Andocides.* Translated by K. J. Maidment. Loeb Classical Library 308. Cambridge, MA: Harvard University Press, 1941.

Arnaoutoglou, Ilias. *Ancient Greek Laws: A Sourcebook.* London: Routledge, 1998.

Bartlett, Robert C. *Plato's "Protagoras" and "Meno."* Ithaca: Cornell University Press, 2004.

Beaumont, Leslie. *Childhood in Ancient Athens: Iconography and Social History.* Abingdon, UK: Routledge, 2012.

Cantarella, Eva. "Gender, Sexuality, and Law." In *Cambridge Companion to Ancient Greek Law*, David Cohen and Michael Gagarin, eds. Cambridge: Cambridge University Press, 2005, 236–253.

Davies, John. "The Gortyn Laws," *The Cambridge Companion to Ancient Greek Law*, 305–327.

Demosthenes. *Orations, Volume VI: Orations 50–59: Private Cases. In Neaeram.* Translated by A. T. Murray. Loeb Classical Library 351. Cambridge, MA: Harvard University Press, 1939.

Denyer, Nicholas. *Plato's Protagoras.* Cambridge: Cambridge University Press, 2008.

Hunter, Virginia. "Did the Athenians Have a Word for Crime?" *Dike*, 2007, 10, pg. 5–18.

_____. *Policing Athens: Social Control in the Attic Lawsuits*, 420–320 B.C. Princeton, 1994.

Lysias. *Lysias.* Translated by W. R. M. Lamb. Loeb Classical Library 244. Cambridge, MA: Harvard University Press, 1930.

Gagarin, Michael. "Athenian Homicide Law: Case Studies." in Adriaan Lanni, ed., "Athenian

Law in its Democratic Context" (Center for Hellenic Studies On-line Discussion Series). Republished in C.W. Blackwell, ed., Dēmos: Classical Athenian Democracy (A.

Mahoney and R. Scaife, eds., The Stoa: a consortium for electronic publication in the humanities [www.stoa.org]) edition of March 27, 2003.

Golden, Mark. *Children and Childhood in Classical Athens.* Baltimore: Johns Hopkins Press, 2015, 2nd ed.

Ogden, Daniel. *Greek Bastardy in the Classical and Hellenistic Periods.* Oxford: Oxford University Press, 1996.

Macurdy, Grace. "Apollodorus and the Speech Against Neaera," *The American Journal of Philology*, Vo. 63 no.3 (1942): 257–271.

Maffi, Alberto. "Family and Property Law." In *Cambridge Companion to Ancient Greek Law*, David Cohen and Michael Gagarin, eds. Cambridge: Cambridge University Press, 2005, 254–266.

Nails, Deborah. *The People of Plato.* Indianapolis, ID: Hackett Publishing Company, 2002.

Noy, David. "Neaera's Daughter: A Case of Athenian Identity Theft?" *The Classical Quarterly*, New Series, Vol. 59, No. 2 (Dec., 2009), pp. 398–410.

Ogden, Daniel. *Greek Bastardy in the Classical and Hellenic Periods.* Oxford: Oxford University Press, 1996.

Parker, Robert. "Law and Religion." In *Cambridge Companion to Ancient Greek Law*, edited by David Cohen and Michael Gagarin. Cambridge: Cambridge University Press, 2005, 82–96.

Plastow, Christine. *Homicide in the Attic Orators: Rhetoric, Ideology, and Context.* Abingdon, UK: Routledge, 2020.

Scaltsas, Patricia Ward. "Virtue without Gender in Socrates." *Hypatia* 7, no. 3 (1992): 126–37.

Stauffer, Devin. *The Unity of Plato's* Gorgias: *Rhetoric, Justice, and the Philosophic Life.* Cambridge: Cambridge University Press, 2006.

Townsend, Mary. *The Woman Question in Plato's* Republic. Lanham, MD: Lexington Books, 2017.

Weiss, Roslyn. Virtue in the Cave: Moral Inquiry in Plato's Meno. Oxford: Oxford University Press, 2001.

NOTES ON THE CHARACTER OF CALLICLES

Kevin S. Honeycutt

> So great a man he seems to me, that thinking of him is like
> thinking of an empire falling.
> —Thackeray on Swift[1]

Who is Callicles?[2] It is a question clearly critical to the meaning of
the *Gorgias*. Callicles utters the opening words, "war and battle" (*polemou kai maches*); his house is the dramatic setting; his name is the
last word of the dialogue; and his conversation with Socrates com-
prises most of the text.[3] Though we know of the other characters in
the *Gorgias* from other Platonic dialogues and from sources other
than Plato, we possess almost nothing about Callicles except for
what is found in the *Gorgias*.[4] Thus, we can only understand the

---

[1] I would like to thank Kathryn Honeycutt, Charlotte Thomas, Anthony
Jensen, Charlene Elsby, Anna Bates, and Preston Earle for feedback on previous
versions of this essay.

[2] All Greek citations are from E. R. Dodds, *Gorgias: A Revised Text with
Introduction and Commentary* (Oxford: Clarendon Press, 1990 [1958]). All English translations are from the Loeb Classical Library edition of the *Gorgias* (Cambridge: Harvard University Press, 1996 [1925]), trans. W. R. M. Lamb. Translations are occasionally modified.

[3] Dodds, 15n3, notes that the dialogue may have even sometimes gone by
the title of *Callicles* in antiquity.

[4] Almost nothing and perhaps nothing at all. As I will explain below, I make
use of Douglas MacDowell's emendation of Andocides 1.127.5 in order to claim
that Callicles is a member of the Ceryces clan. It is the sole piece of information
that does not come from the *Gorgias*. Regarding the other characters in the dialogue, Gorgias is mentioned at *Meno* 95c; *Philebus* 58a, c; *Symposium* 198c; *Phaedrus* 261c and 267a; and *Apology* 19e. Compare the possibly spurious dialogues,
Greater Hippias 282b, d; and *Theages* 127e–128a. See also Aristotle, *Rhetoric*,
1404a; and Xenophon, *Symposium* 1.5 and *Anabasis* 2.6.16. Polus is mentioned at
Phaedrus 267b-c; and *Theages* 127e–128a. See also Aristotle, *Metaphysics*, 981a
and *Rhetoric*, 1400b. Chaerephon is mentioned at *Apology* 20e–21a and 28a; and
Charmides 153b. See also Xenophon, *Memorabilia* 1.2.48 and 2.3.1; and *Apology*,
14. Chaerephon was the one who asked the Delphic Oracle whether anyone was

Platonic Callicles by looking at the text.[5] As space precludes a comprehensive response, I have speculated on four aspects of his character that remain underappreciated (at least as far as I can tell): his deme; his clan; his known associates; and his misquotation of Pindar. What follows is a series of sketches or vignettes that are intended to provoke rather than to explain.

---

wiser than Socrates; this fact is surely crucial to the dramatic action of the *Gorgias* (see for instance 447a and 447d–448a, where he is called "responsible" [*aitios*]). Chaerephon was also frequently ridiculed by comedians (e.g., Aristophanes, *Clouds* 104, 144ff, 502-504, 831 and 1465; *Birds*, 1296 and 1562–64; and *Wasps* 1413). Catherine Zuckert provocatively notes that "[w]hen or even whether Chaerephon went to Delphi is unclear." See Zuckert, *Plato's Philosophers: The Coherence of the Dialogues* (Chicago: University of Chicago Press, 2012), 205n47. For a more comprehensive treatment of these characters, see Dodds 6–12; and Debra Nails, *The People of Plato: A Prosopography of Plato and other Socratics* (Indianapolis: Hackett, 2002), 86–87, 156–58, and 252.

[5] The vast majority of Platonic characters have historical verification outside of the dialogues. But Callicles is not alone in his lack of external evidence; the same is true for Philebus and Protarchus in the *Philebus* and for Diotima in the *Symposium*. There may be others that I am not aware of. At any rate, it has been conjectured that Callicles is a symbol for any number of figures: Charicles, Critias, Alcibiades, Isocrates, Demos, or Polycrates. Dodds believes that Callicles might have been an actual politician who died young as a result of being so ambitious and frank. See Dodds, 12-13, for a summary of these views. Werner Jaeger argues that Callicles is Plato himself, or, rather, a Presocratic Plato—a Plato minus the influence of Socrates, a Plato who "lies deeply buried beneath the foundations of the *Republic*." See Jaeger, *Paideia: The Ideals of Greek Culture* (New York: Oxford University Press, 1943), 2.138. Jaeger is quoted by Dodds, 14n1. See also W. K. C. Guthrie, *A History of Greek Philosophy* (Cambridge: Cambridge University Press, 1969), 3.106 and 106n2; and George Klosko, "The Refutation of Callicles in Plato's *Gorgias*" in *Greece & Rome* 31.2 (Oct. 1984): 134 and 138n15. Nalin Ranasinghe argues that Callicles is a cypher for Athens itself on the basis that his name may derive from a combination of "Callias" and "Pericles." See Ranasinghe, *Socrates in the Underworld* (South Bend: St. Augustine's Press, 2009), 79. Seth Benardete suggests that Callicles' name contains "the beautiful" (*kalon*) and "the naming of the beautiful"—the latter insofar as *kles* is a suffix from the same root as the word for glory (*kleos*), which became "contaminated" very early with *kalein*. See Benardete, *The Rhetoric of Morality and Philosophy* (Chicago: University of Chicago Press, 2009), 63; and Zuckert, 551n70, who also alludes to Benardete.

Before we turn to Callicles, I should say a word about why I have chosen to focus on him in a volume dedicated to ancient tyranny. The *Gorgias* was considered to be one of the most important of the Platonic dialogues in antiquity, especially on moral and political matters.[6] Moreover, it is an ancient work that remains especially relevant insofar as it treats two contemporary topics: how to control the power of propaganda or rhetoric in a democratic society; and how to reconceive moral standards in a world in which the traditional accounts of meaning have disintegrated.[7] And with respect to these topics, Socrates' most formidable, or at any rate most persistent, opponent in the dialogue is neither the titular rhetor, Gorgias, nor his student, Polus. Rather, it is Callicles, who has been taken to exemplify Plato's "tyrannical man"—the figure from the *Republic* who is at once a product of democracy and its deadliest enemy.[8]

That is why we take him up in this essay. If Callicles is intended by Plato to represent the tyrannical life, then an examination of the nuances of his character may help us to better understand the nuances of the Platonic view on tyranny.[9]

---

[6] Cicero makes Lucius Licinius Crassus claim to have carefully studied the *Gorgias* in Athens (*De Oratore* 1.47). Aelius Aristides reports that some readers admired the *Gorgias* more than any other work of Plato (II.6 Dindorf). And for the Neoplatonists, it was one of the dozen or so dialogues that were regarded as central and regularly taught; one began with the *Alcibiades* as an introduction to Plato's thought, after which one immediately took up the *Gorgias*. For these claims and for a fuller history of the *Gorgias*' reception, see Dodds, 62–66 and Index I.

[7] Dodds, 387, calls these the "central problems" of our time. See also Ranasinghe, 7: "…in an era where nihilism replaces totalitarianism as the main challenge facing humans, it is the *Gorgias*…that will help us to gain strength from the origins of the Western tradition."

[8] *Republic* 565d. See Dodds, 13, for this particular formulation as well as Nails, 75, who quotes Dodds.

[9] For explicit mentions of tyranny in the *Gorgias*, see 470d–473e and 510a–c. James Arieti suggests that Socrates himself is responsible for transforming Callicles from a "patriotic, well-meaning man into a tyrant-loving, antiphilosophical man." See Arieti, *Interpreting Plato: The Dialogues as Drama* (Savage: Rowman and Littlefield, 1991), 90.

The Man from Acharnai

Although it is difficult to establish Callicles' precise age because the *Gorgias* has an indefinite dramatic date, he is certainly older than 18 (because he has seen combat; 498a) and probably older than 30 years of age (because he desires to begin a career in politics; 515a).[10] He is a member of the Ceryces clan and the deme of Acharnai (495d).

Let us begin with his deme and with a brief word about the Cleisthenian reform of 508/7 BCE. In order to break up the power of aristocratic families and also to generate common concerns, Cleisthenes made demes, or villages, the foundational population unit of Attica. Demes were assigned to one of thirty trittyes or "thirds," which corresponded to the roughly geographical divisions of the Attican peninsula: the coast, the countryside, and the urban city of Athens. Each of the ten tribes was composed of three of these thirds—one from each of the geographical divisions. The basic idea was that citizens would have local concerns through the deme, regional concerns through the trittys, and national concerns through the tribe.

Acharnai was apparently enormous even in the late sixth-century and remained conspicuously prominent in the Cleisthenian arrangement.[11] It was in fact the largest of the Attican demes; its nearest rival, Lamptreis, was less than two-thirds as large.[12] Acharnai had a bouletic quota of twenty-two, which was by far the highest of

---

[10] I believe the dramatic date to be intentionally indefinite due to its incoherent historical references, but others have seen fit to assign it a concrete date, e.g., 405 BCE. On the contentious issue of the dramatic date of the *Gorgias*, see Dodds 17–18; Nails, 326–27; Benardete, 7; and Zuckert, 9 and 483n2. On the age of Callicles, see Nails, 75.

[11] David Whitehead, *The Demes of Attica* (Princeton: Princeton University Press, 1986), 397; and Sterling Dow, "Thucydides and the Number of Acharnian Hoplitai" in *Transactions and Proceedings of the American Philological Association* 92 (1961): 71.

[12] Dow suggests that Lamptreis was "actually two demes perhaps topographically distinct" (72).

any deme and almost half of the representation of its tribe, VI Oineis.[13]

Deme affiliation was inherited by sons from their fathers, and change of residence did not change one's deme or tribe.[14] Callicles has a house in Athens (447b), where he is hosting Gorgias and which is the dramatic setting of the dialogue. But it was common for citizens to have a house in the city and also one in a rural deme, providing two sources of income.[15] So he might also have had a residence in Acharnai. We don't know. We also don't know who his father was; Callicles is identified with his demotic name ("...of Acharnai") rather than his patronymic ("son of..."). So we could only speculate as to how Callicles spent his childhood; to what extent he grew up in Acharnai; and to what extent he "feels" Acharnian. But since Socrates calls him by his demotic, it is reasonable to conclude either that Callicles chose to be known this way or that Socrates wants to highlight Callicles' deme (495d).[16] And it is noteworthy on this point that Callicles is the only citizen from Acharnai in all of the dialogues.[17]

Therefore, while it is speculative, it is also reasonable to assume that it is important to the dramatic action of the dialogue that Callicles is from Acharnai. But how? Aside from its size, Acharnai was unusual in other ways. It was an area heavily exposed to Spartan raids, for one thing, and was thus noted for the proud belligerence and fierceness of its inhabitants.[18] It gave cult to Ares and Athena Areia.[19] It contributed 3,000 hoplites to the Athenian cause during

---

[13] Whitehead, 397. Acharnian citizens composed 44% of VI Oineis and thus 4.4% of the Attican citizenry as a whole.

[14] Nails, 349

[15] Ibid. Nails notes that this is the arrangement prescribed in *Laws* 745e.

[16] Callicles immediately responds by calling Socrates by his demotic. Nails notes—in an elaboration of Whitehead, 71, and with reference to *Laches* 179a–181c—that an individual's choice of demotic or patronymic could be an expression of class, status, and political values but "it need not be" (348).

[17] Nails, 352.

[18] Arlene Saxonhouse, "An Unspoken Theme in Plato's *Gorgias*: War," *Interpretation* 11.2 (May 1983): 141–142; and Benardete, 68.

[19] Whitehead, 399.

the Peloponnesian War, which was a tenth of the entire army, and approved of the aggressive prosecution of Athenian war efforts.[20]

This martial character was recognized by ancient Greek contemporaries. Pindar writes his second *Nemean Ode* to celebrate the victory of Timodemos of Acharnai in the pankration.[21] Thucycides portrays no other individual deme *qua* deme as a prominent actor in the events of the war except for Acharnai. Furthermore, the scene explicitly concerns the aforementioned number and profile of the Acharnian fighters.[22] And Aristophanes in several of his plays captures the collective Acharnian stereotype: veterans of Marathon; tough as oak or maple; wild, rough, vigorous, and unyielding.[23] In short, while it was unusual for martial traditions to be so closely attached to a specific deme, Acharnai was the notable exception.[24]

Callicles' views on nature may help us to see a connection between him and the militaristic timbre of Acharnian life. E. R. Dodds associates Callicles with Hippias' understanding of nature because Andron sits with Hippias in the *Protagoras* and because Andron is associated with Callicles in the *Gorgias*.[25] We will discuss Andron in more depth below. But this connection to Hippias, especially on such grounds, has rightly been called "something of a stretch."[26] Instead, perhaps we can understand Callicles' view on nature as a domestic rather than a foreign one. In other words, perhaps Callicles thinks of nature in the way that he does because he is Acharnian,

---

[20] Thucydides 2.20.4; and Saxonhouse, 142. Thucydides' report of 3,000 hoplites has been disputed, though it seems clear that the manuscript tradition upholds this number, rightly or wrongly. See Dow, 76; and Whitehead, 397–399.

[21] Whitehead, 399.

[22] Thucydides 2.19ff, as noted by Whitehead, 399.

[23] Whitehead, 399–400. See Aristophanes, *Acharnians* 178–185, 204–236, 280–365, and 665–675. On the Acharnian women, who were known as proud and formidable in their own right, see *Lysistrata* 61–63; and *Thesmophoriazusae* 563–563.

[24] Whitehead, 399, reporting K. J. Dover's assessment in A. W. Gomme, *Historical Commentary* (Oxford University Press: Oxford, 1970), 4.446.

[25] Dodds, 282.

[26] The phrasing is that of Nails, 75.

not because he is associated with sophists—whom he calls "worthless" (520a).

Callicles has seen combat or at least has seen cowardly men run in war (498a). He parses strength, insofar as it embodies natural justice, as political intelligence on the one hand, and as courage (or manliness; *andreia*) and firmness of resolve on the other (491a–d). He attacks "softness of soul" (*malakian tes psyches*; 491b). He also deems it so slavish and "unmanly" for an adult to practice philosophy that such a man deserves a beating (485c–d). Socrates says that Callicles has what many in Athens would call a "sound education" (487b), but what this means is unclear. And the above views are not obviously sophistical positions to me. In fact, the thesis he proposes regarding the *nomos / physis* distinction would have been extreme even for a sophist of the late fifth century.[27] Callicles' views sound instead like something that one might reasonably expect from a no-nonsense type of aristocratic Acharnian who has harsh views of justice due to his wartime experiences, and who consequently seeks as much pleasure as he can.

What is the basis of Callicles' hedonism? Some scholars hold that his worldview is derived in various ways from Gorgias' teaching.[28] But there may be other foundations for his position.

---

[27] Dale Grote, "Callicles' Use of *Nomos Basileus*: *Gorgias* 484b" in *The Classical Journal* 90.1 (1994): 22. Regarding extremity, Raphael Woolf wonders whether Plato invites the reader "to regard Socrates' worked out views as more radical (or 'extreme'), relative to everyday thought and practice, than [those of] Callicles.'" See Woolf, "Callicles and Socrates: Psychic (Dis)Harmony in the *Gorgias*" in *Oxford Studies in Ancient Philosophy* 18 (2000): 16n21. Arieti claims that Socrates and Callicles represent "polar extremes" (82) but that "Plato wants us to reject *both* ways" (92; original emphasis). Zuckert claims that "Callicles puts forth a more decent view of politics than does Gorgias or Polus" (546). Devin Stauffer suggests that Callicles is provoked by Socrates into offering a more extreme view than he actually holds. See Stauffer, *The Unity of Plato's* Gorgias (Cambridge: Cambridge University Press, 2006), 115–16.

[28] On this possible connection, see for instance Dodds, 15; Eric Voegelin, *Order and History* (Baton Rouge: Lousiana State University Press, 1957), 3.28; and Roslyn Weiss, *The Socratic Paradox and its Enemies* (Chicago: University of Chicago Press, 2006), 69–70.

Thucydides' report of the plague that struck Athens in 430 BCE is an interesting analogue. The plague was devastating not simply because of the physical debilitation, and indeed death, which it caused; there were also severe social ramifications. "Men did just what they pleased," Thucydides says, "coolly venturing" in public what once they did only in private. And "they resolved to spend quickly and enjoy themselves, regarding their lives and riches as alike things of a day...Fear of gods or law of man there was none to restrain them."[29]

It is noteworthy with respect to these effects of the plague that Callicles is praised for saying what others think but will not say in public (492d); that he says that luxury (*tryphe*), license (*akolasia*), and freedom (*eleutheria*) lead to virtue and happiness (492c); and that he derides the laws and conventions (*nomoi*) of human beings as so many frail and worthless fabrics (483b–484b and 492c). Perhaps Callicles suffers from a plague of his own: the sickness of injustice (*nosema tes adikias*; 480b), which, if left untreated, could become an incurable spiritual cancer.[30] But perhaps he simply detects the disintegration of civic life brought on by the war, feels his old, aristocratic way of life under threat as Athens increasingly moves toward naval fighting, and has decided that all bets are now off.[31]

---

[29] Thucydides 2.53.1–4. The translation is that of Richard Crawley in *The Landmark Thucydides*, ed. Robert B. Strassler (New York: Free Press, 2008).

[30] Voegelin, 5.60. Voegelin notes that the Athenian Stranger speaks of a similar man who lets his soul become inflamed (*phlegetai*) to a state of self-assertive inflation (*exartheis*), such that he no longer believes himself to be in need of guidance (*Laws* 4.716a). See also Voegelin, 2.45: "the criterion of the curable soul" is that it experiences itself "permanently in the state of judgment."

[31] Here my position bear similarities, at least in the broad strokes, to that of Zuckert (and thus secondarily to the positions of Benardete and Saxonhouse, with whom she explicitly aligns herself on this point). Zuckert believes that Callicles' "character mimics and so reflects the regime under which he has grown up, Athenian democracy during the Peloponnesian War" (546n63). Zuckert also suggests that Callicles' "resistance to reason" is not simply a matter of seeking pleasure or avoiding pain; it also involves "our fear of death" (556). Compare Ranasinghe, who notes that by the end of the war someone from Acharnai might be "bitter, bellicose, and cynical" (95n5).

The Ceryces

The identity of Callicles' clan, like his deme, is also suggestive.[32] The Ceryces clan derives its name and its lineage from the god Ceryx, who was the son of Hermes and Aglaurus. Aglaurus was the daughter of Cecrops, the mythical first king of Athens. Members of the Ceryces thus believed themselves to be tied to the very beginning of Athens (via Cecrops) and to a certain kind of office (via Hermes). In the Homeric era, a *ceryx* was a herald, messenger, or attendant; Hermes was the *ceryx* of the Olympian gods.[33] His sons, that is to say his descendants, thus became the Ceryces for human beings.

This sense of divine obligation was maintained in the fifth century BCE. In Callicles' time, the Ceryces were a powerful aristocratic clan who held the privilege—along with one other clan, the Eumolpidae—of supplying lifetime-appointed priests for the celebration of the Eleusinian mysteries.[34] There is no explicit mention in the dialogue that Callicles is a priest or is even especially religious; he appeals to divinity only in passing.[35] Nonetheless, the fact that he is of the Ceryces means that his very presence likely bore an aristocratic, and perhaps even arrogant, stamp. The fact that he is of the

---

[32] His membership in the Ceryces is asserted by Nails on the basis of an emendation by Douglas MacDowell of Andocides 1.127.5. See Nails, 76. Without getting too much into the argumentative weeds, I will only note that I find the emendation plausible and have made use of it here. But it is worth noting that Callicles is not a Ceryces on the basis of the *Gorgias* text alone; the Ceryces connection stands and falls with MacDowell's emendation. See also MacDowell's similar, though less convincing, emendation of Lysias 30.14.6. Both emendations can be found in *Andokides on the Mysteries*, ed. Douglas M. MacDowell (Oxford: Clarendon Press, 1962), 153–54, which is the basis of Nails's aforementioned assertion.

[33] Hermes' *caduceus* is a Latin corruption of the ancient Greek *kerykeion*, which was a herald's staff.

[34] Xenophon, *Symposium* 8.40; and Nails, 70.

[35] Callicles never address the gods at length but does swear occasionally and generically: in excitement "by the gods" (458d) during Socrates' conversation with Gorgias; in frustration "by Zeus" during his own conversation with Socrates (489e and 511c [2x]); in frustration "by the gods" (491a); in confusion "by Zeus" (498d); and so forth.

Ceryces also ties him to the founding of Athens and to Hermes; and it is noteworthy on this point that Socrates calls him not only a touchstone—that is, a stone used to test for the presence of gold (486d–e)—but literally a gift of Hermes (*hermaion*; 486e and 489c).

Viewing Callicles primarily as an Acharnian Ceryces—rather than as the result of foreign influence—may help to make sense of some of his well-known peculiarities. His aristocratic concerns are clear: though his political career (515a) means that he must pay heed to the people (*demos*; 481d–e), he thinks of them as weak (483b) and little more than a rabble (489c). He looks with scorn on professionals and laborers (512c). He is repeatedly rude (e.g., 489b, 490e, and 497b–c), and he is not above an almighty sulk that threatens to derail the rest of the dialogue (505c–d).[36] He calls sophists worthless in front of Gorgias, which charitably means that he does not consider Gorgias to be a sophist,[37] or that he loves the truth more than his friends.[38] Taken uncharitably, this statement makes Callicles appear to be an uncouth and even haughty host.

His domestic concerns are clear, too, especially with respect to a fellow citizen. Although these statements are sometimes interpreted as ironic, Callicles seems to like Socrates (485e) and repeatedly offers concerns for Socrates' safety that are plausibly sincere (485e, 486ab, 511b, and 521c).[39] And in responsive statements which are also sometimes interpreted as ironic, Socrates says that Callicles is very clever (481d); that he possesses what many in Athens would call a sound education (487b); and that he is brutally honest, even to a fault (487a and 492d). Socrates goes so far as to address Callicles in the name of friendship twice (500b and 519e; compare 499c).[40] Socrates clearly sees something of importance in Callicles

---

[36] Dodds, 14.

[37] Dodds, 7; and Nails, 75–76.

[38] Aristotle, *Nicomachean Ethics* 1096a and *Metaphysics* I.9.

[39] Dodds, 14. Contrast Jaeger, who speaks of the "brutally menacing tone of Callicles" and the "irreconcilable spiritual enmity between the protagonists of each side" (141). Zuckert believes that the friendship that Callicles claims to feel for Socrates "masks a kind of contempt" (550).

[40] Woolf, 11.

and is at great pains to distinguish the nuances of their respective positions, which is one reason why the *Gorgias* is as long as it is.[41] It is important for philosophy to distinguish itself from sophistry, surely. But it is also important for philosophy to distinguish itself from revelation.

What do I mean here? As I noted above, Callicles professes to be a type of hedonist: he says that true happiness consists in allowing one's appetites to grow as large as they can without restraint (491e) and in having as much as possible flowing in (494b).[42] He also explicitly connects the value of one's existence to the pursuit of power. But here he is not as clear as in his remarks on the pursuit of pleasure, which has led to a surfeit of interpretative results—none of which has been conclusively demonstrated. He has been called both an immoralist and an amoralist, for instance.[43] He has been deemed something of a postmodern nihilist.[44] And he has been compared to Thrasymachus in the *Republic*, to the Unjust Speech in Aristophanes' *Clouds*, and even to Nietzsche.[45] Regardless of the relative merits

---

[41] The *Gorgias* is longer than all other Platonic dialogues except for the *Republic*, *Timaeus*, and *Laws*.

[42] Benardete cryptically suggests that Callicles' hedonism "is not the opposite of morality but derivative from morality" (79).

[43] On Callicles' purported immoralism, see for instance Paul Shorey, *What Plato Said* (Chicago: University of Chicago Press, 1968), 154. Shorey says that Callicles presents "the most eloquent statement of the immoralist's case in Western literature." Shorey is quoted by Dodds, 266; Charles Kahn, *Plato and the Socratic Dialogue* (Cambridge: Cambridge University Press, 1998), 126n1; and Devin Stauffer, "Socrates and Callicles: A Reading of Plato's *Gorgias*" in *The Review of Politics* 64.4 (Autumn 2002), 627n2. See also Klosko, 126. On Callicles' purported amoralism, see for instance Bernard Williams: "Once at least in the history of philosophy the amoralist has been concretely represented as an alarming figure, in the character of Callicles." Williams is quoted by Kahn, 126n2. Contrast Stauffer: "Callicles is not simply amoral, despite his efforts at times to present himself that way..." ("Socrates and Callicles," 640-41). Zuckert likewise argues that "Callicles is not simply immoral or amoral" (546n63; see also 553).

[44] Ranasinghe, 77, 84, and 95.

[45] For a good summary of these views, see Stauffer, "Socrates and Callicles," 627n1. Both Dodds (14–15) and Woolf (33n47) note that Callicles' position

of each characterization, it is not hard to see why these sorts of comparisons are made. Callicles' own words invite them. But are they correct accounts? As Seth Benardete points out, Callicles does not claim that he himself is the naturally superior man described in his opening speech to Socrates. In fact, he goes so far as to say that he would be one of the slaves of such a man were he to arise (483e–484a).[46]

I agree that Callicles is not the naturally superior man. We might say that he is instead the prophet of such a man's coming. As Devin Stauffer notes, Callicles' language in his speech to Socrates is at least evocative of something hopeful; as Dodds notes, it may also be evocative of something revealed.[47] It is noteworthy that Callicles almost immediately makes nature the ground of his disagreement with Socrates. He says that "Nature herself" will "reveal" that what the many call injustice is in fact justice. He appeals to the neologism of the "law of nature" (*nomos tes physeos*; 483e) and speaks of the "justice of nature shin[ing] forth" (484a–b).[48] He talks of his teaching as something that can be known if one takes up "greater things" than philosophy (484c), and he claims that he speaks the "truth" (492c). Perhaps, in the end, Callicles looks like a Ceryces priest after all—one revealing a hitherto veiled mystery. The mystery concerns the nature of nature, which is why Socrates must so forcefully take it up.

---

differs from that of Thrasymachus. See also Dodds' appendix on Nietzsche and Callicles.

[46] See Benardete, 65, who also draws attention to Aristophanes' *Frogs* 1431–32. Contrast Ranasinghe, who claims that "Callicles aspires to be the strongest beast amid chaos" (95).

[47] Dodds, 266–67; and Stauffer, "Socrates and Callicles," 634n9 as well as *Unity*, 88.

[48] On the *nomos / physis* distinction, which Callicles elides in novel fashion, see Guthrie 3.55–134; Voegelin 2.379–386; and G. B. Kerferd, *The Sophistic Movement* (Cambridge: Cambridge University Press, 1981), 111–130.

Friends and Lovers

I should note at the outset of this section that it is the one most sparsely sprinkled with conclusions. It may read like a detective's report of the detritus of a crime scene—bereft of immediately obvious meaning but dutifully recorded in the event that it somehow matters. Perhaps it does not. But if it does, hopefully I have carried the case far enough for another to bring it to fruition.

We are told in the text that Callicles counts among his associates Andron, Tisander, and Nausicydes—a group which Socrates calls "partners in wisdom" (487c). We are also told that Callicles is the lover of Demos, the son of Pyrilampes. Ideally, we could learn something about Callicles by examining these connections.

There is little concrete information to be gleaned about Tisander of Aphidna. His father may have been Cephisodorus, which would mean that Tisander was a member of one of the wealthy and well-known families of his deme. Tisander may also have been a member of the Thousand in 380 BCE.[49] Aphidna itself was one of the twelve ancient towns of archaic Attica and was where Theseus was said to have left Helen of Troy.[50] And Gorgias wrote an *Encomium to Helen* in which he implies something of the thesis that Callicles maintains: that it is not natural for the stronger man to be hindered by the inferior man. As interesting as this elliptical connection may be, however, it is difficult to see how it shines light on Tisander or, indirectly and more importantly for our purposes, on Callicles.[51]

Nausicydes of Cholargos, according to Xenophon's Socrates, was a miller and holder of foreign slaves who remained in the city under the Thirty.[52] As with Callicles, it is unclear who his father was. Nausicydes rose to the liturgical class due to his mercantile

---

[49] Nails, 294–95

[50] Plutarch, *Theseus* 31.1–3.

[51] Unless the (oblique) implication is that Callicles did in fact take his philosophical bearings from Gorgias, in which case it would militate against my suggestion that he may have taken them from his aristocratic and wartime experiences.

[52] Xenophon, *Memorabilia*. 2.7.5–66; and Nails, 210.

success; he apparently grew so wealthy from making barley flour that he could keep herds of cattle and pigs and still have enough money left over for liturgical purposes (which he was reluctant to fund, though obliged in principle). Athens was largely dependent on foreign trade for the grain necessary for breadmaking, so grain trading was highly regulated.[53] Nausicydes may have attained some of his wealth through exploiting this system. With respect to Cholargos itself, it is noteworthy that Pericles also hailed from it. It was also one of the few demes which had its own Thesmophoria, the annual religious festival devoted to Demeter and Persephone. Finally, it belonged to a city trittys despite being located away from the city itself. But what to make of these facts? As with the penumbral details concerning Tisander, this information about Nausicydes is interesting but hardly demonstrative of anything concrete with respect to Callicles.

But maybe this is part of Plato's point. Three of the group (Callicles, Tisander, and Nausicydes) are identified by their demotics by Socrates; only Andron is identified with a patronymic. This might suggest that Andron is somehow a special case.

Andron was the son of Androtion and a member of the Four Hundred in 411 BCE.[54] He was of the Gargettos deme, which (like Aphidna) is connected to the legend of Theseus.[55] At some point later in his life, Andron was prosecuted for debt.[56] And after the collapse of the oligarchy, he denounced former colleagues regarding the sacrilege of 415 BCE—perhaps to save his own skin, as he himself had been implicated.[57] More provocatively, Andron is the only member of the four who appears in another Platonic dialogue. We

---

[53] Xenophon, *Symposium* 2.20; and Nails, 211.

[54] Nails, 28–29. Nails reports that Andron's son, Androtion II, was a wealthy Atthidographer who studied under Isocrates. However, she also attributes these qualities to Andron's father, Androtion I, in what seems to be a conflation. Compare Nails, 29 and 332.

[55] Gargettos is where Theseus turned the tables on some would-be ambushers during his war with the Palantidae. See Plutarch, *Theseus*, 13.1–3.

[56] Demosthenes, Oration 22 (*Against Androtion*).

[57] Dodds, 282; and Nails, 29.

find him in the house of Callias as one of three named characters, along with Phaedrus and Eryximachus, who gather around Hippias in the *Protagoras*.[58] He is thus the common link between this notable group and the partnership in wisdom in the *Gorgias*. It is difficult to know what to make of this connection, however, aside from the aforementioned and (I think) dubious supposition by Dodds that it consequently connects Callicles to the teachings of Hippias.

As if this paucity of useful detail were not enough, there do not seem to be any meaningful patterns in the residences of the partners in wisdom. Callicles and Nausicydes are from a city trittys; Tisander and Andron are from an inland one. None of them is from a coastal trittys. None of them is a member of the same tribe.[59] None of them is a sole member of their respective tribes in the dialogues. It is note-worthy that Callicles, Tisander, and Andron are the only members of their respective demes in the dialogues.[60] But while this fact was interesting with respect to Callicles, it is unclear what to do with it when it is shared among the three of them. In the end, perhaps we simply do not have enough historical information to make many ventures about the partners in wisdom. Or perhaps someone else will see something that I have missed.[61] The main point might be simply that Callicles has friends at all, since both Plato and Xenophon make it clear that the tyrant has no real friends.[62]

---

[58] *Protagoras* 315c. That Phaedrus and Eryximachus were very close is clear from other places in the Platonic corpus such as *Phaedrus* 268a and the whole of the *Symposium*.

[59] Acharnai was part of VI Oineis; Aphidna was part of IX Aiantis; Cholargos was part of V Akamantis; and Gargettos was part of II Aigeis. See Whitehead, 369–373.

[60] A handful of other characters in the Platonic corpus fulfill this condition. See Nails, 352–56.

[61] Saxonhouse asserts that Aristocrates was another "friend of Callicles," but I have found no evidence for this claim, in the text or out of it. Aristocrates is mentioned only once in the dialogue (472b) and not obviously as a friend or even associate of Callicles. See Saxonhouse, 144.

[62] Plato, *Republic* 575e–576a; and Xenophon, *Hiero* 1.37–38, 3.1–9, and 6.4–5.

Let us turn now to an examination of Callicles' lover, whose identity is divulged by Socrates. In his opening speech to Callicles, Socrates draws a commonality between them: that of pain. They each suffer the pain of erotic longing for two objects that they consider beautiful.[63] Socrates is a lover of philosophy and of Alcibiades; Callicles is a lover of the people (*demos*) of Athens and the son of Pyrilampes (who happens to be named Demos; 481d and 513b). Here we are interested only in Callicles' love for Demos. But because Demos is not named but rather indicated by his parentage, it is worth examining both him and his father.

Demos, whose name obviously calls to mind the people or *demos*, is the first man to be attested by that name in the historical record. Aristophanes calls him beautiful (*kalos*) in 422 BCE; a year later Eupolis implies that Demos may have been intellectually slow or at least hard of hearing.[64] Demos became Plato's stepbrother at seventeen when Pyrilampes married Plato's mother (and his niece), Perictione. Pyrilampes was thus Plato's stepfather (and great-uncle). He was also a personal friend to Pericles, an ambassador to Persia, a veteran of Delium, and a very handsome man himself. He started an aviary that included prized peacocks and that Demos subsequently maintained for many years.[65] But perhaps the most important thing about him with respect to the action of the *Gorgias* is that he was often absent on state business.

---

[63] Benardete, 62.

[64] Aristophanes, *Wasps* 98 and Eupolis, fragment of *Poleis* (213 Kock). See Nails, 124–25 and 258; and James H. Nichols Jr.'s translation of the *Gorgias* (Ithaca: Cornell University Press, 1998), 71n65. Nails and Ranasinghe follow Dodds in suggesting that Demos was stupid, but Ian Storey suggests that Demos' "wax in the ears" might instead refer to a hearing deficit which caused one to miss verbal subtlety. Compare Dodds, 261; Nails, 124; Ranasinghe, 78; and Ian Christopher Storey, *Eupolis: Poet of Old Comedy* (Oxford: Oxford University Press, 2009), 226. Lastly, Demos is a friend of the speaker in Lysias' Oration 19 (*On the Property of Aristophanes*; 25–26) but cannot be the same Demos in Aristophanes' *Knights*, who is an old codger. See Nails, 125 and 232.

[65] Dodds, 261; and Nails, 258.

Why would this be important? In the *Laws*, Plato gives examples as to how the absence of fathers leads to political ruin.[66] In the *Laches*, Lysimachus, son of Aristides the Just, speaks for himself and Melesias when he informs Nicias and Laches: "we blame our fathers for allowing us to take things easy when we were growing up, while they were busy with other people's affairs."[67] And one might also think of the *Odyssey*, where not only the 108 suitors but also Telemachus effectively grow up without fathers in the static frustration of Ithaca. With respect to the *Gorgias*: Callicles is the lover of Demos, implying that Callicles is the older man. Perhaps Plato is asking us to reflect upon the fact that Callicles may have been something of a father figure to Demos in the absence of Pyrilampes. Would it be worse to grow up in a family without a father or with a bad one? Would it be worse to grow up in a polity without a ruler or with a bad one, i.e., a tyrant? Does Plato deem the regime itself, rather than any particular individual, the best surrogate for fatherless men?

The Misquotation of Pindar

In a key moment of his opening speech to Socrates (484b), Callicles incorrectly recites one of the most famous fragments in Greek lyric poetry: Pindar's fragment 169, which concerns one of the labors of Heracles. Martin Ostwald notes that the fragment was widely quoted in antiquity and attained the status of a proverb, perhaps even in Pindar's own day and certainly by that of Callicles.[68] In other words, it is likely that most, if not all, of the people in the *Gorgias* who are listening to Callicles would have recognized his error. Here is what Callicles supposedly says:

> "*Nomos*, the king of all mortals and immortals"; and this indeed, he says, "leads, making what is most violent just, with highest

---

[66] *Laws* 682d–e and 694e–695a.

[67] *Laches* 179d. The passages from the *Laws* and *Laches* are cited by Nails, 258.

[68] Martin Ostwald, "Pindar, *Nomos*, and Heracles" in *Harvard Studies in Classical Philology* 69 (1965): 109. The fragment is correctly quoted by the Athenian Stranger at *Laws* 715a. Compare *Laws* 890a.

hand; I judge so from the works of Heracles, since—without payment—..." he says something like this—for I do not know the ode...

In all of the primary manuscripts that have come down to us, Callicles does not actually say "making what is most violent just," which are undoubtedly Pindar's actual words. Callicles instead says something like "making what is most just violent."[69] In other words, whereas Pindar says that *nomos* renders just that which is most violent, Callicles says that *nomos* renders violent that which is most just.

Scholars have long suspected that, from what else we know of Pindar, he is badly misrepresented by Callicles.[70] However, all of the primary manuscripts contain the misquotation; thus, while it is possible that the misquotation is a scribal error, it would then be an error in every primary manuscript in the direct tradition.[71] Only a single marginal note in a single manuscript has the reading accepted by most editors.[72] Thus, since the error is found so widely, perhaps the misquotation is not a scribal spoonerism at all. Perhaps Plato intended Callicles to misquote Pindar in order to display something about Callicles' character.

---

[69] I say "something like" because the phrase under consideration is notoriously problematic (along with other aspects of the fragment). Concerning what I take to be the factitive character of the relevant verb, see H.W. Smyth, *Greek Grammar* (Cambridge: Harvard University Press, 1974), §866.3, to which Grote, 22n3, also appeals in his similar account of the passage. See also Marian Demos, "Callicles' Quotation of Pindar in the *Gorgias*" in *Harvard Studies in Classical Philology* 96 (1994): 94–95 and 106n79.

[70] For instance, Hugh Lloyd-Jones insists that Callicles' phrasing "cannot be what Pindar wrote." See Lloyd-Jones, "Pindar Fr. 169" in *Harvard Studies in Classical Philology* 76 (1972): 48. Regarding the history of the fragment, see Marcello Gigante, *NOMOS BASILEUS* (Naples: Saggi, 1956).

[71] MSS B, T, P, and F. Regarding the possibility of a scribal error, see Dodds, 270–72; and Ostwald, 132n8.

[72] V, Parisinus 2110. This rendering is attested in the scholion on Pindar's *Nem.* 935a, as well as in Aelius Aristides and the corresponding scholion (*orat.* 24 [2.68 and 3.408 Dindorf]). But scholia do not have the same authority as primary manuscripts. See Dodds, 34–67, for both the direct and indirect traditions of the text.

Wilamowitz, the contemporary of Nietzsche, was the first scholar to propose that the misquotation was intentional.[73] Over time, his line of reasoning has been criticized on various grounds.[74] Furthermore, when relevant sections of the Oxyrinchus papyrus were published in 1961 by Lobel, a fuller version of the poem certi-fied that the Platonic quotation differed from the original.[75] One might think that this discovery would settle the matter. Indeed, for many editors, it has. In modern English translations that I have examined, with a single exception, Callicles' words are altered to Pindar's actual phrasing without any editorial comment whatsoever.[76] But surely the issue at least deserves comment, if not additional scrutiny, and not merely because the error is found in all of the primary manuscripts. Immediately after the misquotation, Callicles admits that he *does not know the ode*. This piece of evidence alone should give one pause. And, as it turns out, the misquotation of Pindar is

---

[73] His main argument concerns Libanius, a fourth-century CE teacher of rhetoric. Wilamowitz showed that Libanius has the misquotation in his manuscript of the *Gorgias* and that he paraphrases it in his own *Apology of Socrates*, a fictitious account of the trial (*Apology* 87). Furthermore, Libanius accuses the fourth-century BCE rhetor Polycrates of an intentional misquotation in the latter's lost *Accusation of Socrates*; Libanius accuses Polycrates of making Anytus alter Pindar's phrasing. Why? Libanius asserts that Polycrates did this in order to call attention to Plato's previous and intentional misquotation of the same passage in the *Gorgias*; and to support the claim that Socrates abused the poets. On this view, Plato's intentional misquotation in the *Gorgias* (via Callicles) provokes Polycrates' intentional misquotation (via Anytus) in the *Accusation*. See Ulrich von Wila-mowitz-Moellendorff, *Platon* (Berlin: Weidmannsche Buchhandlung, 1920), 2.95–105. See also Dodds, 271; Lloyd-Jones, 48; and Demos, 102–106. Regarding Anytus, compare Plato, *Apology* 23e.

[74] See for instance Dodds, 28–29 and 271; and Lloyd-Jones, 49.

[75] "P.Oxy. 2450" in *The Oxyrinchus Papyri* XXVI, ed. E. Lobel (1961): 141, with Plate XVa and b.

[76] The exception is James Arieti, who surely knows about the problem via Grote, a former student. See Arieti and Barrus' translation of the *Gorgias* (Newburyport: Focus, 2007), 91n95. In fairness to translators, I should point out that Burnet's OCT offers the corrected reading. It does, however, also note the original reading (i.e., that of B, T, P, and F) in the critical apparatus. Dodds, 270–72, discusses the issue in depth in his more recent edition of the text.

but a single instance in a series of interpretative errors made by Callicles.[77]

What is the evidence for the possibility of an intentional misquotation? In other words, what are Callicles' other interpretative errors? The first concerns the very story of Heracles that Pindar describes. Here is (1) the passage from the *Gorgias* again (with Callicles' original words); (2) a rendering of the fuller version of the Pindaric passage to provide context that Callicles omits; and (3) Ostwald's reconstruction of the additional material found in the Oxyrinchus papyrus:

(1) *Nomos*, the king of all mortals and immortals leads, making what is most just violent, with highest hand; I judge so from the works of Heracles, since—without payment—..."

(2) *Nomos*, the king of all mortals and immortals leads, making what is most violent just, with highest hand; I judge so from the works of Heracles, since he drove the cows of Geryon, which were not for sale and for which no payment had been paid, to the Cycloplean entrance-way of Eurystheus.

(3) He also stole the horses of Diomedes, after he had subdued by the Distonian marsh the monarch of the Kikones, the marvelous son of bronze-corseleted Enyalios, who resisted the great son of Zeus not by reason of greedy insolence but because of his valor. For it is better to die in defense of one's property when it is being robbed than to be a coward. Having stealthily entered the great palace at night, he [Heracles] found the road of violent force of hands. He seized one man high in the air and cast him in the stone mangers to satiate the most brutal hearts of the

---

[77] I have learned the most about these errors from the aforementioned work of Grote and Demos. It seems to me that they have essentially (and, as far as I can tell, independently) revived the spirit of Wilamowitz's thesis, shorn of the Libanius connection. For older works concerning the various guises of this interpretation, see Paul Friedlaender, *Plato* (Princeton: Princeton University Press, 1964), trans. Meyerhoff, 2.260–261; Éduoard des Places, *Pindare et Platon* (Paris: Beauchesne, 1949), 117ff; Jean Irigoin, *Histoire du texte de Pindare* (Paris: Klincksieck, 1952), 16–17; and A. E. Taylor, *Plato: The Man and His Work* (London: Routledge, 1960), 117n2.

raving mares, and they slaughtered him. And quickly there rang abroad the dull sound of white bones being crushed. Straightway he freed the entwined bronze chain from the cattles' tables throughout their enclosures; with a firm {--} he wore out one mare as she was carrying a leg, one as she was carrying an arm, and another as she was carrying with her teeth the neck, the lower part of the head...[78]

Scholars have largely interpreted this story in the traditional Pindaric manner. *Nomos* makes just what is most violent; though it may be beyond mortal comprehension, it is something like the will of Zeus. It is the king of all.[79] Callicles, however, does not interpret the ode this way. Callicles does not mean the will of Zeus by *nomos*, but neither does he mean human convention. What does he mean by it? And why? Does he misremember the ode? Does he willfully distort it? Does he go so far as to transvalue *nomos* and *physis*? I cannot take a stand on these interpretative issues here due to space. But I will point out that all of these lines of interpretation are congruent with the possibility that the error is deliberate on the part of Plato. And whatever he means by *nomos* here, Callicles also distorts the myth in at least two other ways. He wrongly attributes self-interest to Heracles, who took the cattle not because he desired them or because he was strong but because Eurystheus told him to. And he neglects to mention that Heracles was Eurystheus' servant, if not slave, at the time. Heracles' action was certainly not due to some philosophical conception that the strong should dominate the weak.[80]

Another of Callicles' interpretative errors concerns military endeavors. As evidence of his position concerning natural justice, Callicles cites Xerxes and Darius, even though "countless other such examples" could be mentioned. These are curious examples to choose,

---

[78] Ostwald, 117–18. I have omitted the final few lines of the reconstruction because they do not pertain to the story of Geryon's cattle.

[79] See for instance Lloyd-Jones, 15–17; Ostwald, 130–31; and Grote, 24–25.

[80] Grote, 22; and Ranasinghe, 84.

since both campaigns turned out poorly.[81] Xerxes, despite an overwhelming advantage in manpower and wealth, was ultimately defeated by the Greeks. And Callicles' other example, Darius, is an even worse case; his forces were completely routed in Scythia and barely managed to escape with their lives. Thus, one might imagine that Plato would have expected his audience to recognize that these examples would hardly constitute evidence for Callicles' position; not only do they not evince any notion of the right of the stronger, they are not even military victories.[82]

Thirdly, Callicles refers to the *Antiope*, the lost play of Euripides. No fewer than four passages from it are quoted almost verbatim in his conversation with Socrates.[83] Not only that, but Callicles explicitly compares himself and Socrates with characters in the play (485e), a comparison that Socrates accepts and refines (506b). Callicles and Socrates take on the roles of Zethus and Amphion, the sons of Antiope—the daughter of the late king of Thebes. Callicles is Zethus, a shepherd and a hunter who argues the merits of the active life; Socrates is Amphion, a musician who defends the contemplative life of the artist and thinker.[84] According to Dodds, the

---

[81] Herodotus 4.133–142. Herodotus himself quotes the relevant Pindaric passage when discussing the differences between Hellenic and Kallatiaen burial rites (3.38). Compare Aristotle, *Nicomachean Ethics* 1134b.

[82] Grote, 26; Saxonhouse, 157; and Zuckert, 548n67. Woolf, 5n8 notes that Callicles parses collective conquests in terms of individual rulers.

[83] 484e, 485e–486a, 486b, and 486c. See Andrea Nightingale, "Plato's *Gorgias* and Euripides' *Antiope*: A Study in Generic Transformation" in *Classical Antiquity* 11.1 (April 1992): 122. Nightingale, 129n20 notes that no other dialogue has so many direct allusions to a single literary text. For more on the relationship between the literary forms of dialogue and poetry, see Nightingale, *Genres in Dialogue: Plato and the Construct of Philosophy* (Cambridge: Cambridge University Press, 2000). It is worth noting on this point that Socrates glosses his move from dialogue to monologue in the *Gorgias* by alluding to a scene from a comedy by Epicharmis (505e). As Nightingale points out, Plato calls Epicharmis "the greatest master of comedy" at *Theaetetus* 152e ("Generic Transformation," 132n30).

[84] Nightingale notes that Zethus has a strong "aristocratic temperament" which finds a "parallel in the character of Callicles" ("Generic Transformation," 124). I see this as support for my earlier emphasis upon Callicles' aristocratic bearing as an Acharnian Ceryces.

debate between them was the scene for which the *Antiope* was most remembered in antiquity.[85] Zethus wins the debate, which is surely what Callicles is thinking of when he draws attention to the poetic parallel. But he forgets or distorts certain other features of the play. For one thing, Zethus, unlike Callicles, is averse to pleasure.[86] For another, it is in fact Amphion's music that rebuilds the walls of Thebes and restores order to the polity in the end. So Callicles misinterprets who ultimately triumphs in the dialogue, especially with respect to the restoration of the city. And it is noteworthy on this point, and in light of the fact that Callicles is a Ceryces, that it is Hermes who gives Amphion his lyre and who ultimately vindicates him.[87]

In summary: in the overall context of these other errors, Callicles' misquotation of Pindar can reasonably be taken as deliberate. The error would then be intended by Plato as commentary on Callicles' character rather than the result of a scribe's errant pen. But what would be the commentary? Plato (and this section) invites, rather than answers, that question.

Conclusion

The *Gorgias* bears the subtitle *peri rhetorikes* in Diogenes Laertius and in the medieval manuscripts; and it remains uncontroversial to claim that the dialogue concerns rhetoric.[88] It is more controversial, though not uncommon, to claim that the deeper concern of the dialogue is not really rhetoric but rather the question of the best existence according to nature.[89] Though this latter view is not without its

---

[85] Dodds, 276; and Nightingale, "Generic Transformation," 122.

[86] Nightingale, "Generic Transformation," 126n15.

[87] Not only that, but Hermes speaks more lines to Amphion (7.5) than he does to Zethus (1.5). See Nightingale, "Generic Transformation," 130n25. I believe this poetic resonance is also foreshadowed at 482b–c, where Socrates notes that he would rather have an out-of-tune lyre than internal discordance.

[88] Diogenes Laertius 3.59. See Dodds, 34–67, for the manuscript tradition.

[89] See Dodds, 1n2, who notes that this theme was readily recognized by ancient commentators such as Olympiodorus. See also Christopher Rowe, *Plato and the Art of Philosophical Writing* (Cambridge: Cambridge University Press, 2007),

detractors, the overall importance of the question is suggested by the fact that Socrates highlights this issue at least eight times.[90] In the *Gorgias*, the question "what is rhetoric?" gestures, if it does not reduce, to the question "what is nature?" And on this question Socrates' most implacable foe in the dialogue is surely Callicles.

When Socrates insists that Callicles must refute philosophy or else face psychic discord, he certifies this claim with an extremely strong Egyptian oath: "By the dog, god of the Egyptians"—the Egyptian god of the dead and discernment that the Greeks called Anubis (482b).[91] The suggestion is that the conversation is a matter of life and death; and that truth is at stake. Socrates utters this oath in the *Gorgias* more times than in any other dialogue; only in six other dialogues is it uttered at all, and only in the *Republic* more than once.[92] There is something particularly important, perhaps in the whole of the corpus, about Socrates' battle with Callicles. In this essay, I have offered four speculations in order to better provoke our engagement with that battle, if not our understanding of it. It may be that I have settled no disputes. But then, as Ann Hartle always

---

198; Terence Irwin's translation of the *Gorgias* (New York: Oxford University Press, 1979), v; and Voegelin, 3.24.

[90] 458b, 472b, 472d, 487b, 487e, 492d, 500c, and 527b–e. Dodds notes that it is possible that the two themes are distinct strands that are interwoven throughout the text. See Dodds, 1–5, especially 3. For a dissenting opinion, see Nichols, viii.

[91] Socrates also cites this oath at 461a, 466c, and 466e, although only at 482b does he append "God of the Egyptians" to it. See Russell Blackwood, John Crossett, and Herbert Long, "*Gorgias* 482b" in *The Classical Journal* 57.7 (April 1962): 318–19; and Robert G. Hoerber, "The Socratic Oath: By the Dog" in *The Classical Journal* 58.6 (March 1963): 268–69. These authors collect eight additional instances of the oath between them: *Lysis* 211e; *Phaedrus* 228b; *Phaedo* 98e; *Apology* 22a; *Cratylus* 411b; and *Republic* 399e, 567e, and 592a.

[92] There are perhaps other kinships between the *Gorgias* and the *Republic*, especially Book 1. Callicles is the third of Socrates' interlocutors in the *Gorgias* and, though there are important differences, clearly brings to mind Thrasymachus, the third interlocutor in Book 1 of the *Republic*. The names of Polemarchus ("war maker" or "warlord") and Thrasymachus ("bold in battle") also resonate with the first words of the *Gorgias* ("war and battle"; *polemou kai maches*).

used to say, good philosophy is like good theology. It does not dispel mystery. It only deepens it.

GORGIAS AS REDUCTIO AD ABSURDUM ARGUMENT: SOCRATES, TRUE POLITICIAN BUT FAILED TEACHER?

Jeffrey Dirk Wilson

The *Gorgias* examines the relationship between politics and philosophy and the relationship of rhetoric to both. The longest of Plato's undivided works, E. R. Dodds notes its tragic and even bitter tone,[1] but what tragedy and why the bitterness? I suggest that this dialogue is colored by Plato's own disillusionment with the flawed character of human nature and the inability of his beloved teacher to overcome that human frailty with his teaching. I shall examine the final quarter of the dialogue (503c-527e) where the role of political leader as magistrate, i.e., as chief teacher of virtue in the political community, is considered. Throughout the dialogue, Socrates offers the refrain to his interlocutors, "Refute me, or be refuted!" After coming to the conclusion that the four truly great political leaders of Athens had failed as teachers of virtue and despite his insistence on rational refutation, Socrates closes his account of political truth with a myth that has the character of a folk story (523a-526d). This juxtaposition of rational argument and a folkloric myth is itself aporetic because myth is aimed at that part of human nature which is below rationality, namely the imagination. It might be argued that Plato's myths are rational myths as distinguished from Homeric myths which are poetic, but myth taken *qua* myth is non-rational in its character. They are, in the final account, stories. This *aporia* of rational refutation juxtaposed with myth is not discussed by Socrates, but is, rather, enacted by him. What is the relationship of human rationality to the non-rational aspect of human nature? In the dialogues that

---

[1] Eric Robertson Dodds, "Introduction" and "Commentary" in Plato *Gorgias: A Revised Text with Introduction and Commentary*, ed. Eric Robertson Dodds (Oxford: Oxford University Press, 2001), 19.

conclude with explicit *aporiai*, the *aporia* itself sheds light on the theme of the dialogue. The closing *aporia* to the *Gorgias* sheds such light on Plato's lending a tragic and even bitter tone to the *Gorgias* and, thereby, also invites a reconsideration of the dialogue as a whole. Before this proposed resolution to fundamental questions about how to read the *Gorgias* can be concluded, however, another question must be considered, namely: Does the modern, i.e., post-Cartesian, understanding of the intellect in relation to the imagination inhibit an accurate reading of Plato's representation of their relationship?

Juxtaposition of Rational Refutation and Myth

Three-quarters of the way through the *Gorgias*, Socrates challenges Callicles to name political orators in Athenian history who truly cared for the citizenry. Callicles names four: Themistocles, Cimon, Miltiades, and Pericles (503a-c). The first duty of anyone concerned with the public trust is to make the citizenry as good as possible (513e-514a). Socrates proceeds to demonstrate the failure of the Four as political orators because, in each case, the people turned against them, i.e., the people became worse rather than better during the guidance of those statesmen (e.g., 515a-b, 519b-d). A shepherd who cannot lead his sheep is a failure as a shepherd. If Pericles and the others failed as statesmen because the Athenians became worse instead of better during their tenure, then by implication Socrates— who claims to practice "the true politics" (521d) [2]—must be a failed teacher for the same reason. That conclusion, however, is absurd because Socrates was the greatest of teachers, and yet, if that is so, how could Athenians not have been improved by his teaching? The *Gorgias* (especially 503b-527e) is viewed here through the lens of this *aporia*.

It is impertinent, perhaps, to suggest that one has gotten the point Plato was making that so many better scholars have missed. I do think, however, that Professor Dodds trips over the point of this

---

[2] Plato, *Complete Works*, ed. John M. Cooper (Indianapolis: Hackett Publishing Company, 1997), 864; hereafter, Cooper, 864.

extended argument, and his citations of others who criticized the argument in antiquity evidences a long history of tripping over the very point Plato was trying to make. Dodds comments:

> This passage was much criticized in antiquity, as appears not only from Aristides' extant *Defence of the Four* (*orat.* xlvi) but from the ἀπορίαι recorded by Ol [Olympiodori in *Platonis Gorgiam Commentaria*, ed. W. Norvin (1036)] (192. 3ff.) and the somewhat embarrassed apologia he offers. People asked whether Socrates had made Alcibiades and Critias better men, whether Dionysius II a better man, and the Athenians' treatment of Socrates did not disprove his claim to be a statesman. To the last point the answer no doubt is that Socrates was not a statesman and did not pretend to know how to teach ἀρετή; if Plato makes him claim to be a true πολιτικός (521d), it is only in the sense of claiming to know the general principle on which the statesman should act. But the argument of the passage is in any case a weak one.[3]

Dodds goes on to provide various reasons for the failure of a statesman and even of the citizenry (355-56), but here, again, he misses the point. After all, if we take Socrates's argument and challenge him on the same points on which he criticizes the Four, we can reasonably ask, did Socrates improve Callicles, or Charmides, or Alcibiades, or even his devoted disciples in the *Phaedo* whose passions are so to the fore and their rationality so in retreat that they weep and wail as Socrates, the model for the later Stoics, prepares to die?

At a very minimum, the discussion suggests the question of why is it that the political craft is unlike any other? One possible answer to that question—an answer that Dodds does not include in his list of possible explanations for the failure of the Four—is that politics has to do essentially with the human's soul and only accidentally with the material realm. It is, indeed, the material realm in which politics is played out, but it is the human soul that in every case is the motive force. If that is the case, however, then why did Socrates,

---

[3] Dodds, *Gorgias*, 355.

most rational of men, still manage to get himself condemned to death by his fellow citizens?

Dodds rightly notes that "the *Gorgias* stands out among the early dialogues by the tragic tone of its later pages."[4] He is also surely right in claiming that part of the reason for "the tragic tone" is that Plato realized that 404 B.C.—the year of Athens' conclusive defeat by Sparta—marked "the end of an age, and the clock could not be put back."[5] In the aftermath of that defeat Athens betrayed her noblest citizen.[6] However fitting such a lament might be from Plato or any other of the noble Athenians in the decades following that decisive and enduring eclipse, Plato's gaze was directed to the eternal even when he felt most keenly the tragedy of the temporal. I suggest that the tragic tone of the dialogue is due to the realization that by the very arguments presented by Socrates to Callicles—and as rightly observed by ancient critics referenced by Dodds—Socrates himself was a failed teacher. For Plato, that was the *reductio ad absurdum* conclusion which was both nonsense and the necessary conclusion of the argument's logic. If Socrates was the true practitioner of politics, and if Socrates was the wisest of men, and if Socrates was best of men and greatest of teachers—which certainly Plato believed—then why was he unable to make human beings better? Why did the people he sought to improve, in turn, condemn him to death? That was for Plato the truly tragic reality.

While one must apply to Socrates as teacher the same test as he applied to the Four, there are also ways that Socrates can be distinguished from them. Dodds comments on 517a7-518c1: "Plato

---

[4] Dodds, *Gorgias*, 19

[5] Dodds, *Gorgias*, 34.

[6] On 521a2-522e8, Dodds writes: "Here we reach the bitter conclusion of a long debate: Athens has one man who knows what true statesmanship is—and because of his knowledge that man must one day receive his death-sentence at the hands of 'a jury of children.' In choosing the manner of life Socrates chose also his manner of death, and chose it with his eyes open....For Plato the trial of Socrates was, as Friedländler has said, 'the crucial experiment' which tested the worth of the two opposed ways of life and set the seal of authority on Socrates' mission." Dodds, *Gorgias*, 368.

recognizes that what the Four Men did, they did well. The fault, in his view, lay not in their incompetence, but in their misconception of the statesman's task, which is primarily educational—he defined it in the *Laws*...(650b6)."[7] Zuckert comments on this point as well, "Persuasion, and thus the power of rhetoric, is not simply a product of the skill of the speaker; it also depends on the relation the speaker has to the audience and thus on the character of the audience."[8] Both Dodds and Zuckert show that the "Four Men" did as well as could be done with the vision they had and with the tools at their disposal. The work of chief magistrate as teacher is all too easily forgotten, neglected, or missed altogether in the first place, and yet it is as teacher that the statesman can affect the political community most. But by the standard of this realization—the primacy of the teaching role—Socrates is even more culpable than the Four. They did well what they understood to be their duty, but they under-conceived their duty and, thus, only had tools inadequate for their highest task. Socrates understood the character of the people he addressed, and he understood his true duty as a politician, namely to teach the people virtue, and he had the tools of philosophy as well as of rhetoric, and yet he failed as much as the Four.

There is implied here an essential teaching responsibility of statesmen. Political oratory is the primary tool of that teaching responsibility. While Socrates argues that political orators are accountable for the virtues and vices of their citizenry, unanswered is whether a people—the communal citizenry—can be taught virtue (520d). Further, the unasked question is whether Socrates is culpable for not teaching Athenians gentleness. Plato's response to these unanswered and unasked questions is to have Socrates present an eschatological myth at the end of the dialogue, but before he pitches

---

[7] Professor Zuckert cites James I. Kastely for pointing "out that E. R. Dodds, Brian Vickers, and Terrence Irwin all fail to note that Socrates admits that these statesmen were exceptionally able servants, even though they failed to improve the character of the people," but the quotation from Dodds shows that, at least, for him, that is simply not the case. Catherine H. Zuckert, *Plato's Philosophers: The Coherence of the Dialogues* (Chicago: University of Chicago Press, 2009), 554.

[8] Zuckert, *Plato's Philosophers*, 539

his "refute me, or be refuted" mantra one last time. Is the reader to infer that while there is no earthly way for a political orator to teach the people virtue, there might still be a heavenly way to do so?

The problem of the myth is compounded by two considerations. First, it follows immediately after Socrates' claim to be a true practitioner of politics: "I believe that I'm one of the few Athenians—so as not to say I'm the only one, but the only one among our contemporaries—to take up the true political craft and practice the true politics. This is because the speeches I make on occasion do not aim at gratification but at what's best" (521d).[9] The second is that he goes on to compare his work to that of a physician who might be accused by a pastry chef to a jury of children of not giving them pleasure (521e-522a). This is a moment where the dramatic depth of the dialogue is on full display. Plato has his literary Socrates, putatively years before the trial and death of the historical Socrates, characterizing that trial and death. The presence of Chaerephon at the outset of the dialogue (447a-c) with occasional reappearances (458c and 481b)—lest readers forget that he is present throughout the conversation—serves to remind readers of Plato's *Apology* in which Plato's Socrates, during his trial, makes reference to his late friend's inquiry of the Delphic Oracle whether anyone was wiser than Socrates (*Apology* 21a). The mentions of Chaerephon effectively import the action of the *Apology* into the *Gorgias*, allowing for the implication that Plato, as author, intends readers to identify Meletus, the prosecutor in the *Apology*, as the pastry chef in the *Gorgias* accusing the physician, Socrates, for not giving his patients pleasure.

And yet—the reader must say—children can be very fond of their doctors even though they have at times inflicted pain, say in the sewing of stitches on an ugly wound. This part of the literary Socrates' argument justifying the historical Socrates really does not hold. For all that Socrates has emphasized rational argument, he has committed the logical fallacy of the straw man here, i.e., casting Meletus as a pastry chef. But that too is a standard trick of Plato's Socrates. Homer plays such a role in the *Republic* and in the *Theaetetus*.

---

[9] Cooper, 864.

Heraclitus and especially Protagoras are straw men in the *Theaetetus*, as is even the more favorably depicted Thales. Earlier in the *Gorgias*, Socrates has said that laughter is not an argument (473e), but it is mockery to the end of laughter that Socrates uses against his putative accuser, the pastry chef. It is not rational argument here that Socrates uses, but rather rhetorical sleight of hand—exactly what he says he has no skill in doing. But this too is standard fare in Plato's dialogues: Socrates does what he condemns; it is just that he does it more brilliantly than those he condemns.

The putative commitment of Socrates of the *Gorgias* to *elenchos*, refutation, is specifically reinforced a few lines later, just prior to beginning the myth:

> Now if someone were to refute me and prove that I am unable to provide *this* refutation for myself or for anyone else, I would feel shame at being refuted....If I were put to death for lack of this ability, I really would be upset. But if I came to my end because of a deficiency in flattering oratory, I know that you'd see me bear my death with ease. For no one who isn't totally bereft of reason and courage is afraid to die; doing what's unjust is what he's afraid of" (522d-e).[10]

Socrates of the *Gorgias*, having told his interlocutors that he is the one true practitioner of politics then alive and that he would only be ashamed if he were refuted in a rational argument, immediately thereafter launches into a genre that precisely cannot be refuted because it is not subject to rational argument whatsoever, namely an eschatological myth in which, in a word, he tells us that those who live justly on earth shall be rewarded hereafter while those who live unjustly shall be punished.

This myth, along with its parallels in the *Phaedo* and *Republic*, makes a series of claims about the after-life that simply cannot be tested. Professor Dodds even distinguishes the *Gorgias* version of the myth from the other two versions. He says, "It displays none of the quasi-scientific trappings of the myths in the *Phaedo* and the

---

[10] Cooper, 865 (emphasis in Cooper).

Republic, but has the directness and vividness of folktale, and keeps something of the folktale *naïveté* in its style."[11] Of course, as Professor Dodds also points out, Socrates—and we can add Plato as author—creates some distance from this myth by observing that he had heard it from someone else (524a8-b1).[12] But seven times (at least), Socrates calls this myth a *logos*, three times at the myth's beginning, once in the middle, and—just in case we had forgotten— once more at the end. Indeed, he calls it a very beautiful *logos* (522e5, 523a1and 2, 527b4, c6). Three times (at least)—beginning, middle and end—Socrates affirms that he believes the myth to be true (523a2, 524a8-b2, 526d3), and—as shall be discussed below—still twice more as the dialogue comes to a conclusion. In other words, it is as if Socrates is telling a story to the children of the jury whom Meletus the pastry chef has tried to influence against him, and assuring them that the story is true, in a way not unlike the way parents tell their children about Santa Claus and to the same moral end, namely that the children should, therefore, behave themselves. Socrates doth protest too much, methinks. He has abandoned the rational argument of refutation for a myth that is not subject to refutation and also is not—unlike poor Santa Claus—subject to empirical disproof.

After telling this myth, he acknowledges that some may think it "an old wives' tale" and "feel contempt for it" (527a5-6). The myth complete, he returns to the argument that he claims to be irrefutable: "This one alone survives refutation and remains steady: that doing what's unjust is more to be guarded against than suffering it, and that it's not *seeming* to be good but *being* good that a man should take care of more than anything, both in his public and private life."[13] That statement embodies a range of metaphysical claims, but at present I want to focus on the relationship of the rational

---

[11] Dodds, *Gorgias*, 372-73. Thanks to Dr. Mary Townsend for pointing out the similarly folkloric character of the origins myth presented by Protagoras in the eponymous dialogue and that both myths share a positive view of shame in conjunction with justice (April 6, 2019).

[12] Dodds, *Gorgias*, 373.

[13] Plato, *Gorgias* 527b; Cooper, 868 (emphasis in Cooper).

argument Socrates makes to the myth that he tells and which, multiple times, he calls a *logos*. The myth intervenes between the earlier rational arguments and their final reprise. The myth, moreover, follows more or less immediately on Socrates' claim to be the only true practitioner of politics then living. What is there to make of this?

One cannot remind one's self too often that Plato was not merely a philosophical genius, but also a literary genius and that—to borrow from the title of a book by Seth Benardete—the argument is often in the action.[14] To read Plato's texts well, one must always watch what Plato as author is *doing* as well as to listen to what his characters are *saying*. I suggest that the juxtaposition of Socrates' claim of the irrefutable argument, on the one hand, and the myth, on the other, tells us that the true practitioner of politics will tell myths, myths that reinforce the rational arguments and to tell myths which cannot be refuted by argument because myth as genre is not subject to refutation. There is a sense in which Socrates' steady drumbeat throughout the *Gorgias* of "refute me or be refuted" is a rhetorical ruse. He is guilty of philosophical legerdemain. While he is distracting us with his cast iron rational arguments, he is pulling a myth out of his magician's hat, and a myth which he insists is a *logos* as true as anything that could be said in rational argument.

In fact, though Socrates calls his myth a *logos*, it is not an appeal to the intellect—as rational refutation is—but rather it is an appeal to the imagination. Is there anything earlier in the *Gorgias* that prepares the reader for this juxtaposition of myth and *logos*?[15]

---

[14] Seth Benardete, *The Argument of the Action: Essays on Greek Poetry and Philosophy*, ed. with an introduction by Ronna Burger and Michael Davis (Chicago: The University of Chicago Press, 2000).

[15] In the question and answer period following the presentation of my paper, I actually asked this question. In truth, I posed the question only rhetorically. Nicholas D. Smith, Socrates-like, rose from his seat, and said, "Well, actually there is." He went on to point to passages where Socrates appeals to the imagination, to the passions, of his hearers throughout the dialogue, juxtaposed to the rational arguments he was making all the while. After the conclusion of the formal session. Smith, along with Catherine Zuckert, Alex Priou, one or two others, and I walked together from the room where our formal sessions were held to the hotel. Smith and I continued the conversation, the dialogue, continuing as Socrates with

I suggest that the puzzlement over the myth is, at least, partly due to an implicitly Cartesian reading of the *Gorgias* and of the Platonic texts in general. In order to resolve the *aporia* of *elenchos* versus myth, it is helpful, perhaps even necessary, to de-Cartesianize our reading of Plato.

De-Cartesianizing Our Reading of Plato

It is a commonplace amongst philosophers that Descartes only read one of Plato's dialogues, the *Phaedo*, and that one he read badly. In the *Phaedo*, Plato's Socrates makes some of his sharpest distinctions between body and soul. Speaking approximately, Descartes took those body-soul distinctions and radicalized them, giving us what Gilbert Ryle, in *The Concept of Mind*, denominates, "with deliberate abusiveness, as 'the dogma of the Ghost in the Machine.'"[16] This dogma "is so prevalent among theorists and even among laymen that it deserves to be described as the official theory...which hails chiefly from Descartes."[17] He summarizes the dogma: "Every human being has both a body and a mind....His body and his mind are ordinarily harnessed together, but after the death of the body his mind may continue to exist and function."[18] What I am suggesting takes Ryle's

---

a chief interlocutor and others along the way. I recount the ideas I heard in Smith's words without claiming that I record his speech here. Smith spoke of how Cartesian our readings tended to be, reading with a Cartesian lens that filtered out all that was going on in the Platonic dialogues that did not cohere with the rational argument taking place at the most obvious level. Then, when confronted with something like the myth at the end of the *Gorgias* that did not fit with our reading, we could only be puzzled. The question was what were we going to do, having been confronted with an immoveable obstacle like a myth that was obviously important to Plato's Socrates and which came at the point of the dialogue where one could reasonably expect some kind of resolution, but where we are met with a bigger *aporia* than we had hitherto tackled? This was an epiphanic moment for me, for which I thank Professor Smith. I shall never read Plato's texts the same again. What follows is my own initial response to Professor Smith's challenge. The experience was, for me, like taking a walk in one of Plato's dialogues.

[16] Gilbert Ryle, *The Concept of Mind* (London: Penguin Books, 1968), 17.

[17] Ryle, *Concept of Mind*, 13.

[18] Ryle, *Concept of Mind*, 13.

claims a step further, namely that this Cartesian dogma permeates Western culture to the exist that all of us—philosophers and ditch-diggers alike—are Cartesians.

What I am suggesting is that even the most serious scholar of Plato can give Plato's texts a Cartesian reading without wanting or knowing that that is what one is doing. I am suggesting further, that overtly seeking to over-ride one's Cartesian default setting can lead to a fresh reading of Plato's texts, and in specific here, the *Gorgias*.

How, then, do we de-Cartesianize our reading of Plato's texts?

Thomas C. Brickhouse and Nicholas D. Smith, in their article "Socrates on the Emotions," show that Plato's Socrates recognizes persuasion cannot be complete through rational argument alone, because some of the most deeply held beliefs have a non-rational basis in "our natural attractions and aversions": "The beliefs created by these natural attractions and aversions, because they derive from non-rational processes, are veridically unreliable, but are also to some degree (by their nature as non-rational) resistant to rational persuasion."[19] At the beginning of *Republic* 2, Glaucon asks Socrates, "Do you want to seem to have persuaded us...or do you want to truly convince us?" Socrates replies, "I want truly to convince you."[20] If we take as a general premise that Plato's Socrates wants truly to convince his interlocutors, then it is necessary that he address the whole human person, i.e., the human imagination as well as the human intellect. Brickhouse and Smith do well to call these processes of persuasion "non-rational," rather than irrational, for the imagination *qua* imagination is precisely not part of the human's rational apparatus. It can and does interact with the intellect, but considered unto itself, it is something entirely other than rational. It is only with respect to reason that something can be called irrational, i.e.,

---

[19] Thomas C. Brickhouse and Nicholas D. Smith, "Socrates on the Emotions," Plato Journal, 15, 14-15. Quoted in Jose Lourenço and Nicholas D. Smith, "Socratic Epistemology," in *Knowledge in Ancient Philosophy*, ed. Nicholas D. Smith, vol. 1 of *The Philosophy of Knowledge: a History*, ed. Stephen Hetherington, Nicholas D. Smith, Henrik Lagerlund, Stephen Gaukroger, Markos Valaris (London: Bloomsbury, 2018), 72.

[20] Plato, *Rep.* 2.357a4-b2; Cooper, 998.

contrary to reason. The mistaking of the "non-rational" for "irrational" lies at the heart of Descartes's "Ghost in the Machine." Descartes famously writes, "The soul by which I am what I am, is entirely distinct from my body, and is even more easy to know than is the latter; and even if the body were not, the soul would not cease to be what it is."[21] It would be wrong and even silly to suggest that Plato was not a dualist, but one can conclude from the work of Nicholas Smith and his colleagues, Thomas Brickhouse and Jose Lourenço, that it is correct, obvious, and even sobering to conclude that Plato was not a Cartesian dualist. To employ—as if true—the Platonic insight of Smith and Brickhouse that the beliefs derived "from non-rational processes,…are…resistant to rational persuasion," just because we are shown and perhaps persuaded rationally does not entail dislodging beliefs derived from non-rational processes. In other words, even if we are persuaded rationally that the Cartesian "Ghost in the Machine" is wrong as an account of human being, that alone does not touch our default settings as Cartesians. To change those default settings requires address not only to reason but also to the non-rational processes, in short, the imagination broadly construed, i.e., the imagination of the Divided Line that apprehends reality thrice removed from reality.[22]

---

[21] René Descartes, *Discourse on Method and Meditations on First Philosophy*, ed. David Weissman (New Haven, Conn.: Yale University Press, 1996), 22 (*Discourse*, Part 4).

[22] Plato, *Rep.* 6.509d-510a; reprised in 7.533e-534a. If someone suggests that I have operated by philosophical sleight of hand, importing arguments and ideas from the *Republic* into my argument about the *Gorgias*, I point out that just as Socrates of the *Gorgias* addresses the intellect through argument and the imagination through myth, so does Socrates of the *Republic*. Not only is there the Myth of Er (*Rep.* 10.614a-621b), but the Myth of Gyges (2.359c-360b), and perhaps most tellingly the Myth of the Metals (3.414d-415d). In the dialogue surrounding the Myth of Metals, Socrates actually models Plato's dualism by speaking to the need of addressing both the rational and non-rational faculties of the human being: "I think we must observe them at all ages to see whether they are guardians of this conviction and make sure that neither compulsion nor magic spells will get them to discard or forget their belief that they must do what is best for the city. . . . By 'compelled' I mean those whom pain or suffering causes to change their

In the *Gorgias*, Socrates shows interest in the passions through-out the dialogue. Consider, for example, the way Socrates juxtaposes scratching where it itches with blushing and how these two are em-blems for the hedonistic life versus the philosophical life:

> Socrates: Do carry on the way you've begun, and take care not to be ashamed. And I evidently shouldn't shrink from being ashamed either. Tell me now first whether a man who has an itch and scratches it can scratch to his heart's content, scratch his whole life long, can also live happily.

> Callicles: What nonsense, Socrates. You're a regular crowd pleaser.

> Socrates: That's just how I shocked Polus and Gorgias and made them be ashamed. You certainly won't be shocked, however, or be ashamed, for you're a brave man. Just an-swer me, please.[23]

Socrates gives us a human at the level of a chimpanzee who scratches wherever and whenever it itches. The reaction of the hear-ers is to laugh, as indicated by Callicles. Socrates' words drip with irony, and Callicles tries to give as good as he gets, but he cannot manage it. His words fall flat. Socrates converts Callicles' flat reply

---

mind....The 'victims of magic'...are those who change their mind because they are under the spell of pleasure or fear" (Plato, *Rep.* 3.412e-413c; Cooper, 1049). How does Socrates propose to counteract the compulsion and magic? He elabo-rates the noble lie (414b), addressed not to someone's reason, but to the non-rational imagination.

Emily A. Austin offers a fresh and welcome approach to reading the *Gorgias* and sees Socrates addressing the lingering child, and therefore the non-rational aspect, in all of us. Story plays an essential role in addressing that lingering child. Emily A. Austin, "Corpses, Self-Defense, and Immortality: Callicles' Fear of Death in the *Gorgias*," *Ancient Philosophy*, 30 (2013), 49. Still, she does not address the non-rational aspect as essential to a fully mature adult psychology, again an example of the pernicious influence of implicit Cartesianism. She also seems somewhat puzzled about the role the myth plays in the dialogue. Austin, "Corpses," 50-51.

[23] Plato, *Grg.* 494c-d; Cooper, 837.

into further irony: "That's just how I shocked Polus and Gorgias and made them be ashamed," in other words, by being such a "crowd pleaser." Of course, Callicles is literally correct. Socrates is talking nonsense. Literally, Socrates is saying that he brought Polus and Gorgias to the philosophical moment (the blush) by doing a comedic turn for the *hoi polloi*. That is rubbish, indeed, but literalness has no chance against irony. Now, Socrates goes in for the kill. He says, in effect, that Callicles is in no danger of ever being brought to the philosophical moment. He is too brave for that. Again, utter rubbish, but devastating irony! Socrates has presented two physical states, one a perpetual response to appetites and the other the blush of shame, as emblems of two ways of life, hedonism and philosophy. In this exchange, there is no attempt at rational argument, but is there no *elenchos*? Socrates plays irony as a *logos*, and that irony is an *elenchos*.

At 473e, as noted above, Socrates takes Polus to task for laughing as a response to Socrates' argument: "Is this now some further style of refutation, to laugh when somebody makes a point, instead of refuting him?"[24] Now, however, Socrates himself incites laughter as part of his *elenchos*. The *Gorgias* (525e) and the *Republic* (620c) make reference to Thersites in the concluding myth, and Thersites is named in no other Platonic dialogue. Plato thereby evokes *Iliad* 2.211-277 where Odysseus restores order to the army by making them laugh by mocking Thersites, himself a mocker. As the wily Homeric hero mocked Thersites, so Socrates mocks Callicles. Socrates the philosopher of *elenchos* also persuades by appealing to the human imagination. That is a conclusion that Descartes could not have drawn, nor could we as long as we read the Platonic text with a Cartesian lens.

Now, we can better understand what Socrates was doing when he set up the pastry chef (and thereby Plato set up Meletus) as a straw man, by making us laugh at him. Plato has his Socrates appeal to the human imagination with his brilliant rhetorical flourishes, and thereby to persuade the human imagination of rational truths

---

[24] Cooper, 817.

when he is not able to persuade the human intellect of them.[25] All of a sudden, the mule-driving, sheep-leading analogies become clearly applicable. The human is a *rational* animal, but still an *animal*. Socrates prepares his listeners—Plato, his readers—for this epiphany, but the Cartesian lens prevents us from attending properly. For example, in 517b, Socrates praises the good qualities of the Four "in redirecting its [the city's] appetites and not giving into them, using persuasion or constraint to get the citizens to become better."[26] The non-rational faculties are not susceptible to rational argument. For that reason, rational argument has to be translated into forms of non-rational address to the non-rational of human faculties.

The human must both think truth right with the intellect and also feel truth right with the imagination. This insight derives from what I described at the outset as the dialogue's closing *aporia*.

---

[25] My view is partly in agreement and partly in disagreement with that of Jessica Moss: "Appetite is not subject to positive moral education, and thus can play no positive role in virtue, because it is not possible to 'redirect' appetitive desire towards the good. Both Callicles' speech and the *Republic's* programme for musical education show that unlike desires for pleasure, feelings of shame and admiration *are* [her emphasis] subject to morally useful redirection." Jessica Moss, "Shame, Pleasure, and the Divided Soul," in David Sedley, ed. *Oxford Studies in Ancient Philosophy*, vol. 29 (Winter 2005) (Oxford: Oxford University Press, 2005), 168. While I have largely addressed the imagination and passions, thus approximately her "thumoeidic part of the soul" (168), I also hold that Plato's Socrates believes the passions for pleasure and even the appetites can be directed toward virtue. Two successive examples from the *Republic* will suffice to establish my point when Socrates proposes that desire for sex be teleologically ordered to the good of the city. First, "the best men must have sex with the best women as frequently as possible" (459d), and, second, "Among other prizes and rewards the young men who are good in war or other things must be given permission to have sex with the women more often" (460b). Cooper, 1087. There is nothing quite like doing your patriotic duty by having sex.

[26] *Grg.* 517b-c; Cooper, 860. Terrence Irwin uses this speech as a basis for attributing "authoritarian views" to Socrates. Terrence Irwin, "Notes," in Plato, *Gorgias*, trans. with notes, Terrence Irwin (Oxford: Oxford University Press, 1982), 236. My argument provides an alternative reading to his notion that Socrates advocates coercion.

Socrates' modelling of how to address imagination as well as intellect is performative rather than discursive pedagogy. Socrates set up the contrast of the physician and the pastry cook and claims that in a contest with children, the pastry cook would always win (464d-e). There is a sense, however, that Gorgias has made a point early in the dialogue which is not entirely invalid, namely that the rhetorician can persuade someone to undergo medical treatment when the physician cannot (456b-c). Employing the language of Socrates' analogy of philosopher to physician so is rhetorician to pastry cook, by spinning a myth to his readers, Socrates the physician has offered them a pastry as reward for submitting to their vaccination or stitches—a healthy pastry, to be sure, perhaps an oatmeal cookie.[27] There is, after all, some quality of the pastry chef in the best of doctors: children and adults must not only think the medicine good for them, they must feel it good for them too.

Earlier I said that in light of the myth which follows, it was a problem when Socrates of the *Gorgias* claims: "I believe that I'm one of the few Athenians—so as not to say I'm the only one, but the only one among our contemporaries—to take up the true political craft and practice the true politics."[28] With a de-Cartesianized reading of the text, I now want to suggest that that claim is not the problem, but rather the key to understanding the relationship of *elenchos* to the myth. Just as Socrates addresses the human intellect with rational argument, so he addresses the non-rational imagination with myth. A good story persuades the feelings analogous to the way that

---

[27] While Jessica Moss has other points to make, still I have her to thank for the juxtaposition of 456b-c and 464d-e. Jessica Moss, "The Doctor and the Pastry Chef: Pleasure and Persuasion in Plato's *Gorgias*," *Ancient Philosophy* 27 (2007), 235. She is tempted to draw a conclusion parallel to my own, but rejects it in the end: "Perhaps there could be a way of persuading people to pursue virtue as *pleasant* [her emphasis], and vice as painful—a way of using appetites as a tool of moral persuasion. A careful reading of doctor/pastry chef analogies indicates that although the dialogue does raise this suggestion, in the end it rejects it." Moss, "Doctor," 246. What Moss misses by attending only to what the dialogue says to the neglect of what it does is that the dialogue concludes with Socrates bringing the discussion to an end with a pastry, a myth with the character of an old wives' tale.
[28] Plato, *Grg.* 521d; Cooper, 864.

rational argument persuades the intellect.[29] The device is one used by parents perhaps since Adam and Eve of first explaining to a child why something must or must not be done, and then spinning a story in which the moral lesson becomes the moral of the story: the *logos* of *elenchos* becomes the *logos* of *mythos*. Because Socrates knows he must speak both to the intellect and to the imagination, he is one of the few "to take up the true political craft and practice the true politics." He cannot merely replace Homeric myth with dialectic, he must also simultaneously fight myth with myth.[30]

"But Socrates still gets himself killed," you reply. And here we see the tangle of the historical Socrates and Plato's literary creation, the literary tangle also of bitterness and epiphany. If the *Gorgias* be read with Zuckert (i.e., in her version of the dramatic order),[31] then,

---

[29] As an example of a Cartesian rationalization of the myth's juxtaposition to *elenchos*, Irwin comments on 527a-b: "But just as the *elenchos* seeks the most coherent selection from our moral beliefs, we also seek to make our moral beliefs coherent. And since we have better warrant—Socrates assumes—for our moral beliefs, we should select those religious traditions which fit our moral beliefs. The policy is not foolproof; but Socrates claims that it is the most reasonable option in the present state of our knowledge." Irwin, "Notes," 248. Indeed, his entire assessment of the myth (242-49) is rationalist. Perhaps Professor Irwin has done the best that anyone can do while reading the text through a Cartesian lens.

[30] Here, I disagree with Matthias Vorwerk. He asks whether rhetoric has any role at all to play in persuading someone. As part of his answer, he sees the myth as showing that in this life, rhetoric serves "nur zur Verschleierung von Unrecht und zur manipulieren." He concludes, "Sie [die Überzeugungskraft] will nicht durch emotionale Argumente manipulieren, sondern durch die Vernunftsgründe zur Erkenntnis der Wahrheit führen." Matthias Vorwerk, "Der Arzt, der Koch und die Kinder: Rhetorik und Philosophie im Wettstreit," in *Gorgias-Menon: Selected Papers from the Seventh Symposium Platonicum*, eds. Michael Erler and Luc Brisson (Sankt Augustin, Germany: Academia Verlag, 2007), 301-02. Thus, he argues for the essentially rational character of the myth which Socrates himself has acknowledged to be folkloric, the myth that, I argue, is aimed at the imagination. Vorwerk's analysis is an example of the implicit Cartesianism that I am arguing against. In a sense, I am arguing that the work of rhetoric is precisely to manipulate the non-rational faculties of the human in order to align them with the rational faculties.

[31] "If we list the dialogues in the order of their dramatic dates, we see not only that the dialogues featuring Socrates can be so ordered, but also that the non-

yes, Socrates still gets himself killed. If, however, the *Gorgias* be read with Kahn,[32] then the writing of the *Apology* is well behind Plato as he inscribes the *Gorgias* into the wax. Though the tone of the *Gorgias* is bitter and though Socrates of the *Gorgias* is feisty and defiant in his arguments, still in the end he relents and becomes conciliatory in a way that he does not, for example, in the *Apology*. Smith and Brickhouse would argue that Socrates does appeal to the non-rational faculties of humans in dialogues commonly taken to be "Socratic": "Non-rational appeals and extra-logical rhetorical devises of various sorts are nonetheless abundant in the relevant group of dialogues."[33] They give numerous examples from several dialogues, one of which is the *Apology*.[34] What is different is that Socrates of the *Apology* is feisty and defiant to the last line, while in the *Gorgias*, Socrates spins a myth as *logos*. After recounting the myth, Socrates delivers a gentle homily derived from the myth, addressed to Polus and Gorgias as well as to Callicles and, presumably, to others like Chaerephon who were present.

The final page of the *Gorgias* has the character of a philosophical altar call. Like many a preacher who has held up a vision of final judgement to his hearers, Socrates launches from the myth to call his hearers—and Plato, his readers—to a new way of life, the life of

---

Socratic dialogues can be ordered into the narrative that emerges on the basis of the dramatic dating." Zuckert, *Plato's Philosophers*, 8-9.

[32] Professor Kahn reads the *Gorgias* as representing an intermediate stage in Plato's development: "The *Gorgias* thus lies on a direct line of moral concern that leads from the *Apology* and *Crito* to the *Republic*." Charles Kahn, *Plato and the Socratic Dialogue: The Philosophical Use of a Literary Form* (Cambridge: Cambridge University Press, 1999), 127. At the same time, he regards the *Gorgias* as prior to the *Republic*, but not proleptic to it. Charles Kahn, "Prolepsis in *Gorgias* and *Meno*?" in *Gorgias–Menon: Selected Papers from the Seventh Symposium Platonicum*, eds. Michael Erler and Luc Brisson (Sankt Augustin, Germany: Academia Verlag, 2007), 325.

[33] Thomas C. Brickhouse and Nicholas D. Smith, "The Myth of the Afterlife in Plato's *Gorgias*," in *Gorgias–Menon: Selected Papers from the Seventh Symposium Platonicum*, eds. Michael Erler and Luc Brisson (Sankt Augustin, Germany: Academia Verlag, 2007), 137.

[34] Brickhouse and Smith, "Myth," 137.

virtue: "It's not *seeming* to be good but *being* good that a man should take care of more than anything, both in his public and his private life."[35] In fact, Plato casts the voice of Socrates here as if he spoke from the grave: "So, listen to me and follow me to where I am, and when you've come here you'll be happy during life and its end, as the account [λόγος] indicates."[36] Where is Socrates that he beckons his hearers to join him? The historical and literary Socrates are melded into one. Socrates who died ventriloquizes Socrates in the dialogue. As such, he refers again to the myth as a *logos*, and he does so still one more time: "So let's use the account [λόγος] that has now been disclosed [παραφανέντι] to us as our guide, one that indicates to us that this way of life is the best, to practice justice and the rest of excellence both in life and in death." Dodds notes, "παραφανέντι adds a touch of vividness and perhaps of religious solemnity: the word could be used of the epiphany of a god."[37] A revelation has been received. Socrates has been merely the means of that revelation. He calls his hearers to become followers of this best way of life.

Plato's literary Socrates comes to know some things of which the historical Socrates really was ignorant. One of Plato's aims as he built his literary corpus and taught in the Academy was how to be a philosopher without getting killed. Plato's Socrates knows that stories can calm and perhaps persuade the non-rational irritation and even fury aroused by rational refutation: story and argument alike are essential to the political craft.[38] This dialogue, however, ends not

---

[35] Plato, *Grg.* 527b; Cooper, 869 (emphasis in Cooper).

[36] Plato, *Grg.* 527c4-6; Cooper, 869.

[37] Dodds, *Gorgias*, 386. The atemporal or paratemporal or transtemporal aspect of the *Gorgias* is evidenced by the difficulty or even impossibility of establishing a dramatic date for the dialogue (contra Zuckert). Dodds writes, "In what year are we to imagine the conversation as taking place? If Plato ever asked himself this question (which may perhaps be doubted), his answer must have been 'In no particular year.' For, as Herodicus of Babylon already noticed . . . no ingenuity can reconcile the various chronological data which he has obligingly supplied." Dodds, *Gorgias*, 17.

[38] My own conclusion is at odds with that of Lourenço and Smith: "Several indications in our texts show that Socrates believes his elenctic refutations of others can also address faulty cognitive processing of this non-rational sort."

only with a story, but with a moral to the story. Where another dialogue may end in defiance (e.g., *Apology*) and some in befuddlement (e.g., *Lysis, Hippias minor*), or in amity (e.g., the *Republic*) the *Gorgias* concludes with an invitation.

Conclusion

Socrates the literary figure, the true practitioner of politics, characterizes the jury as children who found the historical Socrates guilty, and then the literary Socrates tells a folktale fit for children. The conclusion I draw from this is that though the true practice of politics should be obedient to reason, the inability of the mass of human beings to obey reason—even in such a noble city as fifth century B.C. Athens—implies the necessity of telling myths, and not just any old myths, but eschatological myths in which the just are rewarded in the afterlife and the wicked are punished. Setting aside the question of the metaphysical claim, Socrates of the *Gorgias* seems to suggest that the telling of eschatological myths is politically necessary to the maintenance of virtue amongst the citizenry even of a remarkable political community.

This is a claim that must ring dully in the ears of an increasingly secularized society in which the meaning of "the separation of church and state" is debated in and out of the courts. Nevertheless, the conclusion I have drawn has unlooked for support from a philosopher unlikely to agree much with Plato. I mean David Hume who proposes a similar conclusion in his *Enquiry Concerning Human Understanding*, Section 11 entitled, "A Particular Providence and a Future State." This section of the *First Enquiry* is unlike the other eleven in that it is written as a dialogue, and bears a relationship to his *Dialogues Concerning Natural Religion*. Hume as an agent in the world was surely an atheist, certain that at death he would become

---

Lourenço and Smith, "Socratic Epistemology," 80. I would suggest that their arguments in this article actually lead to the conclusion I have formulated rather than the one they propose.

mere atoms in the void,[39] and yet Hume the political philosopher says to his interlocutor in Section 11:

> You conclude, that religious doctrines and reasonings *can* have no influence on life, because they *ought* to have no influence; never considering, that men reason not in the same manner you do, but draw many consequences from the belief of a divine Existence, and suppose that the Deity will inflict punishments on vice, and bestow rewards on virtue, beyond what appear in the ordinary course of nature. Whether this reasoning of theirs be just or not, is no matter. Its influence on their life and conduct must still be the same. And, those, who attempt to disabuse them of just prejudices, may, for aught I know, be good reasoners, but I cannot allow them to be good citizens and politicians; since they free men from one restraint upon their passions, and make the infringement of the laws of society, in one respect, more easy and secure.[40]

Hume recognized what Plato had long before seen and that Socrates of the *Gorgias* clearly establishes: the general run of citizens will not stay the course of reason. They need stories that reinforce reason and in that respect are rational even though in genre they are not arguments at all and, thus, not subject to rational scrutiny or refutation. Hume, in response to Descartes, was a pre-eminent philosopher of the imagination and, therefore, of sentiment. Curious as it may seem, Hume might assist in recovering to our reading of Plato what we lost with Descartes.

Human beings are not mules to be driven, nor sheep to be led, but we are still animals, though rational animals. Because we have

---

[39] David Fate Norton writes, "A few weeks before his death Hume was able to satisfy Boswell that he sincerely believed it 'a most unreasonable fancy' that there might be life after death." David Fate Norton, "An Introduction to Hume's Thought," in *The Cambridge Companion to Hume*, ed. David Fate Norton (Cambridge: Cambridge University Press, 1993), 32, n. 29.

[40] David Hume, *An Enquiry Concerning Human Understanding, A Letter from a Gentleman to His Friend in Edinburgh, An Abstract of "A Treatise of Human Nature,"* ed. with intro. Eric Steinberg (Indianapolis: Hackett Publishing Co., 1993), 101 (emphasis in Hume).

reason, we are subject to rational persuasion. For all our rationality, however, humans also live in our imaginations and senses, as other animals live all the time. Images must be presented to our imaginations to calm fear and jealousy and to inspire the feeling of having done well. To those imaginative ends, we must be told stories which, in and of themselves, are not rational, but rather appeal to the non-rational side of human being, to the side of imagination and passion. The philosopher who repudiates rhetoric as a philosopher, must embrace it as a politician. Callicles says that he is not convinced by Socrates' arguments, so Socrates tells him a story. Thus philosophy is extended as myth. There is a way in which this too is *elenchos*: argument against argument and story against story. The philosopher who spends many pages running Homer out of town must, as a politician, spin myths of his own.

Professor Dodds quotes the brilliant line of another thinker commenting on the *Gorgias* myth, who plays upon the famous line of Carl von Clausewitz that "war is the continuation of politics by other means," saying that "philosophy was for Plato 'the continuation of politics by other means."[41] For all of that line's elegance, I do not think it is quite right. Based upon my analysis of Plato's juxtaposition of Socrates' claim to be the pre-eminent practitioner of politics to his telling of an eschatological myth, it is myth-telling that is the continuation of both philosophy and politics by other means. Myth, in general, and eschatological myth, in particular, is essential to a durable political community.

Socrates condemns four of the greatest leaders of Athens because the people they sought to teach turned against them. But Socrates stands under the same condemnation. Not only was he condemned by Athens, but he failed to transform even those who deliberately sought to follow him. In that tragic realization, Plato as author has his literary Socrates' claim to be the true practitioner of

---

[41] "As a recent writer has put it, adapting Clausewitz, philosophy was for Plato 'the continuation of politics by other means' (V. de Magalhães-Vilhena, *Socrate et la légende platonicienne*, 128)" Dodds, *Gorgias*, 384.

politics, then to make his irrefutable claim, then to tell his eschatological myth which is a *logos*, and then to make his irrefutable claim
one last time. In the *Gorgias*, the eschatological myth is essential to
the work of Socrates the philosopher as politician. Rational argument is insufficient, no matter how irrefutable. The rational animal
needs a good story as well. While not accepting Plato's metaphysics
or psychology, David Hume, the atheist, agrees that the general run
of humanity needs the story of heaven and hell to maintain civil society. Where the texts of Plato and Hume agree, we neglect their
insights to our peril.

LIBERTY, TYRANNY, AND THE FAMILY IN PLATO AND MACHIAVELLI

Khalil Habib

Introduction: Setting the Stage

This essay explores liberty and tyranny in the reform of marriage and family in Plato's *Republic* and Machiavelli's *Mandragola*. For Plato, Socrates is the embodiment of the just life, and only the just person is truly free. In the *Republic*, Socrates argues that a just city is one in which Philosopher Kings rule a regime, just as reason governs the passions in the soul of a just individual. Thus ordered, the just soul could be said to be free from the tyranny of the passions, or the disharmony that is created when the soul is divided between reason and the passions. As R. F. Stalley observes, Plato "argues that to be free a city must avoid the extremes of liberty and of authoritarianism. The legislator should rely on persuasion, not force, so that people willingly obey his laws. The underlying idea is that we are free if we willingly follow the demands of reason rather than being coerced by external forces or by unruly desires."[1] By contrasting key portions of Plato's reform of the family in the *Republic* with Machiavelli's reform of the family in his comedy, *Mandragola*, Plato's defense of Socrates' life of philosophy and the just life becomes more visible.

Both Plato and Machiavelli treat the family in relation to politics and what is best for the political order. In the *Republic*, Socrates attempts to eradicate divisions within the city by subordinating the love of one's own to the common good. In order to found his unified republic, Socrates reforms, among other things, the family. As Allan Bloom points out,

---

[1] R. F. Stalley, "Plato's Doctrine of Freedom," *Proceedings of the Aristotelian Society* 98, no. 1 (June 1998): 145–158, https://doi.org/10.1111/1467-9264.00029.

Socrates…recognizes that there must be a revolution in the family in which its functions are transferred to the community, so that women will not have to bear the double burden of career mothers. Day-care centers, abortion, and the desacralization of marriage are only a few of the easily recognizable elements of this revolution in favor of synthesizing the opposites man/woman into the unity, human being. Some activists even find Socrates' analysis too radical, sacrificing all the charms of family ties to rational considerations of justice. Reason, it seems, is corrosive of the mysteries of human connectedness.[2]

The radicalism of Socrates' proposals, what he refers to as "waves" in Book 5 of the *Republic*, must take place in order for such a city to become reality (449a–480a). Socrates proposes three such waves, or policies, that are intended to create a city that recognizes and respects the rule of reason over the passions, and where the love of one's own family branches out to and includes all members of the city.

In the *Mandragola*, Machiavelli, like Plato before him, also desacralized the family and sexuality, but not in order to discipline the passions through reason or to unite the city around the theoretical life. In the prologue to *Mandragola*, Machiavelli proclaims that there are certain "tricks to the world" that can be used to help the audience achieve their desired ends, which he primarily associates with pleasure.[3] Once his audience learns these "tricks," he explains, it is possible for anyone to satisfy their desires while maintaining order and a good public reputation.[4] The "trick" is knowing how to successfully satisfy one's desires by learning how to help others satisfy theirs. Such a scheme works, Machiavelli suggests, so long as everyone conspires together to keep up appearances by maintaining publicly

---

[2] Allan Bloom, preface to *The Republic of Plato*, originally written by Plato (New York: Basic Books, 1991), ix. All references to Plato's *Republic* refer to this translation. References to the dialogue itself will be indicated by the Stephanus numbers.

[3] Niccolò Machiavelli, *Mandragola*, trans. by Mera J. Flaumenhaft (Prospect Heights, IL: Waveland Press, 1981), 7.

[4] Ibid.

respectable decorum and refusing to upset the political order. In the *Mandragola*, Lucrezia is able to provide her sterile husband with an heir by sleeping with a younger man. A community of women and children, so to speak, is formed in order to provide an old man with an heir that fortune deprived him of. The community of women and children in the *Republic*, by contrast, is designed to ensure that the parts of the city resemble the soul perfected through virtue (427c–445e). Whereas Plato's city ultimately supports the theoretical life, Machiavelli's emphasis is on the things useful to the world, such as conquering chance (lack of an heir in this case) and satisfying desire through cunning or intelligence.

I

Plato's *Republic* is set during the Peloponnesian War, just prior to the rise of the Thirty Tyrants, who briefly ruled Athens in 404–03 B.C. The argument and the action of *Republic* are also framed within a metaphor of Socrates' relationship to politics. A group of young Athenian men playfully attempt to coerce Socrates, the embodiment of the life of reason, to attend a party. Like a democracy, the boys appeal to majority rule and insist that Socrates ought to join them and come along to the party.[5] The will of the majority, rather than the rule of reason, ought to prevail, according to these young men. Socrates eventually acquiesces, but only after they promise him that, at the party's conclusion, they will all attend a torch race that will be put on for the first time in the Piraeus. Socrates is now interested: "On horseback? [Socrates] said. That is novel. Will they hold torches and pass them to one another while racing the horses, or what do you mean?" (328a–b). Having found common ground (the torch race), the will of the majority and Socrates temporarily unite. We note, however, that while Glaucon wanted Socrates to remain in the Piraeus, it is Socrates' insatiable thirst for novelty, particularly his desire to examine what new gods Athens is now introducing

---

[5] Plato, *The Republic of Plato*, 327a–338c.

amidst the decline and decay of its own civilization, that moves him to attend the party.

Upon arriving at the gathering, we are introduced to Cephalus, the host of the party. Cephalus is an old religious patriarch whose body is now in decline.[6] Cephalus greets Socrates warmly and says that Socrates should visit more often, since Cephalus is now too old and feeble to make a trip himself. He informs Socrates that he is interested in speeches now that his body is old and he can no longer enjoy the pleasures of his bygone youth. When he was younger, Cephalus partied, drank, and chased women.[7] Now that he is old and his body is in its decline, he claims he is interested in philosophical discussions, which explains why he invited Socrates to his home. We learn from his dramatic entrance and what he says about the gods and religion that he is now also quite pious. He is at the threshold of old age and takes more seriously the stories about the afterlife and clearly fears the possibility of eternal punishment. Cephalus has no interest in engaging Socrates directly in conversation. He instead invites Socrates to discuss philosophy with the youth in attendance and perhaps others, such as Thrasymachus.

As we shall soon see, Cephalus turns to philosophy as a means of distracting himself from the fear of death in his old age. From the outset of the interaction between Socrates and Cephalus, the conversation takes a direction unforeseen by both Cephalus and the gathering of young men in attendance at the party. Cephalus has just returned from having performed religious sacrifices.[8] Cephalus, accustomed to the respect of all around him by virtue of his age, wealth, and status as a religious patriarch, intends initially to be entertained by Socrates. The patriarch has no interest in engaging the philosopher directly. Rather he asks Socrates to converse with his guests who have gathered at his home. Socrates ignores Cephalus' demand and subjects the poor old man to scrutiny. The philosopher poses four seemingly simple questions that soon have Cephalus

---

[6] Ibid.

[7] Ibid.

[8] Ibid.

voicing his innermost fears and doubts about his existence and the meaning of justice, around which Cephalus' hopes for a just treatment in the afterlife depend. Within a brief span of time the elder patriarch retreats in near panic from his own home, ostensibly to offer further sacrifices to the gods, and he is never seen again.

Plato thus presents Cephalus as a man whose mind and existence revolve around his body. Even his personal attachments, such as his family and his estate stem from or are associated with his body. While he was young, his mind and his imagination were directed toward sexual desire and money making. Now that he is frail, his mind is dominated by the fear of death and the afterlife. Even in his interaction with Socrates, Cephalus expects Socrates to revolve around his old decrepit body and interact with the passionate youth for his own amusement. The same, however, cannot be said of Socrates, whose mind—it appears—is always sovereign over his desires, a glimpse of which we will see once Socrates constructs the city in speech where philosophers rule the parts of the community like the mind rules over bodily desires of the just person. Even though Socrates has yet to control the discussion and influence those present, the city in speech that he later constructs is nevertheless a model of what politics might look like if the parts that constitute the city learn to listen to, appreciate and serve the life devoted to contemplation. Furthermore, unlike Cephalus, Socrates is evidently comfortable with raising troubling questions about death.

Socrates responds to Cephalus' warm welcoming greeting with the first of the four questions. His initial question to Cephalus concerns the perspective on life as seen through the eyes of one on "the threshold of old age."[9] Socrates asks: what is it like to be face to face with death? Cephalus is immediately on the defensive as the subject raised by Socrates causes Cephalus to probe his own fragile existence and his self-awareness is soon brought into full view for all to see. Where Cephalus intends to convey cavalier self-assuredness, having supposedly been freed of the pursuits and temptations of the flesh, he instead sounds like an old man reminiscing over capacities lost

---

[9] Ibid., 328c.

but still coveted. Cephalus claims he is no longer obsessed with sex as he was when he was younger.[10] Yet, he spends most of his time responding to Socrates' question about death by retelling, and perhaps reliving, stories of his sex-crazed youth while trying to convince himself and others around him that—unlike his old peers—his old age is not a burden to his family because he is a man of good character. Indeed, the old man intimates that it is due to the strength of his own character that he is not a burden to his family and that he finds the encroachment of old age and the approach of death "only mildly troublesome."[11] Apparently he has forgotten that he admitted early on that he is only now interested in philosophy, or listening to others philosophize, because he can no longer perform sexually.

Cephalus' pronouncement that he does not fear death because of his good character rings hollow. As we soon discover, Cephalus is indeed up at night troubled by the thought of the possibility of punishment in the afterlife. He clearly does not believe he has always lived a life of good character. Allan Bloom argues:

> Cephalus' youthful passions, however appealing, seem to have led him into activities that are contrary to justice, and his old age is spent worrying about them and atoning for them. Thus, from the point of view of justice, eros is a terrible thing, a savage beast. For a man like Cephalus, life is always split between sinning and repenting. Only by the death of eros and its charms can such a gentleman become fully reliable, for his eros leads neither to justice nor philosophy but to intense, private bodily satisfaction.[12]

As the conversation between Socrates and Cephalus unfolds, however, it becomes obvious that Cephalus' former sex life is not what keeps him up at night. Something else does, and it centers around questions related to property, justice and the fear of death.

Cephalus tells Socrates about the time when he overheard someone once ask Sophocles if he can still perform sex with women

---

[10] Ibid.

[11] Ibid.

[12] Allan Bloom, Interpretive Essay in *The Republic of Plato*, (New York: Basic Books, 1991), 313.

now that he is old. Now that Cephalus is old himself and can no longer engage in sexual activity himself, he finds the wisdom of Sophocles consoling. He reports that when the poet was asked if he could still have intercourse, Sophocles responded that he is relieved to be free from sex, that "frenzied and savage master."[13] Sophocles' claim that freedom from eroticism is a blessing is reassuring to Cephalus now that his family and its continuance is what Cephalus largely has to live for. Cephalus is hopeful that old age brings peace and freedom, even though, as we shall shortly see, Cephalus is hardly at peace or free from troubles and anxiety.

Socrates pounces again, this time drawing together Cephalus' awareness of death and his relationship to property: "Did you earn or inherit your wealth?"[14] Cephalus answers that he inherited some and earned enough money to restore some of what his father, who had also inherited, had wasted. Socrates gets Cephalus to recognize that attachment to wealth seems to alternate in generations depending on who earned or inherited their money. Those who make it, are more attached to it, which would indicate that Cephalus' sons are less likely to be as attached to the wealth that Cephalus has spent his life accumulating. Socrates also lets something troubling slip into the exchange: those who earned their money are more attached to it than those who inherited, just as parents are more attached to their offspring. By implication children, who obviously did not make their parents, are less attached to their parents, their parent's wealth and their father's pursuits. The observation that children are less attached to their parents than parents to their own children is confirmed later in the dialogue when, after Cephalus leaves his own

---

[13] Ibid., 329c.

[14] Ibid., 330a. Plato draws our attention to the significance of property, broadly construed, to Cephalus *vis a vis* his awareness of mortality by using the Greek word *ousia*, meaning being, to denote property. The suggestion seems to indicate that Cephalus believes he can live on through his property, and even that his children are his property in so far as they constitute a part of his being. As the discussion on property shows, Cephalus is more interested in continuing his family's name and wealth than in the mere accumulation of wealth as such. Hence Socrates' observation that Cephalus is not just simply a moneymaker.

party and is never to be seen again, Cephalus' son, Polemarchus, offers a definition of justice very different from that espoused by his father. Partly because he is liberated from the need to earn money, and partly because of his own nature, Polemarchus is far more political than his father, whose entire existence is centered around his family and his possessions.

Polemarchus defines justice as helping one's friends and harming one's enemies.[15] He defines one's friends in terms of those who belong to his nation, and his enemies as those who do not. Polemarchus' definition of justice reflects the character of a patriot, rather than a man concerned merely with the continuity of his family's name and wealth. Like his father, however, Polemarchus still defines his own existence and sense of justice in terms of birth; the only difference is that he extends membership to include his compatriots. The nation is, so to speak, an extended family for Polemarchus. In order to get him to think more philosophically, however, Socrates must persuade Polemarchus to define friends in terms of those who are good and not just those who merely appear to be good. Polemarchus' definition of justice is too rooted in nationalism, for it overlooks the possibility that enemies, as defined by patriotism, may only appear to be bad, while friends merely appear to be good. Socrates eventually gets Polemarchus to admit that the just man harms no one, thus undermining the definition of justice as harming one's enemies.

Let us, however, return to Cephalus. Socrates' next question to Cephalus concerns the good enjoyed through the possession of great wealth. What is the greatest good enjoyed by money, asks Socrates?[16] Cephalus' response is that money enables him to avoid injustice and impiety. Socrates asks a series of follow up questions intended to expose Cephalus' misgivings about his ill-gotten gains, the true source of the patriarch's anxiety about the afterlife. Socrates draws out the effect that the acquisition of wealth has had on

---

[15] Ibid., 332d.
[16] Ibid., 329e.

Cephalus' life and character. This serves to further disconcert Cephalus as he is called upon to reflect on the unflattering deeds that the rich man may have carried out in the pursuit of his prestige and worldly possessions. Cephalus says that, when a person becomes older, they start to pay more attention to stories about the afterlife and ponder whether they will be punished. Clearly Cephalus does not find the stories about the afterlife comforting. It is obvious that he has committed injustice in his youth, perhaps related to how he may have treated or cheated others along the way to his financial independence, since the context in which Cephalus offers his admission of fear of the divine retribution involves his wealth. Now that he is pious, or thinks he is, Cephalus is hoping to buy himself some peace of mind. Socrates' analysis of Cephalus' definition of justice is within the context of the latter's belief in the gods.

Plato completes his portrayal of Cephalus with the discussion of justice in relation to property and telling the truth. To draw out Cephalus' conception of justice, Socrates proposes the hypothetical situation of returning a confiscated weapon to a friend who has gone mad.[17] No rational person would return a dangerous weapon to a friend who could possibly cause harm to themself or others. We may draw two conclusions from this thought experiment: Justice, then, does good, not harm. Furthermore, the example suggests that ownership is not merely a legal title to a possession, but rather the possession of reason or sound mind is the legitimate standard of ownership. In the example just provided, justice demands that reason is a prerequisite for ownership of property, as indicated by the conclusion that someone gone mad ought not to have his weapon returned to him and, therefore, ceases to own it upon no longer knowing how to use it well. This line of thinking may help us to understand what keeps Cephalus up at night: perhaps his unfettered pursuit of wealth may have harmed others. Motivated to regain the wealth of his father, who squandered his inheritance, Cephalus now hopes wealth can help him to be pious and avoid injustice. Furthermore, in so far as justice means property belongs to those who can reason, and not

---

[17] Ibid., 331c.

simply those with a title to it or claim to own it on the basis of inheritance or birth (recall, for example, how Cephalus counts his family as in some measure property), Socrates' example of the weapon and a mad "owner" implies Cephalus' authority over his property and children is questionable, or at the very least must have its basis in reason, and not convention. Socrates, however, does not let Cephalus off the hook. Socrates is unwilling to allow Cephalus to subordinate reason to fear, ownership of property, wealth, the continuity of property, and confused notions of piety.[18] If anything, Socrates attempts to subordinate the private to philosophy or the life of reason as much as possible, as evidenced later in the three waves in Book 5, reforms that are intended to lay the foundation for a just city ruled by philosopher kings who govern in accordance with reason.

In his conversation with Cephalus, Socrates seems to anticipate a part of John Locke's theory of private property. According to Locke, "Every man has a *Property* in his Person. This no Body has any Right to but himself." And should this be? According to Locke, the natural law, which he identifies with the law of reason, dictates a right to private property on the basis of reason. "God gave the World to Men in Common," Locke claims, "but since he gave it to them for their benefit, and the greatest Conveniences of Life they were capable to draw from it, it cannot be supposed he meant it should always remain common and uncultivated. He gave it to the use of the Industrious and *Rational*...and not to the Fancy."[19] Both Socrates and Locke reject claims to property that are based merely on birth (or divine right of kings in Locke's case). Socrates, however, goes further than Locke. Socrates prepares the community of property and philosopher kings in his exchange with Cephalus. According to Socrates, property belongs to you if you have the wisdom to

---

[18] As we shall see later, Machiavelli is unwilling to subordinate his republic to wealth, piety, and private life. But his reasons are not in order to support the theoretical life, but what is effectual rather than merely contemplative.

[19] John Locke, *Second Treatise on Government*, in *Two Treatises of Government*, ed. Peter Laslett (Cambridge University Press, 1991), 196, 291.

make good use of it. In Socrates' city, property belongs not to those who are most industrious but those who are most rational.

Having been made more aware of the fragility of existence, his life's work and legacy in the pursuit and enjoyment of wealth, his perception of justice, and the attendant relationship to the gods, Cephalus finds his views completely undermined by Socrates' four simple questions. He then makes a hasty retreat from the gathering, offering the transparent excuse that he must depart to pay further homage to the gods. If Socrates is to derive anything positive from this gathering at the party, such as gaining the ability to influence the young and still-impressionable minds of the city's best and brightest, he must rid the discussion of the oppressive presence of the elder patriarch. Cephalus must be removed in order for Socrates to introduce reason into the upcoming debate and subsequent discussion of justice without the oppressive presence of tradition, piety, and authority established through wealth and old age. The ease with which Socrates disquiets, exposes, and panics Cephalus is an indication of just how frightened the old man feels when he is stripped of his faith and worldly trappings and is called upon to review his life's pursuits and outcomes in the harsh light of reason. The dialogue between Socrates and Cephalus does not indulge the passions that reaffirm the family, as the tragic plays of Sophocles do, but rather tames them through dialectic. The audience is left wanting more and it is easy to forget as the dialogue continues that it even takes place within the home of a pious, rich old patriarch. Let us now turn to Book 5 of the *Republic* to see how Socrates reforms the family in order to orient the parts of the city toward the theoretical life.

II

At the beginning of Book 5 of the *Republic*, Adeimantus puts forth a challenge. Adeimantus says to Socrates: "we've been waiting all this time supposing you would surely mention begetting of children—how they'll be begotten and, once born, how they'll be reared—and that whole community of women and children of which you speak. We think it makes a big difference, or rather, the whole difference, in a regime's being right or not right."[20] Socrates responds to Adeimantus by discussing his first wave, first asking his companions whether or not males and females should do things in common. Rather than thinking of Socrates' waves as three distinct items or policies, it is better to think of them as ramifications of each other.

The First Wave proposes equality between the sexes.[21] Socrates asks: "Do we believe the females of the guardian dogs must guard the things the males guard along with them and hunt with them, and do the rest in the common; or, must they stay indoors as though they were incapacitated as a result of bearing and rearing the puppies, while the males work and have all the care of the flock?"[22] When Glaucon replies that men and women should do everything in common, Socrates logically states "If, then, we use the women for the same things as the men, they must also be taught the same things" and "these two arts [music and gymnastic], and what has to do with war, must be assigned to the women also, and they must be used in the same ways."[23] Socrates then argues that women should perform the same jobs as men, including being guardians, if their natures suit them to being guardians, and that a woman's gender should not automatically exclude her from performing these jobs. Socrates argues that a woman's gender should not exclude her from performing a job when she shares the same characteristics of soul as men:

> if either the class of men or that of women shows its superiority in some art or other practice, then we'll say that that art must be assigned to it. But if they look as though they differ in this alone, that the female bears and male mounts, we'll assert that it has not thereby yet been proved that a woman differs from a man with respect to what we're talking about.[24]

---

[20] Ibid., 449d.
[21] Ibid., 451d.
[22] Ibid.
[23] Ibid., 452a.
[24] Ibid., 454e.

Socrates then argues that a woman's nature should determine what job she performs: "there is no task of a city's governors which belongs to woman because she's woman, or to man because he's man; but the natures are scattered alike among both animals; and woman participates according to nature in all practices, and man in all."[25] After thus arguing that each woman has a particular nature that suits her for performing a particular job (in other words, some women have natures that suit them for being rulers, some have natures that suit them for being guardians, etc.), Socrates asks "There is, therefore, one woman fit for guarding and another not? Or wasn't it a nature of this sort we also selected for the men fit for guarding?"[26] When Glaucon answers "Certainly," Socrates logically concludes: "Men and women, therefore, also have the same nature with respect to guarding a city, except insofar as the one is weaker and the other stronger....Such women, therefore, must also be chosen to live and guard with such men, since they are competent and akin to the men in their nature."[27] After thus arguing that women who have natures that suit them for being guardians should serve as guardians, Socrates proceeds to state that female guardians, like male guardians, must participate in any naked exercise: "the women guardians must strip, since they'll clothe themselves in virtue instead of robes, and they must take common part in war and the city's guarding."[28] If women are to do the same work as men, they must be given the same training as men, including exercising naked as a part of their guardian training, if they have natures that suit them for such work. If female modesty is a virtue connected to the exclusivity of love and the family, Socrates' proposal that female guardians exercise naked with the males is intended to eliminate love and family by ridding it of its centerpiece (modesty). The elimination of the family, which follows from the destruction of modesty, leads to Socrates' Second Wave. The elimination of the family means that both the female and male

---

[25] Ibid., 455d.
[26] Ibid., 456a.
[27] Ibid., 456b.
[28] Ibid., 457a.

warriors can devote themselves to the city. The elimination of shame purifies their duties from private attachments by attaching them to the city. Socrates' proposals liberate female warriors from their subordination to men and the household only to reattach them to the city. In other words, Socrates does not liberate the females from the household and the authority of their husbands in order to allow them to pursue any career they may choose. Rather his aim is to undermine the morality surrounding modesty and the traditional family in order for devotion to the city to take root. The females are liberated from the claims of the household, but not from the claims of the city, to which they are to be devoted. This brings us to the Second Wave.

Socrates' quest to eliminate attachment to the family and the private realm continues. Socrates' Second Wave, like his first, addresses Adeimantus' challenge regarding the community of women and children in the ideal city. Socrates suggests that no traditional nuclear families should exist in the city. Socrates claims "[a]ll these women are to belong to all these men in common, and no woman is to live privately with any man. And the children, in their turn, will be in common, and neither will a parent know his own offspring, nor a child his parent."[29] Indeed, Socrates details how in the ideal city, children would immediately be taken from their mothers and predominantly cared for by nurses employed by the city, stating:

> [A]s the offspring are born, won't they be taken over by the officers established for this purpose....they will take the offspring of the good and bring them into the pen to certain nurses who live apart in a certain section of the city....Won't they also supervise the nursing, leading the mothers to the pen when they are full with milk, inventing every device so that none will recognize her own?...And won't they supervise the mothers themselves, seeing to it that they suckle only a moderate time and that the wakeful watching and the rest of the labor are handed to wet nurses and governesses?[30]

---

[29] Ibid., 5.457d.
[30] Ibid., 460b–460d.

Naturally, if children do not know who their parents are and vice versa, such a system would risk incestuous pairings. If parents cannot tell who their children are, what is to stop them from accidentally sleeping with their children? Glaucon asks: "But how will they distinguish one another's fathers and daughters and the others you just mentioned?"[31] Socrates, apparently not overly disturbed by the idea that incest would occur under his proposed system, replies "Not at all."[32] After discussing a complex rule that would in theory prevent people from engaging in incest, Socrates ultimately concedes that incest would likely occur when he claims that it would be permissible in certain instances. According to Socrates, "The law will grant that brothers and sisters live together if the lot falls out that way."[33]

Socrates' Second Wave is more radical than the first wave in that he champions the elimination of the nuclear family. Socrates reasons that, in order to unify the city around the common good, all of the city's citizens are to be subordinated to the city as one large family. Unified by their loyalty to the city, families would have to be totally eliminated so as to prevent the love of one's own from competing with the loyalty to the city. Families would have to be subordinated to the city because loyalty to one's own kin divides a population into small, tight knit groups that result in a society in which people are loyal and devoted to their family members rather than to their city. In Socrates' ideal city, the city's population would no longer be divided between private devotion and public duty. Citizens would be unified by sharing in common an absolute loyalty to the city. Socrates stresses the need for unity in the city and explains his belief that factors (i.e., families) that divide a city's population are evil:

> Have we any greater evil for a city than what splits it and makes it many instead of one? Or a greater good than what binds it together and makes it one?...Doesn't the community of pleasure

---

[31] Ibid., 461d.
[32] Ibid., 461e.
[33] Ibid., 461e.

and pain bind it together, when to the greatest extent possible all the citizens alike rejoice and are pained at the same comings into being perishings?...But the privacy of such things dissolves it, when some are overwhelmed and other overjoyed by the same things happening to the city and those within the city?...Doesn't that sort of thing happen when they don't utter such phrases as 'my own' and 'not my own' at the same time in the city, and similarly with respect to 'somebody else's?'...Is, then, that city in which most say 'my own' and 'not my own' about the same thing, and in the same way, the best governed city?...Then is that city best governed which is most like a single human being?[34]

The Third Wave that Socrates discusses is the one that is met with the most hostility. Socrates proposes that it would be ideal for philosophers to rule as kings over the city. According to Socrates, "Unless...political power and philosophy coincide in the same place...there is no rest from ills for the cities, nor I think for human kind, nor will the regime we have now described in speech ever come forth from nature."[35]

Socrates' proposed city is paradoxical and ironic. Socrates casts doubts upon his own city by asking whether his proposals are both possible and desirable. At the very least, based on the reaction to the third wave, we may safely assume that the answer is a resounding "no," which calls into question how seriously Socrates intends these reforms. What we can say confidently is that the *Republic* is a thought experiment intended to show and justify the theoretical life, as embodied by Socrates, by painting a picture of what a city might look like in which philosophers rule his or her own passions through reason.

III

Machiavelli's ultimate aim in the *Mandragola*, in contrast to Plato's, is clearly political reform. A short chapter in the *Discourses* helps to reveal the elusive relationship between this play and his political

---

[34] Ibid., 461b–461d.
[35] Ibid., 473a–e.

thought. In Book 3 chapter 26 of the *Discourses*, entitled, "How a State is Ruined Because of Women," Machiavelli explicitly references the Roman Lucretia, whose similar-sounding name to Lucrezia draws our attention to the relationship between his comedy and his political writings.[36] In the context of discoursing on how dangerous private life, particularly marriage and violations of female virtue are to the order of a republic, Machiavelli cautions the reader on the dangers of female virtue: if not properly dealt with, as he says, love, marriage, or the violation of a virtuous woman could ruin a state. Here is an abridgement of the chapter:

> In this text are several things to be noted. First, one sees that women have been causes of much ruin, and have done great harm to those who govern a city, and have caused many divisions in them. As has been seen in this history of ours, the excess done against Lucretia took the state away from the Tarquins; another, done against Virginia, deprived the Ten of their authority. Among the first causes Aristotle puts down of the ruin of tyrants is having injured someone on account of women, by raping them or by violating them or by breaking off marriages, as this part is spoken of in detail in the chapter where we treat conspiracies.
>
> I say thus that absolute princes and governors of republics are not to take little account of this part, but they should consider the disorders that can arise from such an accident and remedy them in time so that the remedy is not with harm and reproach for their state or for their republic, as happened to the Ardeans. For having allowed that rivalry to grow among their citizens, they were led to divide among themselves; and when they wished to reunite, they had to send for external help, which is a great beginning of a nearby servitude.[37]

As the contents of this chapter make clear, Machiavelli is not interested in female virtue for its own sake. Rather, he treats marriage, love, and even the violation of an honorable woman's virtue in

---

[36] Niccolò Machiavelli, *Discourses on Livy*, trans. by Harvey Mansfield and Nathan Tarcov (Chicago: University of Chicago, 2009), 272–273.

[37] Machiavelli, *Discourses on Livy*, 273.

terms of their effects on the stability of the republic. Like Plato, Machiavelli, as this passage suggests, seeks a unified city in which marriage and female virtue do not upset the order of the republic. Read in light of the passage quoted above, the *Mandragola* is part of Machiavelli's "remedy" to help eliminate or moderate love and or marriage as sources of conflict within a republic. The play seeks to desacralize female virtue by reducing sexual desire to a harmless itch to be scratched in order to subordinate the private to the public good. By justifying adultery and emphasizing the good effects it can produce, namely the birth of an heir, Machiavelli loosens the church's authority over marriage and undermines the notion that marriage is a holy sacrament. Machiavelli redirects the passions connected to the family and marriage to stable republican government. He enlists reason to aid the passions, rather than directing the imagination and reason to the life of Socrates, as Plato does in the *Republic* through rule of Philosopher Kings. Nor does he respect the church's teaching that love and marriage belong to a divine order.

As I mentioned previously, in the prologue to *Mandragola*, Machiavelli proclaims that there are certain "tricks to the world" that can be used to help people achieve their desired ends.[38] These tricks require the use of the mind to satisfy desires, the direct opposite of Socrates' model of the good life. For our purposes, I will briefly examine the characters of Callimaco, Friar Timoteo, Lucrezia, and Messer Nicia and show how each uses their own "tricks" to achieve the outcomes each desires. And desires it is. It is important to note at the outset that the play concludes by avoiding the dangers to the republic Machiavelli mentions in Chapter 26 of Book 3 of the *Discourses*. By the end of the play, it appears that everyone is more or less satisfied with the outcome. Sexual desire is tamed, not through good character, but simply through easy satisfaction. In the end sexual desire is much ado about nothing, a passion certain to destroy one's life over or upset the political order in search of cosmic meaning behind human eroticism.

---

[38] Machiavelli, *Mandragola*, 7.

In order to understand how each character manipulates the other to get what they want, one must first understand what each person desires in the end. Callimaco wants to sleep with Lucrezia but must overcome the fact that she is an honorable woman who is also married.[39] Lucrezia wants to provide Messer Nicia with an heir, but also wants to have an affair with a young lover without her husband knowing.[40] Friar Timoteo wants to make money from the whole situation but also to maintain his reputation within the community.[41] Messer Nicia wants an heir, but he is sterile.[42] Once there is an understanding of what each wants from the situation, it is easy to see how they manipulate one another and are still able to maintain the appearance of moral decency.

From the beginning of the play, Callimaco is determined to sleep with Lucrezia and devotes all of his time and effort into finding a way to achieve his goal. He enlists the aid of Ligurio, who helps him come up with the idea of using mandrake root as the means by which he can achieve his end.[43] The two decide to tell Nicia that mandrake root will guarantee his wife's fertility, but that it will kill the first man she sleeps with immediately afterwards. Callimaco knows how desperate Nicia is for an heir so he suggests that Nicia allow Lucrezia to sleep with a random man off the street, which will ensure that Nicia will have an heir and not die in the process. Of course, Callimaco knows that the "man off the street" is actually himself in disguise. Once Nicia agrees, Callimaco then moves on to the next phase in his plan, which is to convince Lucrezia to follow along. In order to convince Lucrezia to follow the plan, Callimaco knows that he must first convince her mother. To accomplish this first step, he uses the aid of Timoteo, the local priest. Once Timoteo convinces Sostrata, Lucrezia's mother, she in turn convinces Lucrezia. Callimaco knows that in order for his plan to work Sostrata is

---

[39] Ibid., 13.
[40] Ibid., 52.
[41] Ibid., 52.
[42] Ibid., 14.
[43] Ibid., 15.

the most important link, so he uses Timoteo to help manipulate her into getting her daughter to follow along.

Timoteo is only willing to go along with Callimaco's plan because he knows there is a monetary reward in doing so. Timoteo is tested by Callimaco and Ligurio when they ask him to perform an abortion on a girl practicing to be a nun.[44] Timoteo knows that this would be scandalous if people found out, so he decides to accept money to cover it up. This test gives us insight into Timoteo's true character: he is a man who is willing to accept money to save face within the community even though he is a highly respected religious authority. Once Callimaco can trust that Timoteo would do something immoral for money, he was confident that it wouldn't be a problem talking Timoteo into convincing Sostrata his plan was for the greater good. Timoteo then uses his position as a church authority to convince Sostrata that she should persuade Lucrezia into going along with Callimaco's plan because it was the right thing to do for everyone, suggesting that her salvation is unharmed in the process.[45]

Lucrezia is not easily convinced by her mother, but after some resistance she realizes that her duty as a good wife is to please her husband by any means necessary. Since the way to please Nicia is by providing him with an heir, Lucrezia decides to go along with the plan to honor her husband by providing him with a child. Callimaco then sleeps with Lucrezia and gets what he ultimately wants.[46] The morning after, he reveals his plan to her. Lucrezia is astonished at how Callimaco was able to pull it off, and she is also resentful at the fact Nicia could be so stupid and so gullible. She uses Nicia's stupidity as a reason to continue to sleep with the young lover Callimaco but is able to maintain face because, in the end, she is able to provide Nicia with the heir he wanted. Although Nicia appears to

---

[44] Ibid., 30–32.
[45] Ibid., 34–36.
[46] Ibid., 54.

be the person who lost out the most in this play, we can infer that he was actually the mastermind behind Callimaco's whole plot.[47]

Nicia knew that he would never be able to bear a child with Lucrezia and, therefore, generate his own biological heir. Instead of allowing fortune to dictate or govern his life and desires, Nicia decided to come up with a plan to actually get the heir he wanted. In the beginning of the play, we learn that a man named Cammillo was the one responsible for Callimaco's desire for Lucrezia, but at the start of the play Cammillo is just a stranger in a bar. However, Cammillo is actually the cousin of Nicia, and once his connection to Nicia is made obvious, we can see how ingenious Nicia's plan actually was. He instructed his cousin to tell the story of his beautiful Lucrezia, understanding that Callimaco would immediately fall in love and pursue her. Nicia turned Callimaco on himself because he knew the end result would lead to the heir of his throne. Nicia spent the whole time playing stupid and going along with Callimaco's plan, when in actuality Nicia is the genius and everyone else turned out to be the useful idiots. In the end, Nicia is the only one who truly gets what he wanted: an heir and the last laugh.

Lucrezia's husband is introduced as a follower of Boetius, a sixth-century Roman philosopher.[48] Unlike the classical Boethius, however, who resigned himself to Fortune and found consolation in God and the theoretical life, Machiavelli's "Boetius" learns how to conquer rather than be governed by fortune. Machiavelli's "Boetius" judges the moral worth of human action on the basis of their effects, even if it means he must knowingly consent to his wife committing adultery. Her adultery is justified on the basis of the fact that it provides him with an heir. The couple maintains a respectable public appearance and benefit from an act done behind closed doors. What is astonishing is how Machiavelli gets his audience to laugh at or at

---

[47] I share Mansfield's thesis that Nicia is the Machiavellian character who brings about a Machiavellian plan in the play. See Harvey C. Mansfield, "The Cuckold in Machiavelli's *Mandragola*." In *The Comedy and Tragedy of Machiavelli: Essays on the Literary Works*, ed. by Vickie B. Sullivan, (New Haven: Yale University Press, 2000) 1–29.

[48] Ibid., 9.

least overlook Lucrezia's infidelity, a violation of a sacrament, while laughing at the church and its priest and representative, Timoteo, who desires worldly, rather than otherworldly, gain. By the end of the play, sexual desire is moderated by satisfying it, and adultery is legitimated by the birth of a child, which is to say the ends justify the means; or, to put it differently, the truth of one's actions are judged by their good effects.

IV

The spirit of the *Mandragola* is reminiscent of the famous story of the Ring of Gyges told in Plato's *Republic,* but with one crucial difference—Machiavelli's stance on liberty vis a vis *fortuna* differs from Glaucon's emphasis on whether or not a good exists that is good in itself. Toward the beginning of Book 2 in the *Republic,* Glaucon, Plato's brother, challenges Socrates to show whether or not there is a good that is good in itself, good for itself and for its consequences, or just good for its consequences.[49] Socrates says there is a good, presumably philosophy and justice, that is both good in itself and good for its consequences. Glaucon seems to have his doubts and offers his version of the Ring of Gyges story in order to defend not justice, but the life of tyranny or, at the very least, a life devoted to satisfying one's desires while avoiding a bad reputation and punishment. According to Glaucon's telling of the story, Gyges is a lowly shepherd who is able to satisfy his deepest desires while fooling those around him into believing that he is just. Justice, according to this story, is not good for itself, rather injustice is, while liberty is the freedom from constraint and the anguish of unrealized desires, and ultimately even freedom from societal opinions about justice and mores.

It is difficult to miss the similarity between Gyges' story and Machiavelli's own view on liberty. Liberty in Machiavelli has several meanings. One of the most important conceptions of liberty in Machiavelli concerns the liberty of a republic to acquire and

---

[49] Plato, *The Republic of Plato,* 359c–361d.

maintain its dominance over foreign enemies and internal corruption. As Marcia L. Colish notes, however,

> *Liberta* may also mean the freedom of political action enjoyed by a ruler whose country's laws and institutions place him above criticism. The clearest example cited by Machiavelli is the kingdom of France. France, according to Machiavelli, is a "free monarchy" because the Parlement serves as a target both for the insolence and ambition of the powerful and for the fear and hatred of the masses, thus neutralizing the impact of political dissent and permitting the king to pursue his policies untrammelled by the criticism of either group.[50]

As she goes on to explain, "But when most specific, Machiavelli uses the traditional term *libero arbitrio* (free will); and he uses it in one of the best known passages in his work, the chapter in II of [*The Prince*] where he discusses the relationship between *virtu* and *fortuna*."[51] It is on the basis of Machiavelli's understanding of man's free will that he:

> feels compelled to disagree with those who think that Fortune rules all of human existence. It is precisely because he wishes to uphold the dignity of man's free will that he counters with the theory that Fortune rules only half of human life: 'Lest our free will be extinguished...I judge it may be true that Fortune is the ruler of half of our actions, but that she leaves the government of the other half, more or less, to us." That she leaves the government of the other half, more or less, to us.'[52]

As Colish points point, Machiavelli "goes on in this passage to elaborate that man expresses his free will in the face of *fortuna* by the exercise of *virtu*."[53] Virtue in the context of the *Mandragola* is neither a defense of the theoretical life nor the life of moral virtue,

---

[50] Marcia L. Colish, "The Idea of Liberty in Machiavelli," Journal of the History of Ideas 32, no. 3 (July–Sept. 1971): 323–350, https://www.jstor.org/stable/2708350.

[51] Ibid.

[52] Ibid.

[53] Ibid., 325–26.

as understood by Plato in particular, but rather the satisfaction of desire and the conquest of chance through the strength of one's own cunning and one's own will.

For Plato, sexual desire may take on a transcendent meaning as the divine force associated with the life of contemplation. For Machiavelli, eros is reduced to an itch that can be satisfied and drained of its dangerous threats to political order. The differences between the two thinkers are encapsulated in Machiavelli's distinction between imaginary and effectual truths. What is imaginary leads to one's ruin, and what is effectual leads to one's preservation.[54] In the *Mandragola*, ruin is avoided by recasting sexual desire as a private but largely meaningless passion, unlike the cosmic significance placed on marriage and female virtue that threatens the ruin of the state.[55] Socrates also subordinates the family and marriage to the unity of the city, but he does so in order to establish a regime in which philosophers, and not politically ambitious men or common people rule. The tripartite division of Socrates' city mirrors the parts of the soul—desire, spiritedness, and reason. Each part of the city/soul provides the city with a specific motivation to action and an end to strive toward. Desire (Cephalus) seeks preservation and security, particularly in the family and property; spiritedness (Polemarchus) seeks honor and glory, particularly in politics; and the intellect, seeks knowledge for its own sake, particularly through the theoretical life. Plato's city is ruled by philosophers who rule over society as reason rules over the passions. Machiavelli's city, so to speak, is founded on the people and has utility as its primary motive.[56] It is a city or regime devoted to satisfying the desire for acquisition and maintenance.

Socrates' city in speech is intended to show what justice in the soul of the individual looks like. For purposes of viewing what this might look like on "the big screen," so to speak, Socrates proposes

---

[54] Harvey Mansfield, introduction to Niccolò Machiavelli, *The Prince* (Chicago: University of Chicago, 1998) 61.

[55] Machiavelli, *Discourses on Livy*, 272–73.

[56] Machiavelli, *The Prince*, 38–42.

to found a city mirrored on a well-ordered soul in order to see more clearly how justice emerges naturally from human social interaction. Socrates' treatment of Cephalus and the reforms of the family that follow in the construction of Socrates' just city aim to subordinate the private realm, which Socrates largely treats as governed by the passions and powerful attachments, as much as possible to the life of reason. Neither the general will of the majority (Polemarchus and his crew) nor Cephalus' authority (rooted in ancestry and piety) is ultimately successful in subordinating Socrates' intellectual independence to their wishes. The *Republic*, in other words, is an attempt to neutralize the coercive attempts to subordinate Socrates to majority rule, tradition, piety and the family by demonstrating the autonomy of Socrates' mind in his interactions with others and their powerful attachments and passions. It is a city centered on the theoretical, philosophical life of contemplation.

Bibliography

Colish, Marcia L. "The Idea of Liberty in Machiavelli." *Journal of the History of Ideas* 32, no. 3 (July.–Sept. 1971): 323–350. https://www.jstor.org/stable/2708350.

Machiavelli, Niccolò. *Discourses on Livy*. Translated by Harvey Mansfield and Nathan Tarcov. Chicago: University of Chicago, 2009.

———. *Mandragola*. Translated by Mera J. Flaumenhaft. Prospect Heights, IL: Waveland Press, 1981.

———. *The Prince*. Translated by Harvey Mansfield. Chicago: University of Chicago, 1998.

Plato. *The Republic of Plato*. Translated by Allan Bloom. New York: Basic Books, 1991.

Stalley, R. F. "Plato's Doctrine of Freedom." *Proceedings of the Aristotelian Society* 98, no. 1 (June 1998): 145–158. https://doi.org/10.1111/1467-9264.00029.

THE WORST AND THE LESS HUMANE WAY: THE PLATONIC CONDEMNATION OF A CRIMINAL JUSTICE SYSTEM LIKE OURS

Jennifer Baker

A musical performance without a prelude would begin abruptly. We can imagine not being ready for it. Some of us might not know what is coming and lose time getting accustomed to the notes. Even those of us hearing familiar music could use a bit of notice in order to settle in to attend to the performance. This seems a sound rationale for musical preludes, an ancient practice that is still common today. Are musical preludes analogous to what is missing in our current approach to criminal law? Was Plato right to suggest in the *Laws* that we should not think that laws require preludes, that they should not merely "explain straight away what must and must not be done, add the threat of a penalty, and turn to another law, without adding a single bit of encouragement or persuasion." (*Laws* 720a1–2)? I want to consider Plato's reasons for suggesting as much.[1] And, though I borrow less than he has on offer, his reasons highlight the paucity of our own thought on the impact of criminal law on lawbreakers. Our own thought depends upon distinctly non-Platonic ethical assumptions, I suggest. I think these assumptions are rarely examined and, upon examination, require improvement.

It may seem unlikely, for all manner of reasons, that Plato's recommendations have relevance for us now. We neither share the goals nor the setting for which Plato developed political philosophy.

---

[1] Julia Annas points out that, despite it not being a proposal that caught on (Cicero seems approving, Posidonius seems to have mocked it), the idea that laws should have preludes is "original" to Plato and an idea about which he is "clearly proud." Julia Annas, *Virtue and Law in Plato and Beyond* (Oxford: Oxford University Press, 2017) 91.

Yet despite this, we have borrowed quite a bit from his proposals: due process including the right to question witnesses; levels of review; punishing the agent and not his family; the use of juries.[2] Similarly, I want to suggest that Plato's own focus on preludes to law can serve as a model for us. It is a feature we do not include in our approach, and this encourages us to consider whether we, then, in our approach to criminal law over-rely on coercion alone (both in the justification and application of these laws). Legal theorist Chad Flanders recently argued that contemporary political theory, though it "would seem to be the place to address questions of the power of the state and the limits of that power, especially when it comes to the use of force against its own citizen," has largely been silent on this issue.[3] Not even our major theorists treat criminal justice as if it features in an account of justice generally. John Rawls devoted only five pages to punishment in his lengthy *A Theory of Justice*. As Flanders also explains, despite his emphasis on our shared circumstances when it comes to distributive justice, Rawls declares that citizens who break our laws experience "misfortune" based on "their natures" or "the kind of persons" that "they are." As Flanders writes, "in one place Rawls suggests that the only solution for dealing with such people (whose nature is their misfortune) is to ramp up the punishments for them."[4] When it comes to law-breakers, Rawls demonstrates no commitment to "shared citizenship and solidarity," Flanders concludes.[5] In the *Laws*, Plato assumes citizens will break laws and continues to assume these citizens ought to still be regarded and treated as "free." His focus on the perspective and readiness of our citizen criminal defendants, the law-breakers being faced with "the

---

[2] R. F. Stalley, *An Introduction to Plato's* Laws (New York: Hackett Publishing Company, 1983).

[3] Chad Flanders, "Criminals Behind the Veil: Political Philosophy and Punishment," 31 BYU *Journal of Public Law* (2016) 83.

[4] Ibid, 84. John Rawls, *A Theory of Justice* (Cambridge: Harvard University Press, 1971) 576 *supra* note 7.

[5] Some political theorists have attempted to develop Rawlsian accounts of punishment, but have done so, as Flanders also points out, by ignoring these passages by Rawls, *A Theory of Justice*, 84.

music," can be seen as a result of this. It may not be that we have read and accepted Rawls. It is more likely that he is reflecting the utter lack of concern we maintain for the perspective of a lawbreaker (or potential one). Plato's diagnosis of this would be that this is due to our relying on force alone in the application of law.

Some recent scholarship has made Plato's recommendation of legal preludes more palatable as a positive example. In the past philosophers were concerned that preludes were plain attempts to deceive the citizenry.[6] Since then there have been arguments that suggest preludes were instead stand-ins for informed consent, or an early strike for the explicit and rational justification of state power.[7] Work by Julia Annas and Melissa Lane emphasizes instead the way the preludes are not rational argument but instead representative of a kind of approach to lawbreakers.[8] The approach is not necessary to the justification of state power for Plato, or the recognition of individual rights, they argue, but instead necessary to recognizing the "dignity" of all citizens, even those who might break the law. The "dignity" of a free citizen, she explains, means they are entitled to know "what the point is of their laws."[9]

We have notions of dignity today at play in several of our practices. And it can, at first, seem hard to reconcile the idea that preludes provide a recognition of dignity with the content of the preludes Plato offers. In the *Laws* he provides many examples of the kind of rationales, stories, and motivations he had in mind. He suggests preludes for the law on marriage (773a–e), for the law on temple robbery (854a–c), on homicide (869c–870d), assault (879b–c), atheism (888a–907d) (Book 10 invents a type of cosmology to this end), the selling of adulterated products (916d–917d), and for

---

[6] Karl Popper, *The Open Society and its Enemies*, Vol. 1 (London: 1962) 270.

[7] Christopher Bobonich, *Plato's Utopia Recast: His Later Ethics and Politics.* (Oxford University Press: 2002).

[8] Melissa Lane, 'Persuasion et force dans la politique platonicienne,' translated into French by Dimitri El Murr, in *Aglaïa: autour de Platon. Mélanges offerts à Monique Dixsaut*, eds. A. Brancacci, D. El Murr and D. P. Taormina (Paris: Vrin), 133–66.

[9] Annas, *Virtue and Law*, 105.

various responsibilities concerning the family. These laws certainly reflect a context we can scarcely imagine today, but the warnings in the preludes often resemble the advice nervous parents still give, sometimes even to their adult children: do not go there, you could get kidnapped. Be sure to marry! Murderers will be haunted by the ghosts of their victims.

The nature of this guidance is interpreted by Christopher Bobonich has a recognition that in the *Laws* Plato thinks (even) non-philosophers can come to "appreciate and respond to genuine value," though "partially and imperfectly."[10] But I will stick with those who do not see Plato's preludes as having content that can be seen as diluted versions of more rational appeals. Plato's own medical example suggests that in medicine today, we use a similar approach to what he was suggesting in regard to law.

II. The Free Doctor

In a second analogy to criminal law, Plato provides further context on the issue of mere command. We are asked to consider commands when it comes to medical care. Scholars have noted that in this case Plato is not using the example of a physician to emphasize the nature of expertise. Instead, he portrays, and still relevantly the bioethics literature would suggest, that medical care improves with patient co-operation.[11] The passages:

> Athenian "Shall I give an illustration of what I mean? There are men that are doctors, we say, and others that are doctors' assistants; but we call the latter also, to be sure, by the name of "doctors." These, whether they be free-born or slaves, acquire their art under the direction of their masters, by observation and practice and not by the study of nature—which is the way in which the free-born doctors have learnt the art themselves and in which

---

[10] Christopher Bobonich, *Plato's Utopia Recast: His Later Ethics and Politics* (Oxford University Press: 2002) 7–8.

[11] Raina RS, Singh P, Chaturvedi A, Thakur H, Parihar D. "Emerging ethical perspective in physician-patient relationship." *J Clin Diagn Res.* 2014; 8(11):XI01–XI04. doi:10.7860/JCDR/2014/10730.5152

they instruct their own disciples. Would you assert that we have here two classes of what are called "doctors"?

You are also aware that, as the sick folk in the cities comprise both slaves and free men, the enslaved are usually doctored by slaves, who either run round the town or wait in their surgeries; and not one of these doctors either gives or receives any account of the several ailments of the various domestics, but prescribes for each what he deems right from experience, just as though he had exact knowledge, and with the assurance of an autocrat; then up he jumps and off he rushes to another sick domestic, and thus he relieves his master in his attendance on the sick.

But the free-born doctor is mainly engaged in visiting and treating the ailments of free men, and he does so by investigating them from the commencement and according to the course of nature; he talks with the patient himself and with his friends, and thus both learns himself from the sufferers and imparts instruction to them, so far as possible; and he gives no prescription until he has gained the patient's consent, and only then, while securing the patient's continued docility by means of persuasion does he attempt to complete the task of restoring him to health. Which of these two methods of doctoring shows the better doctor, or of training, the better trainer? Should the doctor perform one and the same function in two ways, or do it in one way only and that the worse way of the two and the less humane?" (720a–720e)

Annas explains that in these passages, "the difference between law with, and without, an added persuasive element (a prelude) is compared to the difference between two types of doctor." The type of care offered by the free citizen doctor includes visiting the sick person and talking with "him and with his friends in order to investigate the ailment from its beginning and discover its nature. The doctor does not give a prescription until the patient is persuaded that it is the right one for his condition, one that he will go on taking until he is cured."[12]

---

[12] Annas, *Virtue and Law*, 91.

Current practices and mores in the United States place us under the "less humane" category, the approach taken by the doctors for the enslaved. This is not to deny our many procedural checks and protections (nor even the significant fact that our inmates do get treated medically while incarcerated). It is instead to focus on how we do not in any way think it is even right to wait to sentence defendants until they are "persuaded" of anything particular about their condition and its remedy. Our system would be regarded by Plato as one invoking an "unmixed," rather than his recommendation of a "mixed," method of justice.[13]

Of course even in an ancient context Plato's recommendations raise questions. Is he suggesting we ought to know as much as our doctors or lawyers? Surely not all citizens are expected to approximate the understanding the training in medicine and law provides. Plato does not see this challenge as a *reductio*, and instead seems to maintain that in a sense yes, citizens must understand the criminal law that applies to them. What must they understand? Is it enough to have meaningfully granted consent to either the law or the procedure?

Annas and Lane give us the resources to answer "no" to this question. Lane concludes that Plato is merely suggesting that is better to rule over or treat people who have become willing, and that, for rulers, it is simply better, more advised, perhaps, more respectable, to make a person willing by persuasion rather than force. There is no doubt, of course, that physicians are going to have medical knowledge they cannot transfer to any non-trained patient, nor even to a physician trained in another specialty. But there are ethical downsides to ignoring patient autonomy that we recognize today, and our practices include listening to patients about even issues that the physician recognizes are irrelevant to the underlying medical issue. Patients are often not corrected on these matters but gently redirected, or issues put in terms that, though not strictly accurate, they might understand. The personalized explanations physicians offer are bound to seem very similar to preludes. They, too, are

---

[13] Annas, *Virtue and Law*, 56.

"gentle" and making patients more "willing" if not more educated or virtuous. They are at least being told, in a way that caters to their situation, what "the point" is of a proposed medical treatment. Is the offer of such a measure patronizing?

It is certainly possible that medical practice today remains paternalistic. It depends on informed consent but there are hardly any checks on patient understanding, and so we often pretend what patients do understand amounts to "informed." Plato, of course, had no concerns about paternalism and was not proposing remedies for a liberal society. Before moving on, let us consider how the very idea of preludes for criminal law might be illiberal.

III. Liberal Concerns About (Even) Rehabilitation

Let us grant that, in the context of political philosophy, suggesting that virtue is best for anyone or any society violates facts of pluralism. Let us also grant that given the complexity of the modern-day state, it is anachronistic to propose that there is even "one" explanation for what we are attempting to do with criminal law. There are also warranted and historic concerns about philosophical overreach in criminal justice, concerning for example, ideas that sometimes seem banal, such as the very notion that we should rehabilitate the incarcerated. Court decisions have recognized a right to merely "serve your sentence" rather than meet any (moving and unsteady) set of improvement-criteria. The motivation for lawsuits is not as complicated as the poor justification of "what counts as good," but more easily understood: sentencing based on rehabilitation criteria may never have an end. The Sentencing Reform Act of 1984 replaced previous ideas about the aim of rehabilitating inmates with the right to "a range of determinate sentences." But, of course, the idea that we should have a right to merely "serve our sentence" is supported by the recognition that we neither know how to rehabilitate inmates nor do we have any undisputed authorities on what would count as rehabilitation.

I think there is a way to avoid any tension with liberalism and still use Plato's preludes as a positive example, and that is by using

Plato's ethical assumptions as a contrast to our own. Our own are stubbornly hidden, and if we confront Plato's emphasis on making criminal defendants "willing" we can, at least, recognize that we have many poor reasons for thinking catering at all to the perspective of the law breaker is needless. So this would not be to suggest any agreement on what counts as a good life, the purpose of government, or the appeal of virtue. Let us set any positions on these firmly aside as illiberal in a criminal justice context. And if Plato had recommended preludes for the task of inculcating virtue in citizens, we may need to be more suspect. But note these lesser and more partial aims: preludes are first described as aiming at encouraging *hēmerōteron* (718d4), a well-disposed frame of mind (*eumenesteron*) (4.718d4, d6), and willingness to learn (*eumathesteron*) (718d6). In Book 4 the Athenian explains that a prelude is designed "to make the person to whom he promulgated his law accept his orders—the law—in a more well-disposed frame of mind and because of this more tractable and willing to learn" (723a4–6).

Much depends here on what "willing to learn" concerns, but as both Annas and Lane point out, we are not to think of the preludes as actual means of reducing crime. The preludes are not generated on the basis of what will bring about successful law-following. We would assume Plato would resort to rational arguments in that case and blame those who cannot follow the argument for their irrationality. That they include myths and persuasion that seem plausibly directed at actual defendants, ones who may not be versed in Platonic philosophy, does not mean that they are dependent on their actual uptake. There is no suggestion that you design a prelude until you find one that works. (Just as there is no requirement that physicians actually convince patients to go through a procedure.) Though a prelude could potentially reduce a person's motivation to commit a crime, I, again, see them as representing the actual things physicians actually say to patients faced with a complicated set of medical procedures. This is a very unusual status being described. It is a "bold conceptual move" of Plato's, according to Annas.[14] And that is why I am so confident that it is missing in our approach to criminal law.

Lane puts it in this way: in the *Laws*, despite Plato's comfort with objective moral authority and political necessity, preludes are designed in order to reflect a recognition from lawmakers that they ought to be "not brutal but gentle" (*mē agriōn alla hēmerōn*, 10.885e2). In other words, were we to consider Plato's preludes today, they would work as a check on our understanding *of ourselves* as lawmakers and supporters of our present-day criminal justice system. This is exactly what I think we are not currently encouraged to do. Let me make some suggestions as to how we might think of criminal justice, encouraged by the role social contract thinking plays in our common sense ideas. I am going to argue that the assumptions we make about lawbreakers having broken the terms of our social contract keep us from examining our relationship to criminal law so that we hardly imagine that these laws might change or be overly harsh.

And rather than focus on dignity, a concept that has been borrowed by so many traditions since, the respect in which I want to borrow from the role preludes play in our understanding of our relationship between ourselves and law breakers is *gentleness*. This is importantly not at all the same as the idea of "mercy," which does play a role in our current system. I think regarding ourselves as best gentle would be a new way to think of criminal justice. As with mercy, if you conceive of yourself as gentle, you are, when addressing another about law (or their health) you are making a choice about your mode of approach. And yet mercy is compatible with force and what Plato is proposing is that we mix persuasion with force to generate something different and new. And I want to use Plato in a negative manner, not trying to convince readers that his ethical assumptions are right, but to convince readers that thinking that we only have recourse to force (and then perhaps mercy later) can be associated with poorly justified ethical thought, in contrast to Plato's own.

---

[14] Annas, *Virtue and Law*, 105.

Finally, being gentle with lawbreakers because they are recognized to retain a status as free is not the same as a rehabilitation program (it does not specify or require one) and is not at odds with any of the rights we currently recognize. Instead, recognizing the good of gentleness a) might get us to revisit and revise our commitment to our present-day criminal justice system and b) be a better way to think of ourselves.

IV. Our Current System and Assumptions We Currently Make About Lawbreakers

Experts such as William Stuntz characterize what we have today as a system devoted to "procedural" rather than older notions of substantive justice. Stuntz, author of *The Collapse of the American Criminal Justice System*, painstakingly details the changes that have come about to make our system one that honors procedural justice (over older notions of substantive justice) and have led to our very expansive notion of criminal liability.[15] We have clear rules about process, and we look to have sentences applied in an impersonal manner that seems fair. The extent to which we honor this idea is clear from the falsely accused hoping to identify procedural violations in order to gain an appeal. But this powerful procedural train, capable of being checked for all of the components we consider necessary, has somehow gotten off the rails.

We have the highest incarceration rate in the world by far. We have out-incarcerated even non-liberal countries, ones still dealing with mass political turmoil.[16] We're instead stable and liberal, and even our incarceration rates do not reflect that we keep 1 in 55 of our citizens under probationary surveillance and that we arrest ten

---

[15] William Stuntz, *The Collapse of the American Criminal Justice System* (Cambridge: Harvard University Press: 2008).

[16] "Highest to Lowest—Prison Population Total," Institute for Criminal Policy Research, accessed May 1, 2020, www.prisonstudies.org/highest-to-lowest/prison-population-total.

million people a year in an incredible churn through our jails.[17] This is often pre-trial detention so we are jailing formally innocent people, to the extent that matters. I want to propose that through Plato's eyes, we are a failure. But what are we missing? It is only the motivation to reform.

There is plenty of agreement on the blueprint needed to fix our system, which, I guess, can be seen as a kind of positive. Criminal justice has gotten a rash of attention, and work after work repeats the same descriptions and suggestions. The history of how we got here has been studied and seems well known by a range of experts. Their proposals for remedy are not at odds with each other: they suggest a stripping away of all of the policies that have backfired. It seems their list of proposed changes get more and more similar over time.[18] Criminal justice reform is also an issue on which there is notable bipartisan support.[19]

But there is one aspect necessary to reform that will never be provided by a consensus that that change should happen or even between experts in the system. This is the need to get the public's support for the particular changes being proposed. (Realistically, historically, perhaps this is not always necessary. Perhaps policy changes will be made in a manner where they are simply never announced for public approval.) We can see how our ideas can interfere with changes in the ongoing story of cash bail reform in New York. Cash bail reform is one aspect of criminal justice reform, it is also an issue

---

[17] Survey of State Criminal History Systems, Department of Justice, Accessed May 1, 2020: https://www.ncjrs.gov/pdffiles1/bjs/grants/244563.pdf.

[18] Here is a rough accounting: The drug war needs to end. We need to make sentences shorter. Judicial logic is necessary to change here, we have many repeat offenders and the formula now is: that they need longer sentences each time, so they finally learn. Prosecutorial strategy needs to change. We need to reverse the direction of incentives so that at points in the system there is interest in reducing our numbers and the length of sentences. It also seems to be the case that reforms tend to work, and this too, seems uncontroversial to those in the system, who are well-aware of the situation on the ground.

[19] The Voice of the People Citizens Campaign Survey Results, Accessed May 2, 2020: http://www.publicconsultation.org/wp-content/uploads/2018/08/Sentencing_Slides0818.pdf.

bipartisan insiders support, and it is also easy to recommend using merely liberal and constitutional principles (how is it fair for only the poor or the innocent to be jailed?). Bail reform is a good example of reform approved by those working in criminal justice that is not considered tolerable by the general public. I am suggesting that the difference is that "insiders" as I will call them are more committed or aware of "procedural justice" than us in the general public. In Texas cash bail was challenged in the courts on the basis of violating due process and the Fourth Amendment and found impermissible. Cash bail is a good example of this because insiders realize the impact of it in a way the public does not; they see drug dealers have no problem meeting it, and being incentivized to prepare for it (generating more crime). And yet efforts to reform bond, if they catch the attention of the right journalists, are vociferously opposed by of members of the public. Why would this be? My worry is that the public is not even supportive of the very idea of bond and would prefer to see those arrested for crime detained before trial. I at least want to suggest a possible disconnect between the principles on which we say the justice system operates and our actual preferences.

Grant me just three more possibilities. The first is that even if the public did recognize liberal principles ought to undergird our tactics in criminal justice that this would still not be enough to reduce mass incarceration or solve over-criminalization. This is to be unconvinced by philosopher Luke Hunt, an ex-FBI agent and philosopher who has just published *The Retrieval of Liberalism in Policing*.[20] He carefully argues that we just need to return to the principles of a liberal society. He wants guides to policing that reflect the idea of liberal personhood: we are all free and equal, we must be given dignity, and that any force against citizens must be well-justified—either for an emergency or necessary for the public good. It is a sophisticated weaving together of Kant and more recent work on rule of law, and it updates Locke. And of course it is very good to rule out brutality or the notion that other people can be thought of as

---

[20] Luke Hunt, *The Retrieval of Liberalism in Policing* (Oxford: Oxford University Press. 2019).

brutes or animals while in a liberal polity. But the language, the principles, are so familiar: if you look to any police departments mission statement you will find the loftiest liberal language anywhere. I am concerned, again, that procedural justice got us here, and let me add this: substantive justice, what would really be fair to a victim and a defendant in a particular circumstance, is out of reach, philosophically, for us today.

This is also true for the legal theorists and political philosophers among us. A certain amount of traction can be gained from pointing out the dissonance between our ideals and our practice, but our practices are so degraded (handcuffing, strip searching upon arrest) that the idea that we uphold the "dignity" of even the non-convicted innocent is farcical. And this is true though many theoretical checks can be considered to be done: due process is in place, judicial reviews are ongoing and have been ample. Procedural justice and an expansive notion of criminal liability are, after all, not self-contradictory. They can be fit with the readily endorsable, well-established collective good or value of safety, which has always been associated with coordinated responses to violence, prevention of crime, and the maintenance of the peace.

When procedural justice is prioritized, the consequences of strict liability are not at issue. One who hopes for justice to be established in a case where it was denied has to hope there were clear rule violations, rather than hope that the decision strikes common sense as unfair. This shift has result in some of the unhealthy outcomes we see today. This would account for our being "equal."

As for us being "free," I want to, in conclusion, suggest that the public is very comfortable with the idea that we lose our freedom if we commit a crime. Allow me to tentatively suggest that we, as a public, share vague ideas of being part of a social contract. When this is the case, those suspected of crime have somehow ended the arrangement necessary to secure mutual respect. I do not expect the public to be influenced by more sophisticated forms of social contract thinking but, as we noted, even carefully wrought conceptions like Rawls' are incredibly clumsy when it comes to lawbreakers, since it resigns them to an unsettled outsider role. (With more than 7 million of us under active surveillance, perhaps a theory is inadequate if so many of us are just considered "off the playing board.") In any case, our idea that we lose our freedom upon violating law completely disconnects us from Plato's analogies to medical care and recommendation that we be gentle in our approach, as one's status as free can be lost.

When Stuntz describes the public's concern for substantive justice as what ended our earlier prohibition, he accounts for it as a kind of confidence in common sense about overreach when it comes to criminalization. This type of confidence would seem to me to rely on ethical rather than political assumptions. I think we've lost touch with this confidence in ourselves and in substantive justice as we have adjusted to our system. Can Plato help?

Plato models himself directly questioning the good of systems we are under. But there is a bit of bite in this recommendation as well. If we do not ask and find answers to these questions, we have lessened our own agency. We have made ourselves less rational and we certainly cannot pretend to have moral authority over a system or actions it takes when we do not even understand it. It might seem familiar, if you know Plato, but think of how directly it challenges each of us to get to know and try to directly approve of our criminal justice system. As an example, what if people visited the jail and saw the conditions in which the mentally ill were kept? I would imagine, as it can be seen in interviews with jail guards, that it is nearly impossible to face, and very hard on the guards to live with.

As another example, what if people began to visit circuit court when sentences are determined? I first did this just a few months ago and it was revelatory. I just did not have a good sense of what people were spending time in jail for. I saw three sentences handed down, and I could not have explained "why that sentence" for any of them. One man got 36 months' probation (as you may realize, probation is an extremely demanding and active set of requirements and no one can easily expect to succeed in it) for a workplace time theft that had been repaid, after three months in jail. Another spent months in jail for a defect on his ankle bracelet that was certainly not his fault. Another was released on time served for offering an undercover officer drugs. Can we explain these sentences, or are we operating, like the less humane doctor, without explanations?

The ethical confidence we lack when it comes to what such issues have to do with us might have been abandoned with notions of substantive justice. Is this similar to losing our philosophical confidence more generally? Consider common sense on the drinking age and military service: "A person willing to die for their country ought to be able to have a beer," is an example of a confident ethical claim. Sometimes Plato is not associated with plain thought like this, but his preludes in the *Laws* brings this to light. Finding explanations, even non-ideal ones, that address restrictions being placed on other people are a requirement of being gentle, and ethical, ourselves.

It is unrealistic to think that we might ever organize ourselves to craft preludes for our laws, which would, I think, focus our attention on criminal justice and its aims. But let me end by suggesting that Plato's attention to gentleness and thinking of ourselves as lawmakers might encourage a revision of assumptions that underlie our passivity concerning mass incarceration. One way to recognize our passivity is by noting that we do not share certain Platonic assumptions about others or about justice. I propose that the following more or less characterize common thought about criminal justice today.

Criminal law is not a matter of ethics. It is merely the result of complex political processes in which I play no direct part. My personal ethics need not concern my country's system of criminal justice.

My moral and political status is dependent on my not being incarcerated for any type of crime.

Those who commit any arrestable offense have lost moral and political standing because they have violated a manner of social contract and have become uncooperative. Uncooperativeness threatens the entire social enterprise, and that is plenty of justification for taking you "off the playing board."

Force establishes authority and questioning this diminishes that very authority.

233

What we are not recognizing, for any number of reasons, are the following. These are claims I think Plato's recommendation of preludes encourage.

* Even people who have committed crimes ought to have the point of the law involved explained to them.

* We ought to understand the point of our criminal laws.

* Our laws should be easily understood by people generally.

And these are the views that I think we could import, without violating a commitment to pluralism or other liberal principles, from Plato's own ethical account.

To use force alone to apply criminal law is intolerable, as it is at odds with the very idea that all citizens are free.

There are ethical assumptions implicit in the laws we maintain, no matter how complex and multi-leveled our system becomes. We can always tether it to explanations that work at the level with which we explain our own behavior, as these explanations do not have be descriptive or causal. They are just ethical justifications.

Actions, even taken at the level of criminal justice, require efforts at justification, place-holders if that is all we can do, but crucially we indicate our reasons for policy; if not, we lose intelligibility and any claim to moral authority.

People are not born good and are bound to make mistakes, repeatedly. Knowing this in advance, we ought to have a plan for those who commit crimes in our approach to justice. They, too, are part of our society.

These claims could exist alongside a liberal system of justification, and alongside many other unstated underlying assumptions about personhood and agency. And yet I think they could help, if used to think about our criminal justice system, because they encourage a focus on the ethical nature of criminal justice. The beliefs we tend to share today, those listed above, encourage us to actively dismiss the outlook of lawbreakers, as if they are not to be anticipated and included in our thought. And yet if we consider their perspective, we could recognize that those tempted to disobey law (or sound law anyway) are out of range of something, and not in tune with it, either. I am going to argue that Plato could help us do this by filling out, and in a manner that bypasses the complexities of debates over liberal philosophy, addressing us each as thinkers on what justice requires.

INDEX

Index

149n10, 150n18, 156n42, 157, 157n46, 161n63
Berns, Laurence, 22n1
biology, 127n10, 214
birth, 17, 32, 34, 126, 138n30, 142, 142n37, 201, 203, 204, 207, 211, 215, 222, 223, 234
Blackwell, Christopher, 129n12; *Demos: Classical Athenian Democracy*, 129n12
Blackwood, Russell, 169n91; "*Gorgias 482b*", 169n91
Bloom, Allan, 59n2, 193, 195n2, 199, 199n12
Bobonich, Christopher, 221n7, 222, 222n10; *Plato's Utopia Recast: His Later Ethics and Politics*, 221n7, 222, 222n10
Boetius, 214
Bolotin, David, 113n61; "The Critique of Homer and the Homeric Heroes in Plato's *Republic*, 113n61
Bostock, David, 118n81
Boswell, James, 191n39
boulêsis, bouletai, 48, 49, 51
Brancacci, A., 221n8; *Aglaïa: Autour de Platon: Mélanges offerts à Monique Dixsaut*, 221n8
Brickhouse, Thomas C., 181, 181n19, 182, 188; "The Myth of the Afterlife in Plato's *Gorgias*", 188n33, 188n34; "Socrates on the Emotions", 181, 181n19
Briseis, 115n69
Brisson, Luc, 187n30, 188n32; *Gorgias-Menon: Selected Papers from the Seventh Symposium Platonicum*, 187n30, 188n32
Bruell, Christopher, 99n8; *Aristotle as Teacher*, 99n8
Burger, Ronna, 179n14
Burnet, John, 80n1, 164n76; OCT (Oxford Classical Text), 80n1, 164n76
Butterworth, Charles, 25n4
caduceus (herald's staff), 154n33

calculation (*logistikon*, λογιστική), 40, 46
Callias, 31, 37, 136, 138, 138n30, 140, 147n5, 160
Callicles (interlocutor), xix, 8-14, 15n14, 15n15, 16, 16n15, 17-19, 45, 49, 138, 140n33, 146, 146n4, 147, 147n5, 148, 148n9, 149, 149n10, 150, 150n16, 151, 152, 152n27, 153, 153n31, 154, 154n32, 154n35, 155, 155n39, 156, 156n42, 156n43, 156n45, 157, 157n45, 157n46, 157n48, 158, 158n51, 159, 160, 160n61, 161-163, 163n70, 164, 164n73, 165-167, 167n82, 167n84, 168, 169, 169n92, 172-174, 183, 184, 185n25, 188, 192
Callicrite, 122
Callimaco, 211-214
Cammillo, 214
Cantarella, Eva, 129n12, 129n13; "Gender, Sexuality, and Law", 129n12
cave, allegory of the, 98
Cecrops, 154
Cephalus, 67, 111, 112, 112n58, 113, 197-200, 200n14, 201-204, 217, 218
Cephisodorus, 158
Ceryces, 146n4, 149, 154, 154n32, 155, 157, 167n84, 168
Ceryx (god), 154
ceryx (messenger), 154
Chaerephon, 146n4, 147n4, 176, 188
Charicles, 147n5
Charioteers, xvi
Charmides (interlocutor, historical figure), 39, 40, 41, 173
Chaturvedi, Aditi, 222n11; "Emerging ethical perspective in physician-patient relationship", 222n11
children, 28, 43, 46, 76, 77n29, 92, 96, 98, 103, 110, 111, 114, 127, 128, 130, 131n17, 132n20, 133, 136n26, 138, 140, 142, 150, 174n6, 176, 178, 183n22, 186, 187, 190, 196,

239

Index

Index

PLATONIC DIALOGUES

Index